ATHLII GWAII

UPHOLDING HAIDA LAW AT LYELL ISLAND

Athlii Gwaii—Upholding Haida Law At Lyell Island

COUNCIL OF THE HAIDA NATION

No. 1 Reservoir Road	504 Naanii Street
HlGaagilda, Haida Gwaii	Gaw, Haida Gwaii
V0T 1S1	V0T 1MO

Library and Archives Canada Cataloguing Publication Data
Main entry under title: Athlii Gwaii—Upholding Haida Law At Lyell Island
Diane Brown, Nika Collison, Ernie Gladstone, Guujaaw, Miles Richardson Jr.,
Terri-Lynn Williams-Davidson ... [et al.]
Text in Haida and English
Cataloguing data available from Library and Archives Canada
Hardcover edition published by the Council of the Haida Nation, ISBN 978-0-9694402-1-5
Paperback edition published by the Council of the Haida Nation, distributed by Locarno Press, ISBN 978-0-9959946-6-9

CIP data is available from the Library of Congress
and Library and Archives Canada

Concept: Council of the Haida Nation with special thanks to Huux *Percy Crosby*
Editor: Jisgang *Nika Collison*
Design: Council of the Haida Nation/Haida Laas/Simon Davies
Cover: (left to right, from back cover) Oliver Bell, Martin Williams, Henry Wilson and Christopher Collison
on the line at Athlii Gwaii. Photo: Ann Yow-Dyson.
Copy Editing: Audrey McLellan and Scott Steedman
Photos: All photos by Captain Gold, courtesy Skidegate Band Council, unless otherwise noted.

Published in 2018 by Locarno Press < locarnopress.com >
Printed and bound in Canada by Friesens Corporation.

The Council of the Haida Nation acknowledges the generous support of the Gwaii Trust Society and
Gwaii Haanas/Parks Canada organization.

Locarno Press gratefully acknowledges for their financial support of our publishing program the Canada Council for the
Arts, the BC Arts Council, and the Government of Canada through the Canada Book Fund (CBF).

ATHLII GWAII

UPHOLDING HAIDA LAW AT LYELL ISLAND

CONTENTS

Elders on the line at Athlii Gwaii.
Seated: (L-R) Kamee *Ethel Jones*,
Jaadsangkinghliiyas *Ada Yovanovich*,
Chief Gaahlaay *Watson Pryce*, Giteewans
Aldophus "Fussy" Marks.

Opposite: Injunction papers burning.

UPON THIS GOOD LAND, LET ME LIVE LONG

X̲AAYDA KIL · X̲AAD KIL – THE HAIDA LANGUAGE

Because of the different dialects of the Haida language, the reader will find a variety of orthographies used throughout this book.

Spelling has been provided by the Elders of the Skidegate Haida Immersion Program and through the work of HlG̲awangdlíi Skilaa *Lawrence Bell* with Gulk̲ihlgad *Dr. Marianne Boelscher Ignace*. Spelling of personal names has been provided by name-holders, and place name spellings follow the Council of the Haida Nation maps.

Opposite: Walking to the line at Athlii Gwaii.

Words found in this publication include:

Awaayah: expression of distaste

Chinaay: grandfather, Skidegate dialect

Gaahllns Kun: the name of Raven's uncle who created a big flood

Guuding.ngaay: red sea urchin

Gwaii / gwaay: island

Gwaii Haanas: Islands of Beauty/Wonder

Haawa: thank you

Jiila K̲uns: Greatest Mountain, the common Ancestress of most Eagle clans on Haida Gwaii

Kaagan Jaad: Mouse Woman

K'aaw: herring roe-on-kelp

K̲alga Jaad: Ice Woman

Kilslaay: expression used to address a man held in high esteem

King.gii: a Supernatural Being that is now a mountain living in Gwaii Haanas

Llnagaay: town

Loo Taas: *Wave Eater*, Bill Reid's 50-foot Haida canoe

Naanii: grandmother, Old Massett dialect

Nanaay: grandmother, Skidegate dialect

Nang Kilsdlaas: He Whose Voice Is Obeyed is the first Nang Kilsdlaas or Nang Kilsdlaas in Raven form, depending on the context

SG̲uuluu Jaad: Foam Woman, common Ancestress of most Raven clans on Haida Gwaii

Sgyam Sgwaan: mosquito hawk, also refers to the sparrow hawk

SG̲yuu: a type of seaweed

Slanjaaw: toilet paper

St'aalaa: snail

Ts'iljii: dried fish strips

Tsinii: grandfather, Old Massett dialect

X̲aad kil: the Haida language, Old Massett dialect

X̲aagyah: name of the reef upon which SG̲uuluu Jaad sat

X̲aayda kil: the Haida language, Skidegate dialect

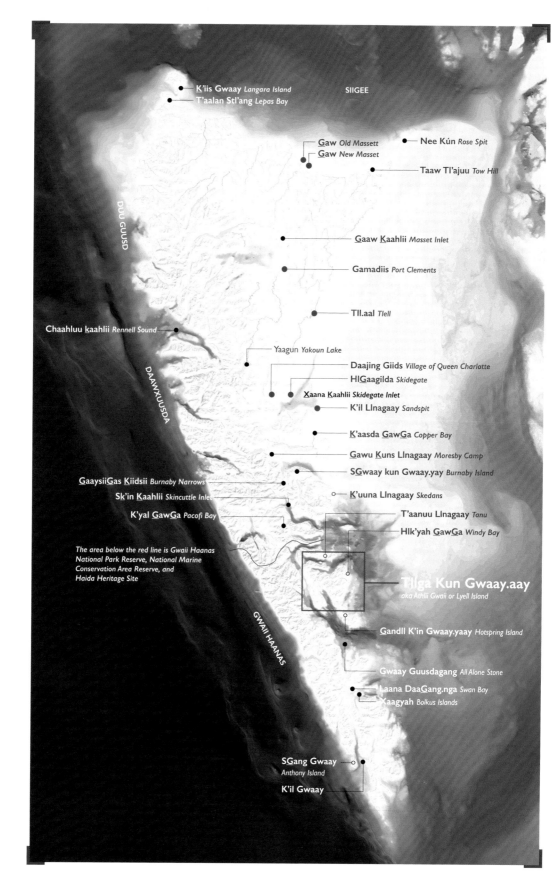

K'iis Gwaay *Langara Island*
T'aalan Stl'ang *Lepas Bay*

SIIGEE

Gaw *Old Massett*
Gaw *New Masset*

Nee Kún *Rose Spit*

Taaw Tl'ajuu *Tow Hill*

DUU GUUSD

Gaaw Kaahlii *Masset Inlet*

Gamadiis *Port Clements*

Tll.aal *Tlell*

Chaahluu kaahlii *Rennell Sound*

Yaagun *Yakoun Lake*

Daajing Giids *Village of Queen Charlotte*
HlGaagilda *Skidegate*
Xaana Kaahlii *Skidegate Inlet*
K'il Llnagaay *Sandspit*

DAAWXUUSDA

K'aasda GawGa *Copper Bay*

Gawu Kuns Llnagaay *Moresby Camp*
SGwaay kun Gwaay.yay *Burnaby Island*

GaaysiiGas Kiidsii *Burnaby Narrows*
Sk'in Kaahlii *Skincuttle Inlet*

K'uuna Llnagaay *Skedans*

K'yal GawGa *Pacofi Bay*

T'aanuu Llnagaay *Tanu*
Hlk'yah GawGa *Windy Bay*

The area below the red line is Gwaii Haanas
National Park Reserve, National Marine
Conservation Area Reserve, and
Haida Heritage Site

Tilga Kun Gwaay.aay
aka Athlii Gwaii or Lyell Island

GWAII HAANAS

Gandll K'in Gwaay.yaay *Hotspring Island*

Gwaay Guusdagang *All Alone Stone*

Laana DaaGang.nga *Swan Bay*
Xaagyah *Bolkus Islands*

SGang Gwaay
Anthony Island

K'il Gwaay

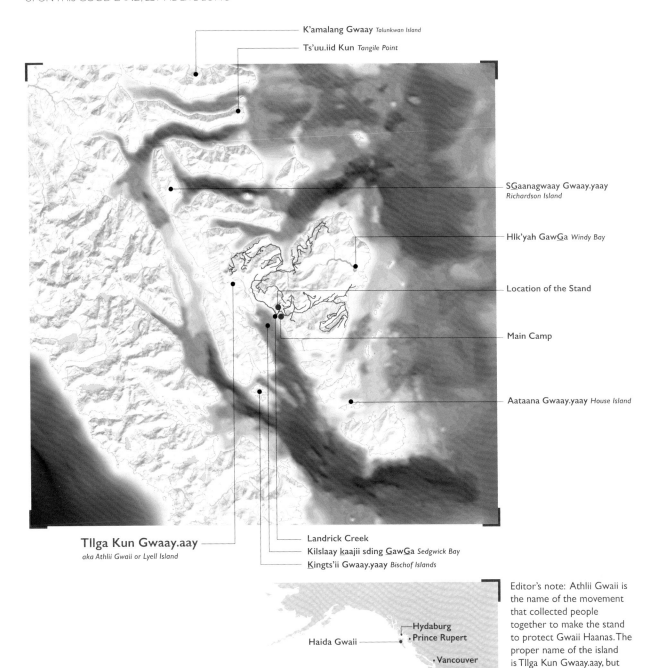

K'amalang Gwaay *Talunkwan Island*

Ts'uu.iid Kun *Tangile Point*

SGaanagwaay Gwaay.yaay
Richardson Island

Hlk'yah GawGa *Windy Bay*

Location of the Stand

Main Camp

Aataana Gwaay.yaay *House Island*

Tllga Kun Gwaay.aay
aka Athlii Gwaii or Lyell Island

Landrick Creek

Kilslaay kaajii sding GawGa *Sedgwick Bay*

Kingts'ii Gwaay.yaay *Bischof Islands*

Hydaburg
Prince Rupert

Haida Gwaii

Vancouver

Los Angeles

Editor's note: Athlii Gwaii is the name of the movement that collected people together to make the stand to protect Gwaii Haanas. The proper name of the island is Tllga Kun Gwaay.aay, but is also referred to as Lyell Island and Athlii Gwaii. The names are used interchangeably in this book.

On the line, around the fire, early in the morning. James Young and Shelley Hageman in the back with Henry "Whip" Williams and Martin Williams in front of the fire.

HAIDA PROCLAMATION
from the CONSTITUTION OF THE HAIDA NATION

HlG̱aagilda Iid kuuniisii asii id gii isda gan. Tllgaay ad siigaay G̱an t'alang aax̱ana ad yahguudang. Huu tllguu G̱iidan hlk'inx̱a gaa.ngang x̱aayda hllng.aay gud giijaagids, gaay G̱aaganuu gam gina daaG̱ang.nga id gwii is hllnga G̱ang ga. Xaaydag̱a Gwaay.yaay G̱aaganuu iid x̱aynanga ga. Asii gwaay.yaay guu, iid kuuniisii x̱aynang.nga, ad siing.gwaa'ad gan. Sah 'Laana Tllgaay G̱aa id gii k̲yaagang.ngaay G̱aaw aan t'ang naax̱ang sG̱waan.nang G̱as ga. Iid sihlG̱a ga x̱aynangas gii t'alang t'aas.slas, asii k̲yang.gaay llgaay 'waagii kilxii gang ga.

G̱aw Iitl' kuníisii áajii gwaayee iitl' ga t'asdlagan. Áajii gwáayee inggu gin 'waadluwaan t'aláng ísdaas G̱an t'aláng yahgudáng-gaa, gin 'waadluuwaan t'aláng ísdaas uu áajii tlagee, isgyaan siis, isgyaan sangee sda isgáagang. Áajii gwáayee k̲iid k̲'úlaas gingaan iitl' xaadaas asán G̱íidang, ahljii ahluu tliisdluu iitl' ga 'wáajaagahls dluu, itl' gwii asán k̲áahlasang. Áajii gwáayee uu iitl' ga x̲íinang-gee ísdagan. Iitl' kuníisii gin G̱aatláandagiinii gingaan uu wéed x̲aadee gin G̱aatláahlaal hlangaas gin G̱an unsadasaang. Áajii gwaayee ingguu iitl' kuníisii x̲íinangaagiinii, wéed áadlan 'l hlG̱íwaawaang. Áajii gwaayee inggu iitl' asán x̲íinangaas k'yaahl gu tlíisdluwaan iitl' asan áadlan hlG̱íwaa'asaang.

English The Haida Nation is the rightful heir to Haida Gwaii. Our culture is born of respect for and intimacy with the land and sea and the air around us. Like the forests, the roots of our people are intertwined such that the greatest troubles cannot overcome us. We owe our existence to Haida Gwaii. The living generation accepts the responsibility to ensure that our heritage is passed on to following generations. On these Islands our Ancestors lived and died, and here, too, we will make our homes until called away to join them in the great beyond.

CHAPTER ONE

WE HAVE A SONG

WHERE THE SCENE IS SET BY LOOKING AT EVENTS
THAT SHAPED TWO NATIONS

THIS IS HAIDA LAND, YOU ALL KNOW THAT, AND WE'RE HERE TO UPHOLD THE DECISION OF THE HAIDA NATION. THIS IS HAIDA LAND AND THERE WILL BE NO FURTHER LOGGING IN THIS AREA.

Kilsli Kaji Sting *Miles Richardson Jr.*

FOREWORD
kil tlaats 'gaa *Peter Lantin*, President of the Haida Nation

I RECALL BEING TEN YEARS OLD, opening up the local newspaper in Ottawa and seeing the headlines about Athlii Gwaii and the stand the Haida Nation was taking against clear-cut logging. I remember feeling very proud when I saw a picture of my Naanii Ethel Jones, who I was very close to growing up. My mother explained to me what was happening, but at that age I didn't understand the magnitude of our stand. After Naanii returned from Lyell Island I asked her over the phone what happened and why she got arrested. She told me, "Peter, we did this for you. One day you will understand and hopefully you will never have to take a stand like we did. Hopefully this will change how people view our land and treat our land." It did.

As president of the Haida Nation I frequently ask myself, "What would our Ancestors think?" I was asking myself this question at Windy Bay when we celebrated the twentieth anniversary of the Gwaii Haanas Agreement and raised the first monumental pole in Gwaii Haanas in over 130 years. There was so much emotion in the air and I remember feeling proud watching everyone witnessing that historic event. It was impossible not to feel proud. This feeling was magnified when I considered the challenges our Ancestors overcame so that the celebration could happen. It is humbling to ponder the sacrifices that were made to protect the lands and waters of Haida Gwaii.

Although rooted in conflict, these sacrifices paved the way to an era of cooperation between the Haida Nation and Canada. It showed Canada that the Rights and Title of the Haida Nation were never extinguished. It was a demonstration of the deep-rooted Haida ways that determine how we treat the lands and waters. The sacrifices of our Ancestors empower us today. They created the pride we felt at Windy Bay and we all honoured them with respect.

The stand at Athlii Gwaii seemed so far ahead of its time. That's why the international community paid attention to the issue. It represented how far the Haida Nation will go to protect our homeland. Our reputation and prominence throughout the world comes from our Ancestors and what they were willing to do to protect our lands and waters. If you listen to our Elders talk about why they were willing to get arrested at Lyell, their answers did not focus solely on Haida people. They were talking about protecting Haida Gwaii for *all* people. The spirit and consequences of their stand are reflected in the Gwaii Haanas Agreement, the Gwaii Trust and the Kunst'aa Guu—Kunst'aayah Reconciliation Protocol Agreement along with many others. Our Ancestors seeded this era of cooperation between nations and it is very important to stop and acknowledge the great work that brought the Haida Nation to where it is today. •

"

Drawing a line is easy, it is holding the line that counts.

Guujaaw, 2016

PROLOGUE
Jisgang *Nika Collison*, **Editor**

In 1985 the Haida Nation rejected the relentless industrial logging practices ravaging Gwaii Haanas. Designating the area a Haida Heritage Site, we drew a line that stands to this day. Guided by Haida law and trusting in our culture, our Nation's responsibility to Haida Gwaii was upheld with unwavering clarity. Canada and BC pushed back, resulting in 72 arrests, including those of Elders.

But the Haida Nation held firm in its stand, and with support from friends around the world, logging was stopped. Negotiations between the Haida Nation and Canada ensued, resulting in the ground-breaking Gwaii Haanas Agreement, in which both nations agree to disagree on Title to the area, and instead focus on its protection for the benefit of all generations.

I was fourteen when everything came to a head. Two months before the stand, my chinaay, Bill Reid, took me out of school and into Gwaii Haanas on Al Whitney's *Darwin Sound II*. We travelled with some interesting characters who were very dedicated to the cause, including author Arthur Hailey and Canada's Opposition Party leader John Turner. Haida Nation President Miles Richardson Jr. joined us at Hotsprings Island. Like everyone in our Nation, when the blockade started, my family helped in any way we could. There were tough times, there were great times. There were magical times. Through the years, I was very honoured to participate in events related to the stand, such as the opening of Looking Around Blinking House, and paddling *Loo Taas* home for what turned into a double-reason celebration. All in all, a pretty interesting and inspiring time for a teenager.

In putting this book together I find myself beyond interested and inspired. I am in awe. In awe of our Elders, whose dignity, grace and wisdom set our path; of our leaders, most of who were in their 20s at the time; of our people in general, who sacrificed more than can be told in this book; of people from around world who joined us in saving Gwaii Haanas. I'm in awe of the loggers, the RCMP and Canadian politicians who played their roles, in their own way standing for Gwaii Haanas. I'm in awe of Gwaii Haanas, all of Haida Gwaii, and the Supernatural, who a long time ago taught us the foundation of co-existence. I'm in awe of our Ancestors. So many stories to tell, so many more to tell.

Tllga Kun Gwaay.aay, commonly known as Athlii Gwaii or Lyell Island, brought the world together, empowering us all to be better people. To have worked with my Nation and friends to share the story of this pivotal moment in history has been a great privilege. The stories are filled with such dignity, love and respect that I have cried many tears while building this book. So many, that I feel like a piece of ts'iljii!

The profound impossibility of what stood in front of our Nation was taken on with integrity, purpose and respect. Those three things encompass a world view that is alive today and part of a through-story that began millennia ago. Athlii Gwaii—Upholding Haida Law at Lyell Island pays homage to Haida Gwaii, the Supernatural, our Ancestors, our people and our friends. It upholds Indigenous Rights and Title, affirms the use of non-violence, and as Guujaaw says, reminds us of the possible.

Opposite: Lawrence Jones standing on the line at Athlii Gwaii with logging company owner, Frank Beban behind.

Editor's note: Athlii Gwaii is the name of the movement that collected people together to make the stand to protect Gwaii Haanas. The proper name of the island is Tllga Kun Gwaay.aay, but is also referred to as Lyell Island and Athlii Gwaii. The names are used interchangeably in this book.

IT WAS TOLD
Guujaaw

At a time before people, it was neither night nor day
... for a long time, the whole world was covered by water.

Supernaturals emerged from the sea to occupy the first rocks.

SGuuluu Jaad *Seafoam Woman* sat on top of Xaagyah, a reef,
while Jiila Kuns and Kaagan Jaad hung on to the edge of her perch.

Opposite: Marchel Shannon and Jennifer
Davidson on the line at Athlii Gwaii.

The first Nang Kilsdlaas showed Raven how to bring forth the nearshore and
faraway lands.

When the great ice covered the continent, more lands emerged,
revealing the tundra plains between here and the mainland.
Our people hunted and lived there in that treeless landscape.
They say that, later on, Kalga Jaad hovered in front of an ice field
in the place now known as Skidegate Inlet.

The Xagi Laanas clan found the first tree, a pine, and claimed it as their crest.

Our relatives told of floods and tidal waves in their time and before.
In one instance, they were saved by the rings on King.gii's hat;
in another, the ones who had dogs on their rafts were not upset by the bears;
in another, they found salvation in the mountains of Duu Guusd.

Mosquitoes flourished in brackish waters after a flood and tormented the people
until the Supernaturals sent Sgyam Sgwaan to ease their suffering.

We have a song of the grizzly bear that came down and raised havoc with the people,
even though grizzly bears aren't supposed to exist here.
We also have a story of a young hero who slays a mountain lion near Copper Bay.

This was all myth, of course, comparable to fairytales put together to make some
sense of things ... at least until a few years ago.

The Tibetans, the Egyptians and the Holy Bible also recount the time when the
world was enveloped in twilight. It was neither night nor day.

Science says there was a meteorite strike that threw water and debris into orbit,
causing a crystal fog mantle that prevented direct sunlight and refracted the light
to the far side, where there was no darkness.

As we have known SGuuluu Jaad,
the Egyptians and the Great Inca Empire knew of a god called "Seafoam" in their own languages.

The Hopi recount the emergence of their people from the ground;
indeed, Nang Kilsdlaas stomped his feet and called the different nations from the Earth.

Scientists have now concluded that there was indeed an ice-free and inhabitable corridor
where Hecate Strait now lies,
and while we were clear of the continental icefield, there were local glaciers,
including those in Skidegate Inlet, where Kalga Jaad flew.

Science has come to see that the ice age came to an end much more abruptly than previously thought,
unleashing torrential meltwaters into the mighty plains now covered by Hecate Strait.
The weight of the ice caused the continent to press down,
while the lands on the edges bulged upward.
Upon the retreat of the ice came the reverse,
and the plains between here and the mainland descended into the briny deep.
We can now look beneath the waters at the sea floor and appreciate the havoc unleashed upon our people
as the lands were swallowed—first by the great thaw and then by the sea.

We all know now that, in addition to floods, tsunamis have been and will continue to be a reality of coastal life.

Scientists now know that our people were here before trees;
in fact, they know the precise sequence of the arrival of plants, and that the first tree was, indeed, a pine.

From our West Coast mountains, scientists confirm the finding of grizzly bear bones, as was told in our songs.
They also learned that, in ancient times, many creatures no longer resident roamed these lands.

Science is coming of age,
and while there is a convergence and a reconciliation of Western academia with our histories,
scientists may have to take our word on certain facts.

It was because Raven fooled around with his uncle's wife
that Gaahllns Kun (his uncle) spun his hat and caused the water to rise, accounting for one of the floods.

Scientists are still trying to figure out how the Sun and the Moon got up there, and while they have theories ...
give them time, as the answers are here,

　　　　because it was told....

Adapted from original text published in *Haida Gwaii: Human History and Environment from the Time of the Loon to the Time of the Iron People.* Daryl Fedje and Rolf Mathewes, editors. Vancouver: UBC Press, 2005.

CHAPTER TWO

UPHOLDING THE LAW

WHERE THE HAIDA NATION MAKES IT KNOWN THAT TREATING THE LAND WITH RESPECT IS THE ONLY WAY

HELD SO DEAR

Kalga *Percy Williams* and Kalga Jaad *Verna Williams* present a pendant to Dave Barrett, Premier of British Columbia (1972–1975) at the Skidegate Community Hall.

We are talking today about an area that has been very dear to me personally, all my life. As a very young child I used to go down there with my grandfather. My grandfather owned a trapline in that particular area. As my grandfather passed away, I believe it was in 1938, my dad took over that particular trapline. I remember during the 1930s ... referred to as the hungry thirties ... that we did not know hunger in this area. There was an abundance of food, abundance of seafood. The best food in the world. I still go back there every year at least once a year to enjoy what our Ancestors once enjoyed....

I became Chief Councillor for 12 years, and in this time our people became very concerned ... there was intensive logging going on in the area, and gradually moving into the area that our people held so dear, the South Moresby area.

Now, in this period while I was Chief Councillor, permission was granted to Rayonier Logging at the time, to log Burnaby Island. They presented a logging plan to the Provincial Forest Industry Service, and they granted permission to log Burnaby Island. And our Band Council objected to this.... We took it to the then Premier ... Mr. Barrett. Dave Barrett is a good friend of mine ... Mr. Barrett came to visit the Islands; he enjoyed the beautiful food that we put before him, and he, through his power, got the logging stopped on Burnaby Island. Now, the logging moved to Lyell Island, and I must say that I was very saddened to see logging going on in that area. •

Kalga *Percy Williams,* testifying at the injunction hearings held at the BC Supreme Court, November 1985.

STANDING FOR GWAII HAANAS
Guujaaw

WHEN ITT RAYONIER CANADA LTD. approached BC to log Burnaby Island in 1974, the Islands Protection Committee (later to become the Islands Protection Society), along with Chief Councillor Percy Williams and the Skidegate Band Council, began lobbying the province for protection of Gwaii Haanas. The premier, Dave Barrett, was invited to meet our people and eat with us. As he returned to Victoria, he promised a five-year moratorium on the logging of Burnaby Island, which would only divert the logging to Lyell Island, and gave no protection beyond the five years.

Clear-cut logging and booming grounds in Gwaii Haanas, circa 1980's.

In our estimation, at the rate of logging set by the province, Gwaii Haanas would be logged off in 12 years.

In 1979, Tree Farm Licence 24 was coming up for "replacement." There was no talking to the province, so we challenged them in their own court. At the time, forestry was the key driver of British Columbia's economy and basically operated with impunity. "Aboriginal Rights" was not in the Canadian vocabulary, never mind a consideration of law, and there was virtually no case law for us to build upon.

Our lawyers, who were working for free, had advised that the first hurdle was to get "standing," meaning the right to even take this case before the court. Enthusiastic with our beliefs in protecting the land, and that the logging proposed was just plain wrong, we brought forward the case that the licence had been managed so badly it should not be replaced.

Gid Ḵun, Nathan Young, went in as a Hereditary Chief and trapline holder; Glenn Naylor as a trapline holder; the Islands Protection Society (IPS) as an advocacy and environmental group; and yours truly as a hunter and gatherer. Nathan gave testimony in Haida; Minnie Croft was his sworn translator, a novel case for the courts all around.

Ultimately, the IPS didn't get standing, but it was the first time that a chief and a hunter-gatherer were given standing, and it opened the courts to a new realm of legal challenges. As we opened that door, it was clear, however, that everything was stacked against us from the beginning, and that winning was somewhat of a longshot.

In the first round of hearings, we argued that the phrase "shall be replaceable" meant the BC Crown still had an option to cancel. The Crown argued it meant that after 25 years it "must be replaced," and that our action was premature, as the licence had not been replaced yet. While BC had already given ITT Rayonier the "offer" of a replaceable licence, and our concerns had been ignored, they said there were still a few days left to consider our interests and encouraged a dialogue and reckoning. The Court encouraged the parties to take the remaining days and try to figure this out.

Though our interest was in stopping the replacement of the licence, we did reluctantly negotiate with the province. The Ministry of Forests eventually accepted eight of the 10 provisions we put forward as changes to the licence. Each one of these provisions would loosen the lock the forest industry wielded. But for the most part, it would restore the Crown's ability to manage—which really wasn't our objective.

As expected, the licence was replaced. We went back to court, where, also as expected, the provincial Crown cited the changes we'd negotiated, and the case was dismissed. The Crown then changed the licence back to what it had been before they'd met with us.

We then tried the BC Court of Appeal, which dismissed the case, saying the licence had already been approved and the action was too late. We then went to the Federal Court, which dismissed our case, saying it was a provincial matter.

While this effort didn't stop the logging, it did put the spotlight on Gwaii Haanas, and over the ensuing years, Gwaii Haanas became a celebrated cause ... and ... the logging was stopped, not by the Court, but by the people. •

TREE FARM LICENCE 24, ed.

BC's Ministry of Forests first awarded Tree Farm Licence 24 (TFL 24) in 1958 to Alaska Pine & Cellulose Ltd. as a 21-year licence. Covering 115,521 hectares of Moresby Island, it came with an Annual Allowable Cut (AAC) of 212,376 cubic metres.

Over the years, the Ministry of Forests (MOF) steadily increased the AAC, so that by 1974 it sat at 436,079 cubic metres. Instead of decreasing over 16 years of unsustainable logging, the AAC had more than doubled in size. Alaska Pine & Cellulose, by then known as ITT Rayonier Canada Ltd., presented MOF with a five-year plan to log Burnaby Island. Haida Gwaii began challenging the Province of BC using Canada's legal system.

In 1979 the original TFL 24 expired, and MOF granted ITT Rayonier a 25-year replaceable licence in the area. The following year, ITT Rayonier became Western Forest Products Ltd. It was this logging company and its contractor, Frank Beban Logging Ltd., who would find themselves caught in the middle of one of the most pivotal moments in the history of Haida Rights and Title, environmental stewardship, and relations between First Nations and Canada.

In 1989, the portion of TFL 24 falling within the boundaries of Gwaii Haanas was removed—shrinking the licence by over half its original size, and lowering its AAC by 73 percent. In 1998, the remainder of TFL 24 became TFL 25, Block 6.

UPHOLDING HAIDA LAW
Kilsli Kaji Sting, *Miles Richardson Jr.*

We wanted Canadians and the world to understand that we were standing on
our Title. Haida Gwaii is ours. We weren't protesting;
we were upholding Haida Law.

THE STAND TO PROTECT GWAII HAANAS was a moment of truth for the Haida Nation. The living generation of our ancient Nation inherited one of humankind's great cultural legacies, but after some mere 200-odd years of the relentless forces of colonialism, our very survival as a people was at stake.

Our Elders counselled that waiting for justice from Canada was no longer a viable strategy: extinction as a people is final; if this happened, it wouldn't really matter whose fault it was. We had to act decisively to protect our Nation and our life source: Haida Gwaii.

To get through times like this, one must remember how to listen. An Elder from the Circle of Traditional Elders, upon hearing my lament that we were losing our stories, our ceremonies, our language and our culture, said: "You know, all those stories and songs and ceremonies and language that you're talking about losing, they haven't gone anywhere. They're still in the places your Ancestors found them, in the forest, in the trees, in the winged ones, in the oceans, in the swimmers and in the four-legs. You've just forgotten how to listen. I have one piece of advice for you: before you take another step forward, take a step back and remember how to listen."

These Islands were designated as our place on Earth. The Supernaturals gave us instructions on how to live right, on how to live properly. Some call this the natural law. Central to this was the understanding of our interdependence with all of Creation. We accepted responsibility for stewardship of Haida Gwaii. This understanding, and our acceptance of this responsibility, underpin Haida Hereditary Title. In Western terms, this equates to sovereignty, ownership and jurisdiction.

On Athlii Gwaii, our people stood in unity to reclaim our inherent responsibility for our homeland, and in so doing breathed new life into our Hereditary Title. We understood that if our Title did not continue to exist in us, then it would no longer exist at all.

Since we first encountered newcomers from the European continent, various colonial agents and the emerging nation-state of Canada have consciously and persistently acted to sever our intimate relationship with, and sense of responsibility to, Haida Gwaii. This manifested politically in a denial of our basic humanity as a people and our Title to our homelands.

Our people originally had hope in the promise of Canada—that Canadians were committed to justice through the rule of law and were a fair and compassionate people. The missionaries had assured our people of this, explaining the Royal

> "
>
> We want to go to work. You're blocking a highway, you're breaking the law ... you're stopping us from going to work and we ask you to step aside....
>
> Frank Beban in *Athlii Gwaii: The Line at Lyell*, Ravens and Eagles Productions, 2003

> "
>
> ... Beban returned to the logging camp, about nine kilometers away, saying, "I don't want to have a confrontation. They are my friends. We're not going to cause violence. We won't log as long as they are stopping us." Chief Collinson said, "Frank's my friend. I told him I don't want to confront him, but I have to. He can't go through us now."
>
> Excerpt from The Sun, October 30, 1985

> "
>
> What resulted was the groundbreaking Gwaii Haanas Agreement, which sees this beautiful piece of the world equally managed by the Haida Nation and Canada. Gwaii Haanas did not become a national park. Instead, it became the Gwaii Haanas National Park Reserve and Haida Heritage Site. The word "Reserve" is very important. It acknowledges that Title to these lands is under dispute. "Reserve" means Canada put aside its unwavering declaration of "ownership" of the area. It is not designated a park under Canada or our Nation. But under Haida law, it remains a Haida Heritage Site, acknowledged as such by Canada.
>
> Kilsli Kaji Sting *Miles Richardson Jr.*

Sitting at the table, (L-R) Percy Williams, Jerry Williams, Chief Chee Xial *Miles Richardson Sr.*, President of the Haida Nation Kilsli Kaji Sting *Miles Richardson Jr.*, Ernie Collison, Pansy Collison, Robin Brown and Charles Wesley. Standing, Charlie Bellis (R) with representatives of the Crown.

Proclamation of 1763 and the British Crown's promise that Haida Title could not be altered or shared without our formal consent, which occurs through a treaty with the Crown. From the early colonial period to the establishment of Canada's Parliament, the settler government seemed to be doing the right thing, negotiating treaties across Canada. These were nation-to-nation agreements establishing the terms of coexistence and sharing, or so the Indigenous people thought. Once the settlers reached the Rocky Mountains, in around 1867, their approach changed dramatically.

When Parliament was established, Canada's policy toward Indigenous people became one of assimilation and denial of fundamental human rights, including those purportedly guaranteed by the British Crown. This approach was implemented through the Indian Act, which attempted to herd us into a generic social category as "Indians," and whose stated purpose was to integrate every "Indian," including those with treaties, into the body politic of Canada.

Our sense of identity, culture and responsibility persisted despite centuries-long efforts to extinguish our Nationhood. Our forebears never gave up. At every opportunity they reminded the Crown that, through due process of international and Canadian law, the Haida Nation still held Title to Haida Gwaii.

Our Nation persisted as an ember and burst into flame when the call of our Elders to protect Haida Gwaii sparked our generation's sense of responsibility and the sure knowledge that Haida Title continued to live within us.

The early 1980s was an intense time in Haida Gwaii. Industrial resource extraction was intensifying and set to devour the last intact parts of our territory, putting the ability of our lands and waters to sustain us in serious jeopardy.

Our Elders made it clear that our first responsibility was to protect Haida Gwaii. To accomplish this, our essential strategy had two elements:

1. Lead our people in a dialogue to develop a contemporary Haida Constitution; and,
2. Design and authorize a Haida land use plan that would uphold our stewardship of Haida Gwaii, consistent with our cultural values.

Iljuuwaas *Bill Reid* with Guujaaw and CBC cameraman, Patrick Bell–the last ones on the line at Athlii Gwaii. Patrick Bell filmed the action from day one, covering the stand until the line came down. Another long-standing media person was Susan Underwood.

Because modern states define their sovereignty and jurisdiction through written constitutions, our challenge was to translate our laws from the oral tradition that we had maintained for generations into a codified, written form. Our Constitution would provide us with the framework for modern decision-making based on our Haida vision and values.

With our Constitution in place, our next step was to authorize a Haida land and marine use plan that would uphold our responsible stewardship of Haida Gwaii, consistent with our cultural values. The first iteration of our plan had six key components:

1. Fourteen protected areas, including Gwaii Haanas and Duu Guusd;
2. Forest lands to be managed with ecosystem-based management;
3. A coastal zone where Haidas live;
4. A highway corridor including most of the fee simple land;
5. The offshore; and,
6. Fisheries, which are so essential to Haida life that they deserve their own designation.

In 1981 we passed the first piece of legislation under our constitution, which declared that all of Duu Guusd would be kept in its natural state, in perpetuity. In 1985 we did the same for Gwaii Haanas, which was our first protected area to be contested by Canada and British Columbia (BC).

In our dispute with the Canadian government over Gwaii Haanas, we took a unique approach. Our goals were to:

1. Keep Gwaii Haanas in its natural state in perpetuity; and
2. Get other governments to respect Haida Title to Haida Gwaii.

By approaching our goals in this order, we could more successfully ensure that Gwaii Haanas would be protected. So long as this was achieved, we could continue to work over time to get Canada to respect the supremacy of our Title over our territories. Many other First Nations have approached these goals in the opposite order, and because Canada

President of the Haida Nation, Kilsli Kaji Sting *Miles Richardson Jr.* and Chief Skidegate *Clarence "Dempsey" Collinson* are interviewed on the beach at Athlii Gwaii.

has traditionally stalled or delayed dealing with Title, protection of key lands and territories has been less than fully successful in many cases. Gwaii Haanas was one of the first examples of "interim measures," meant to protect our territories and resources from development as we continue to resolve the Title dispute.

We were in Vancouver for the offshore oil and gas hearings when the BC government informed us they planned to replace logging permits on Athlii Gwaii (also known as Lyell Island). The BC government's Environment and Land Use Committee had agreed to hold off logging there, but was overruled by the BC cabinet.

Our fundamental premise had been to exhaust all due process with the province before putting our bodies on the line to defend Gwaii Haanas. Now we knew we had to live up to our responsibility to protect our life source by going to Athlii Gwaii and stopping the logging ourselves.

Before we left the offshore oil and gas hearings to return home, we held a press conference to announce our plans. When I returned to Haida Gwaii, I didn't know if many people would turn up for our planning meeting, but when I arrived, it was packed with Haidas from across the Islands. Skidegate Chief Councillor Tom Greene Sr. put down $10,000 to support our efforts on behalf of the Skidegate Band Council. Others started pitching in funds too.

In that meeting, we set up 26 committees, including one to build pre-fab shelters for our time in Athlii Gwaii, and others to manage transportation, media, food, fundraising and so on. We also made three simple rules that anyone who was going to participate had to follow:

1. No violence.
2. No drugs or alcohol.
3. Everyone who went there accepted the responsibility of acting as an ambassador for our Nation.

These rules proved key to discipline and success.

We didn't know what would happen. I was apprehensive. I had heard threats and didn't know if Frank Beban, whose logging company had been contracted to log on Athlii Gwaii, had control over his crews. So we only took the strongest young guys on the boats, though later we found that Roberta Olson and my sister, Waneeta Richardson, had stowed away below deck to ensure we were well fed on our voyage.

It was dark when we left the dock in Queen Charlotte. All along the road to Skidegate, people had turned their cars out toward the ocean, flashing their headlights and honking at our boats as we passed by. Not only Haidas were there; people from across the Islands were there, cheering us on. We passed the front of the Skidegate longhouse, where Bill Reid's pole stood, to see the women and all the young children holding little sparklers, singing Haida songs into the radiophone for us as our crew went by. There was nothing more inspiring or empowering than that.

We got to Sedgwick Bay just before daylight. The first thing we did was run up the road to set up our blockade. We set up a wall of boulders in case any of the logging trucks tried to run us. While we were there, the media choppers came flying up. We were relieved they had come to share our story.

This painting by Iljuuwaas *Bill Reid* adorned the cookhouse and accompanied the Elders on the line.

It was a couple of hours before the loggers showed up. We would not let them go to work, so Beban's logging company and Western Forest Products, the permit holder, each applied for an injunction from the court. They named as defendants: me, as the president of the Haida Nation; Chief Skidegate, Clarence Collinson; Gary Russ; Guujaaw; all members of the Haida Nation; John Doe; Jane Doe; and Persons Unknown.

At the BC Supreme Court in Vancouver, I told the judge, Justice Harry McKay, that I would be representing our people. He tried to turn me away and told me to get a lawyer to represent us. I said, "No, Your Honour. I'm speaking for my people. I've read the injunction and these accusations are so serious that we must speak for ourselves."

COUNCIL OF THE HAIDA NATION

P.O. Box 589   4.4.c
Massett
VOT 1M0

June 20, 1985

The Honorable A.J. Brummet
Minister of Lands, Parks and Housing
Province of British Columbia
Parliament Buildings
Victoria   V8V 1X4

Dear Mr. Brummet:

RE: "South Moresby"

Further to our recent series of meetings, we have given very careful consideration to the issues raised during our discussions.

The Council of the Haida Nation is definite in our position for maximum preservation of 'South Moresby'. We cannot tolerate any further compromise of these lands which, as explained to you, are so vital to the sustenance of Haida cultural heritage and are a unique, irreplaceable world resource important to our common heritage.

The Council of the Haida Nation is certain that maximum preservation can be the most politically beneficial position for your government to put forth. We are willing to work with you to ensure that all legitimate interests are properly dealt with.

We look forward to keeping our dialogue open, as it is important to cooperation and progress. We would be available to meet with your cabinet to discuss these important issues. Also, we would be pleased to meet with yourself or the Minister of the Environment, Mr. Pelton, should you visit our islands.

Sincerely,

Miles G. Richardson
President

MGR:slb

We'd brought down 19 of our best speakers to testify. The judge heard from each person—these were some of the most beautiful speeches I've ever heard. Many of our Elders spoke in Haida; Minnie Croft acted as our interpreter. We were in court every day for a week, and every day our story was the first on regional suppertime newscasts and was also featured on the national networks.

By the end of the week, the judge granted the injunction. He was almost apologetic as he read his decision, saying,

"I have listened with care the last few days. I have never—I have been on the bench a good many years and I can tell you that the last few days have been about the roughest that I have ever had on the bench. Sometimes people think that judges have great powers and we can do what we want. Of course, that is not the case. We must act according to law.... I have concluded, however, that on the law which I am sworn to uphold, I have no alternative but to grant the injunctions sought."

We were not given any jail time; he just asked us not to do it again.

Everyone expected us to be upset about losing, but we had just had the best PR you could imagine for a full week, during which the world heard our story. That was the victory. All of the TV stations and the wire services had reporters there. So as it was all unfolding, everybody knew what was going on, and that made the difference.

And we were not going to let an injunction stop us from honouring our responsibility to Haida Gwaii. Industry assumed that after having our hands slapped, we wouldn't go back. We knew that if we disobeyed the judgment, we would be found guilty of contempt of court, with jail time. But our law and decision were clear: "You're not logging there and we're going to stop you."

When we returned home from court, we decided to relocate the blockade to Landrick Creek. Just weeks before, it had suffered another landslide from clear-cutting, and the salmon were blocked from getting upstream to spawn. John Fraser, the Minister of Fisheries and Oceans, had flown over the creek to inspect the damage and was horrified. The Islands Protection Society sued him over the damage. So it made sense that Landrick Creek would be the best location for the next part of our blockade.

That's when our people started getting arrested.

When the loggers arrived, they came right up to us. We went nose to nose, and then we sang our sad song to them. Just as the song ended, we stepped aside as a show of respect to Judge McKay for hearing from each of us for a week. The next day, we went to the blockades and held the line, and that's when the Elders stepped forward. They wanted to stand to defend our Title and weren't worried about being arrested. They stated, "All our lives we've watched our Islands be destroyed and wanted to do something about it. Don't deny us this moment. We've been waiting for this all our lives." Over the next few weeks there were 72 arrests.

The old Skidegate Band Council office was the main organizing headquarters on-Island. Our people and many other Islanders were emptying their freezers and pocketbooks to support our stand. People from across the Islands and beyond wanted to help down in Athlii Gwaii as well, but we explained we wanted Haidas on the line. We wanted Canadians and the world to understand that we were standing on our Title. Haida Gwaii is ours. We weren't protesting; we were upholding Haida law. There were still a few who did join us on the line, at the invitation of our Elders.

We set up an office in Vancouver for fundraising, and hired Lori Davis as our administrator. A lot of environmentalists got deeply involved, like David Suzuki. Activists like John Broadhead, Thom Henley and Paul George had been involved from as far back as the '70s. Even some Canadian politicians, like NDP MPs Jim Fulton and Svend Robinson, got involved. Several musicians, including Pete Seeger and Bruce Cockburn, held benefit concerts on our behalf. The media was key in spreading the word. We gained support from around the world—people were sending letters, money. There were off-Island rallies and, later on, the cross-Canada South Moresby Caravan.

While the blockade continued, the provincial Crown initiated contempt hearings in Prince Rupert. By the time we went to court there were only charges against a handful of our people. Chief Justice Allan McEachern of the BC Supreme Court heard the charges. There was a battery of lawyers in that courtroom, but again I was our spokesman in court against these contempt charges. After hearing from multiple speakers, the judge called all the lawyers and representatives into his chambers. I went in there with my button blanket as our representative. He said he had precedent to lock us in his chambers until we found a solution; then he told us to figure it out, and left us.

The province's lawyer, Jack Giles, lectured our legal defenders about bringing Canada's legal system into disrepute by defending these "obviously illegal actions." I said to him, "Hold on, Mr. Giles. Explain to me in front of your peers how your client assumed Title, how it took my people's Title away by due process of law. If you think your legal process has such integrity, explain that to me." He said, "Come now, Mr. Richardson, you know I can't do that," and that ended our discussion.

When the judge returned, he was disappointed to find we hadn't come to a conclusion. We went back in the courtroom, where he found our Haida defendants guilty of contempt: Colin Richardson, Lawrence Jones, John Yeltatzie, Diane Brown, Willard Wilson, Guujaaw, Roberta Olson, Michael Nicoll Yahgulanaas, Arnie Bellis and Martin Williams. The judge was considering sentences of six months each, but said he'd give us a chance to purge ourselves if we met three conditions:

1. Say we were sorry.
2. Say we would never do this again.
3. Say we would never return to the site of the blockades.

He gave us a week to consider it.

We noticed there were no media observing our case in Prince Rupert, so we asked the Court if we could do the sentencing in Vancouver, on the premise that it would save them travel expenses. The Court agreed. When we arrived at the Vancouver airport, it seemed like every Indigenous person in Vancouver was there,

I would like to speak on behalf of myself, my history. My grandmother used to tell me that one day I would have to take my place in life, and one day I would have to take my uncle's place—hereditary chieftainship is handed down from uncle to nephew ... I am glad to say in my later years that I took my chieftainship. That's who I am ... Hereditary Chief of the Wolf Clan of the Raven Tribe of T'aanuu....

I was a logger, I cut down many trees. I did every little job in the woods. I worked. But in later years, I realized there was no future—there is no future for our people under that system—that we have to preserve our way of life. A continuity of the Haida way is to me, today, more important than anything. So, therefore, I hope that you would consider in passing your judgement that the future generations of the Haida Nation are dependent on this particular area for their subsistence as well as preserving culture.

This, to me, is more important that the short-term logging of old growth ... This particular area is the most beautiful in the country, I have been around ... going to see different countries, but I can't find anything to match this particular area. So I feel it is very important that you give it your deepest consideration in passing judgement on the plight of our people to preserve this particular area."

Chee Xial, *Miles Richardson Sr.*, testifying at the injunction hearings held at the BC Supreme Court, November 1985.

Clear-cut logging in Gwaii Haanas, circa 1985.

singing and drumming. What a welcome!

We got ready that night. I spoke with each of our people facing sentencing and told them they would still have our full support if they decided to purge themselves and forgo jail time. Court the next day was full of lawyers and Aboriginal leaders. Judge McEachern tried to prevent me from being our spokesman, but our other defendants just stood up and said, "He's the president of our Nation, he is our spokesman."

Then he asked if they would agree to his offer to purge themselves. At home, respected Elders Alfred and Rose Davidson had just passed away, and their funeral was happening the following week. I remember John Yeltatzie standing up and saying he needed to go home for his aunty and uncle's funeral, but that he would serve the six months after that.

When it was time for my summation, I asked the same question of Chief Justice McEachern that I asked of Jack Giles. I said, "Your Honour, you're the Chief Justice of the Supreme Court of BC, a respected institution that stands for the rule of law in this country. Please explain, before you send my people to jail, how you and British Columbia, through the due process of the law you're upholding, acquired our Title." I remember Jimmy Gosnell, the Nisga'a leader, describing McEachern's

reaction to this question later, saying that the judge looked this way and that way, up and down, and then jumped up and ran out of the courtroom. He came back about 10 or 15 minutes later and said, "I don't know why you people thought you were going to jail. Sentence suspended." Svend Robinson had joined us on Athlii Gwaii, and had also been charged. He wouldn't apologize to the court, but agreed not to return to the blockade and was fined $750.

The blockades continued until the Christmas break. In the New Year, it was hard to gather people—the boats were getting ready for the herring season, seaplanes were expensive and many of our people had work to do. Then the whole BC forest industry went on strike, and we were relieved. But the International Woodworkers of America (IWA), who always say how much they support Aboriginal Rights, gave Frank Beban Logging Ltd. an exemption to the strike, saying Beban's loggers had been under so much hardship over the past few months that they could continue logging.

We didn't want to go through all the expense of bringing 20 or 30 people down and going through the same thing again. We tried to think of who could get media attention and help mobilize people, and decided to ask Bill Reid. When my father, Miles Richardson Sr., Chief Chee Xial—Bill's chief—phoned him to ask, Bill said "Yes" right away. We took him down to Sedgwick Camp, carried him in his wheelchair up the muddy trail to the road, built him a little fire and put him on a bench. So Bill Reid is sitting there, in the dark of the morning, and of course he's got his jackknife and a piece of yellow cedar. The trucks come up and see some guy in the middle of the road. The boss jumped out, walked up and realized it was Bill Reid. He said, "Oh, Mr. Reid, what are you doing?" Bill replied, "Oh, just whittling." The guy turned around and went back to his truck. All of the trucks turned around and went back to camp and never showed up again. Bill was the last blockader.

After this victory, we wanted to show the loggers in Sandspit and Sedgwick Bay we weren't their enemies. Our relationship with other Islanders had long been very important to us. We wanted to restore trust and camaraderie between our communities, so we invited them to a feast in their honour. People in Skidegate put the feast together and flew it down to Athlii Gwaii. We made the camp beautiful, with tables and firepits amongst our buildings and the trees. Lots of Elders came down, all of our blockaders, and the workers and their families. It was beautiful to see children from both of our communities running around together. It was a very successful way to rebuild trust and community bonds amongst Haidas and other Islanders again.

We all knew logging was over in Gwaii Haanas, but we needed to formalize this through negotiations and an agreement with the Canadian Crown. There was a lot of back and forth between senior officials in the governments of BC and Canada. In order for Canada to strike a deal with us, it had to first strike a deal with BC. In the "Canadian governance" context, the lands in question were considered BC forestry lands.

In the meantime, we began to build a longhouse at Windy Bay, preparing for the possibility of a new stand. Bob Flitton, BC's Deputy Minister of Lands, said, "If

Opposite: Haida gather and organize to establish the line. (L–R) Henry Wilson, Lawrence Jones, Kilsli Kaji Sting *Miles Richardson Jr.*, Colleen Williams, NDP MP Svend Robinson, Oliver Bell, Arnie Bellis and Brad Collinson.

Opposite: The line is established. (L–R) Christopher Collison, Henry Wilson, Martin Williams, Oliver Bell, Lawrence Jones, Brad Collinson, Colleen Williams, Michael Nicoll Yahgulanaas, NDP MP Svend Robinson, Guujaaw.

(L-R) Valerie Jones and LaVerne Davies on the line with Guujaaw and Chief Chee Xial *Miles Richardson Sr.* supporting.

Frank Baker and Tony Pearson.

you start building that house, we'll be on the beach to stop you." I said, "We'll be there Monday morning." Of course, they never showed up, and the RCMP feasted the house-naming with us in their ceremonial red serge.

The negotiations went on and on into the summer of 1987. Canada identified what they thought was a viable plan: to create a national park and a marine park. We told them that we did not want a park. We had legislated Gwaii Haanas in 1985 and simply wanted Canada to recognize this and stay out of our way.

Eventually Canada and BC made some headway—Jim Fulton, NDP MP for Skeena, let us know he got a call directly from Prime Minister Brian Mulroney to ask him, an opposition MP, to move a motion in Parliament to transfer jurisdiction for Gwaii Haanas (under their Canadian law) from the provincial Crown to the federal Crown. It passed with unanimous support. This is one of the few opposition motions in Canadian history to pass with unanimous support.

That summer, *Loo Taas*, Bill Reid's 50-foot war canoe, was making her journey home after living in Vancouver for Expo '86. When she left Vancouver, we didn't know if she was going to land in Skidegate to a big celebration feast or take a war journey down to Athlii Gwaii. As it turned out, Canada called and said they wanted to join the Haida Nation in protecting Gwaii Haanas. On July 11, 1987, the same day *Loo Taas* arrived home in Skidegate, Prime Minister Brian Mulroney and BC's Premier Bill Vander Zalm signed the South Moresby Memorandum of Understanding (MOU) in Victoria. Then federal Environment Minister Tom McMillan helicoptered into the feast held for *Loo Taas* to announce their commitment.

In the MOU, the governments of Canada and British Columbia agreed to stop logging in Gwaii Haanas. A year later, they negotiated the South Moresby Agreement, a bilateral agreement in which the federal government transferred $106 million to BC to compensate for jurisdiction reserved to the province under Canada's Constitution, which then enabled Canada to negotiate a nation-to-nation agreement with the Haida Nation around land use in Gwaii Haanas.

It was a big moment, but while this commitment met our Nation's first objective—to protect Gwaii Haanas—we told them we did not want a national park, as this did not meet our second objective: gaining other governments' respect for Haida Title.

Authorized by our Nation, we entered into negotiations with Canada to see what was possible. At the core of the negotiating team were Guujaaw and Colin Richardson, assisted by Haida Nation counsel Dr. Andrew Thompson.

Though we sat down with Canada, we did not need an agreement with them. We had our Haida Nation legislation in place, designating Gwaii Haanas under Haida Title; we had Haida Gwaii Watchmen managing the area; and we had the unflinching commitment of our people to protect Gwaii Haanas.

Meanwhile, Canada wanted our agreement to establish a park, so they replaced their negotiating team with the Assistant Deputy Minister (ADM) of Justice, Reg Evans. The previous lower-level staffers had been resistant to all of our terms, but the ADM came with a mandate to reach an agreement and a desire to address even

“

I want to stress to you that the Haida people were loggers a long time before we were introduced to modern ways of logging. The Haida people logged the timber that is rightfully ... ours for the purpose of building canoes, which are famous in the whole of the world. My people logged the timber on the Island for the purposes of building houses....

We are very concerned about what is taking place on our Island. It's been stated not only by ourselves, but people coming from the foreign countries, visiting our Island, refer to it as one of the most beautiful countries ... in the world. And this, Kilslaay, has been destroyed right in front of us. We [had] no say in decision making, and we want to be part of this. We want to be part of making decisions on the land that we rightfully own....

We have children, and our children will have children, and when the logging companies come into our Island, they come in there for a short period of time and they take out what they can and they are gone. We are going to be there a long, long time. And we want to protect what is rightfully ours. With this, Kilslaay, I would like to thank you again for giving us this opportunity to present to the courts our feelings about what is rightfully ours.

Chief Iljuwaas *Reynold Russ*, testifying at the injunction hearings held at the BC Supreme Court, November 1985.

the toughest issues. Canada also wanted us to stop charging visitors to enter Gwaii Haanas and offered to pay all our costs in exchange.

In the lead-up to this nation-to-nation agreement, I was on the phone with Prime Minister Brian Mulroney every day, trying to find solutions. I always thought that if Mulroney could have settled the Title question, he would have. But they were afraid of the ramifications of setting a precedent. They said that if they recognized Haida Title, they'd have to do the same for every Indigenous Nation across the country. But I saw a will there to do the right thing, and we took it as far as we could get it at that time—protecting as much of our Islands as we could.

The issues of Title and jurisdiction had halted many negotiations in the past. What we did differently in this case was agree to disagree on these fundamental positions. It served a very useful purpose: mutual recognition. For the first time, the Haida Nation and the nation of Canada recognized each other at an equal level ... even if it was in the form of a disagreement.

Each found the political will to formally acknowledge our fundamental disagreements, then focus on what we do agree on: protecting the natural and cultural values of one of the planet's, and humanity's, greatest treasures. We focused on our common future, and each gave a little to get there.

What resulted was the groundbreaking Gwaii Haanas Agreement, which sees this beautiful piece of the world equally managed by the Haida Nation and Canada. Gwaii Haanas did not become a national park. Instead, it became the Gwaii Haanas National Park Reserve and Haida Heritage Site. The word "Reserve" is very important. It acknowledges that Title to these lands is under dispute. "Reserve" means Canada put aside its unwavering declaration of "ownership" of the area. It is not

With the courtroom full of supporters, defendants were asked to sit in the jury box throughout the proceedings.

designated a park under Canada or our Nation. But under Haida law, it remains a Haida Heritage Site, acknowledged as such by Canada.

The Gwaii Haanas Agreement also set the stage for our Nation and Canada to protect the waters of Gwaii Haanas together. In 2010, this was formalized through the creation of the Gwaii Haanas National Marine Conservation Area Reserve and Haida Heritage Site.

Another legacy of Athlii Gwaii is the Gwaii Trust and Athlii Gwaii Legacy Trust, created from monies committed in the South Moresby Agreement. These funds are locally managed by the Gwaii Trust Society, whose mandate includes furthering "economic diversification and sustainable development," which, for the record, does not preclude logging. The Gwaii Trust was enabled by an unprecedented Island-wide agreement called the Gwaii Trust Accord, whereby Island communities agreed to a Gwaii Trust board composed of 50 percent Haida representatives and 50 percent Island community representatives, chaired by a Council of the Haida Nation-appointed delegate.

Reflecting on it today, I think there's too much "national park" in the management of Gwaii Haanas, even though it's not a park. I want Haidas living down there again. I want Haidas resurrecting our villages and building economies there. But I can put up with it, because Gwaii Haanas is still in its natural state, it's still protected. We can deal with all those other things as we go along.

And just because we protected Gwaii Haanas from industrial resource extraction doesn't mean we cannot, or will not, use the area. This protection ensures the Haida Nation can continue to use our inherent Rights in meaningful ways; can continue to have an economy; and can continue to be who we are. The Gwaii Haanas Agreement isn't about the creation of a static national park; rather, it's a dynamic relationship intended to evolve over time.

Haida use of Gwaii Haanas must be respected in all its forms. This area has always been an integral part of our way of life and being as a Nation. The Gwaii Haanas Agreement was intended as an interim measure to enable our Haida Nation to resume our stewardship responsibility. According to Canadian law, this agreement excludes the forces of industrial resource development from the area.

The stand at Athlii Gwaii, and the Gwaii Haanas Agreement, were transformative moments, not only for the Haida Nation, but for Canada. This experience helps Canada see what a nation-to-nation partnership with First Nations can look like. We just want to be who we are. We want no more attempts at extinguishing our Title, our Nation or our way of life. It is un-Canadian and it's illegal.

That's what we said on the line, and to see Canadians stand by us in this was beautiful. I believe Canadians are good people who appreciate the importance of humans living in harmony with their place. Canadians are beginning to accept the fact that our people's thriving over thousands of years is not an accident and that our culture guides us in achieving robust, advanced economies without destroying the ecosystem—the basis of our lives. Our cultures remain an integral part of who we are as people and as Nations. Our challenge today as Indigenous Nations is to have the faith, vision and courage to be who we are and not have others dictate

"

It was the most moving and powerful moment at Athlii Gwaii ... Ada Yovanovich, Ethel Jones, Watson Pryce and Adolphus Marks sitting peacefully on the line, strong and dignified, defenders of the Haida Nation. Standing in the trees by the side of the road, Colleen Williams' beautiful clear voice and Guujaaw's drum leading us in song, tears of joy and sadness blurring our vision. Allan Wilson, Native Special Constable, in tears as he led the Elders away.

Earlier, after I flew in to Athlii Gwaii, I had gone up in a helicopter and flown over the barren moonscape of Talunkwan Island, devastated by clear-cut logging. Haida leaders said "never again" will our land be desecrated like that.

Weeks later, there was incredible courage and wisdom in the Supreme Court of BC, as one after another, Haida leaders Buddy (Miles Richardson Jr.), Diane Brown, Roberta Olson, Michael Nicoll Yahgulanaas and others spoke out for the land and the people. Diane explaining to her children that she may have to spend time in jail, but that it was to defend their rights and their future. Huge support from across the country for the stand of the Haida Nation, empowering other Indigenous peoples to also stand up for their rights. The birth of a movement of resistance and empowerment. What an incredible privilege to be able to join my voice with those of the Haida Nation, to stand on the line for justice and dignity and respect.

tyaahlGun Gaada *Svend Robinson*

that. Trusting in our culture was an act of faith. Relying on an agreement with Canada is similarly an act of faith: faith that Canada will live up to its promise of justice, fairness and respect for the rule of law. The stand at Athlii Gwaii was as much about pushing Canada to live up to its purported values as it was about this generation of our Nation taking up the responsibility required to maintain our Hereditary Title. •

CHAPTER THREE

ON THE LINE

WHERE HAIDA LAW IS UPHELD BY PEOPLE
STANDING WITH ONE ANOTHER

FOR THE PEOPLE THAT GO THERE

Gwaay guu anhllns *Robert Cross*

John Broadhead Collection

Chief Skidegate *Clarence "Dempsey" Collinson* at the wheel of the *Haida Raider.*

That first day of the Athlii Gwaii stand, we loaded the wood to build the cabins at Sedgwick Bay at the Charlotte dock on the *Haida Raider* and the *Haida Warrior* and sailed it down. We had lots of help, there were a lot of guys from Old Massett. Arnie Bellis, he was one of the bosses. He was very good at bossing people around, good at organizing workforces.

It was quite the experience because everyone lived at Hotsprings while we were building the cabins in Sedgwick. We used to cart them back and forth every day. As soon as we woke up in the morning we would head to Sedgwick. We would work until dark and then head back to Hotsprings. That probably took a good two weeks, building the cabins. Roberta Olson was the cook. She'd cook for, I'd say, at least twenty people, three meals a day. When the accommodations were ready we phoned up to Skidegate and told them they could start sending more people down. So that's when the blockade started.

I used to go down to Gwaii Haanas all the time with Dempsey (Chief Skidegate *Clarence Collinson*). We'd spend all our time at Hotsprings, every spare chance we got. Even before the k'aaw fishery, we used to go down there just to spend two weeks at Hotsprings. Dempsey would take Albert and Lizzie Jones, sometimes Jack and Millie

Pollard. Our first stop would be the Bischofs. We would go in there and dig half a tote box of clams; another tote box would have abalone and scallops in it. We'd spend two or three days at Hotsprings eating all that food. Then we would set gear to get halibut and snappers. We lived good at Hotsprings.

Albert Jones built the first cabin. They used to go down there in the '40s and the '50s. When we got there in 1972, it was already really old. I think it was built in the '50s. Dempsey and some others beachcombed the logs and split the shakes. It's known as Chucky's Cabin today. In 1978 or '79, Dempsey had his built. Rick Goldson and Norm Bentley Sr. were there. All they brought were their tools. We beachcombed the logs and they milled them up and split the shakes right on the beach. Rick, Norm and Alfie Collinson built the little cement pool beside the cabin, where a little spring comes out. The one up on the cliff was built by the Davies boys—Colin, Glenn and Neil.

Dempsey didn't used to like calling it "his" cabin. He said, "It's a Hotsprings cabin." He built it for the people that go there.

IT WAS FOR ALL OF HAIDA GWAII

Ihldiinii, *John Yeltatzie*

WE WERE ALWAYS WATCHING the log barges go out and it was a real sore point for us. One day we were out fishing, just Sid Davidson and me. We were way the hell out by the entrance to Masset Inlet and this barge was coming in. I thought, "I'm going to barricade it!" We trolled back and forth, back and forth until they got real close. It's a narrow channel and the crew was blasting their horn for me to get out of the way, but in truth I had the right of way, they had to go around me. They were just a few feet from me as they went by—their waves pushed me forward and away from the barge—and there were about four guys way up on the bow of the barge, hollering and swearing at me. I thought once I got back to the village the police would come and arrest me, but nope, no one reported it or anything like that.

(L-R) Fred Davis, Mervin Dunn, John Yeltatzie, Martin Williams and Ron Russ link arms as the RCMP advance.

I sat in the very first meeting called to plan for the creation of the Council of the Haida Nation (CHN). That was in 1972. I'd always visited our Elders in their homes, just sit there listening to them. That's why I sat at these meetings, the Elders had faith in me and kept pushing me forward—I knew I had to be there for Haida Gwaii. I sat there listening to Godfrey Kelley, Chief Gaala (Oliver Adams), Lavina Lightbown and all our other Elders who showed up. I was involved from the start—sitting there, listening at every meeting. The first meetings revolved around identifying all the issues we were dealing with. The big challenge was that we needed money. We invited the Old Massett Village Council to a meeting to ask them help in our moving the CHN forward—to help with things like travel money so our chosen leaders could meet with Canada's politicians, things like that.

By the time Lyell Island started in 1985, I was a CHN elected representative for Old Massett and chair of Forestry. Our Nation was still building, and we still struggled with finding money. Everyone paid all their own gas, all their own food, everything, while doing this work for years. No money, no nothing. Just really dedicated people, a bunch of really concerned people. Daphne White and I used to voluntarily hold luncheons for the Elders, we'd go around and pick them up. That's where I got a lot of my power from, from these Elders sitting together and talking about what we were doing, what their objectives were, all the things they wanted to do with the CHN. I always wanted them to be involved; they're our people and their history is ours. That's why I knew who I could go to when we talked about the Elders coming down to Lyell Island. I went to see Naanii Ethel Jones. She knew everything I was talking about. She was well informed and agreed to go right away. Her son Lawrence Jones was standing there listening to us. She turned to him and said, "Get my stuff ready." He went bustling around to get her stuff ready, and I said to him, "By the way, we need a cook. You better get your stuff, too." And he did—he got his things, he didn't hesitate.

One of the things that's real important to say in this story is that we didn't recruit the Elders to throw them on the line. The intention was to have them with us for moral support. But through a lot of talk and deliberation, it was concluded that we had to respect what the Elders wanted. While we were discussing what could possibly happen, Ethel said, "We aren't going to just sit here, we want to help. We can go on the line, too." It took us about eight or nine hours to get that discussion ended. It was in the middle of the night when we finally said, "Okay."

We didn't want any kind of violence. That was the whole point of things, a non-violent blockade. In our strategizing of the roadblock, I'd figured each person was there by their own choice, so how about each person stood on their own, one after the other, along the road all the way to Landrick Creek—the creek that the landslide slid into because of logging. That landslide killed all the fish that were sitting there dead, in front of our eyes. The point of "one person at a time" was that the RCMP and media would have to move down the road to arrest each one of us. Eventually they'd wind up at Landrick Creek and we'd show the rest of the world why that creek was as it was: because of logging.

The cops began arresting everybody. When they got to where the last few of us were standing along the road—myself, Ron Russ, Fred Russ, Martin Williams and Mervin Dunn—I turned and saw there was only one person left to be taken after us. I said, "Everybody, let's lock arms." We all came together and locked arms. We didn't say anything, we just pointed to the creek. When the RCMP started taking us away, they had trouble pulling us apart. Fred wouldn't let go at all. I leaned over to him and said, "You have to let go." He scowled but he did. They were really forcing his arms. Every time they took one of us away we'd hook to the next person, keeping the line.

So that's how the locked arms came to be. Everybody was very worried when we first did it—worried because we were supposed to be non-violent. Maybe the act seemed aggressive at first, because the police had to pull us apart, but it wasn't. That action wound up making everything stronger. It put the pride into our people that we're not going to take that crap, that we had no choice but to make this stand together. Everybody there was by their own choice. They chose that from their heart. Our people have been ready for a couple hundred years, we just needed to get going.

After the arrests, we were in court in Vancouver. My Aunty Rose and Uncle Alfred Davidson had just passed away back home. When the judge asked if anyone was going to purge themselves, I said I had to go back for their funeral but could go to jail after that. The judge said he could throw us in jail, but if he did he felt there would just be a big uproar and repercussions. And there would have been. He was smart in not doing that. He just suspended our sentences and gave out some fines.

Another thing I would like this story to tell is that, when we initiated Lyell Island it wasn't just for Lyell Island, it was for Haida Gwaii, all of Haida Gwaii, not just Gwaii Haanas. Haida Gwaii is the whole thing, not just certain groups of archipelagos. We didn't do it just to save those areas down there, we wanted to make sure that all of Haida Gwaii was looked after. •

Opposite: Injunction papers served by the RCMP are refused and subsequently burned. Sitting are: Kamee *Ethel Jones*, Jaadsangkinghliiyas *Ada Yovanovich* and Chief Gaahlaay *Watson Pryce*.

WE SLEPT LONG ENOUGH

R CMP Officer: If it comes to a point where we have to make some arrests, then we are going to do so with dignity for everybody concerned, okay? We are going to take two people; Allan Wilson [and] Bob Mills will be involved with two of our regular members....

Kamee *Ethel Jones*: So in other words, you won't ... you'll only arrest those of us that are blocking this road?

Officer: Yes, that's right.

Kamee: ... Tomorrow morning, you would not go down to our camp?

Officer: No, I'm not going to go down to your camp.

Kamee: Okay, we don't mind that. I mean, this is our land and, you know, we definitely ain't afraid of going to jail. Definitely

not—maybe that will open the government's eye—look at this old lady sitting in jail, for what? For protecting their land. We slept long enough.

Officer: Well, as I say, I think that ... and it's totally my opinion, I think your message is coming across, and I think everybody out there knows what is happening here. As I say, we want to do it with dignity. That's what I want.

Kamee: Yes, we can understand that. Well, you can surely expect that from us. We would never do anything ... after all, one of our boys is RCMP. You know, we would never shame that.

Kamee *Ethel Jones* in *Athlii Gwaii: The Line at Lyell*, Ravens and Eagles Productions, 2003.

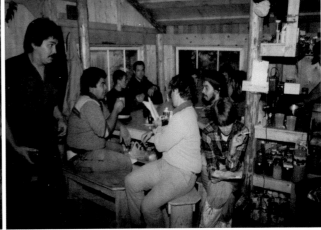

Opposite, clockwise: Loading cedar shakes aboard the *Haida Raider*. (L-R) Steve Samuels and Bert Crosby. • The crew prepping the *Haida Raider*. Al "Partner" Mearns with a halibut to feed the camp. • Materials being readied for loading aboard the *Haida Raider*. • The *Haida Raider* • Colin Richardson, Ernest Davis load trucks to ferry the supplies to the waiting fish boats.

This page, clockwise: The first completed cabin. • In the cabin. (L-R) Lawrence Jones, Miles Richardson Jr., Shelley Hageman, Robert Mills, Michael Nicoll Yahgulanaas, Guujaaw and unidentified. • The work crew. (L-R) Lawrence Jones, Clayton Gladstone, Gary Russ, Mervin Dunn, Steve Samuels, Colin Richardson, Christopher Collison, Miles Richardson Jr., Waneeta Richardson, Ron Russ, Guujaw, Arnie Bellis, Roberta Olson, Robert Cross, John Yeltatzie, Martin Williams, Ernest Davis, Shelley Hageman. • James "Bussy" McGuire splits wood. • The partially finished cabin.

Opposite, clockwise: Assembling on the road. • Heading to the line. Floyd "Sugar" Collinson, Willard Wilson and Colleen Williams. • Logging company owner Frank Beban arrives to serve notice amidst a media scrum, one of many that occurred throughout the stand.

This page, clockwise: The RCMP arrive to manage the site. • A line assembles in the early morning. (L-R) Lawrence Jones, Mervin Dunn, John Yeltatzie, Noel White, Ron Russ, Fred Davis, Andy Edgars, Brad Collinson. • Kathleen Pearson and Shelley Hageman are served. • (L-R) Barry Bell, Bunty Greene, Randy Pryce, Alfie Setso and Floyd "Sugar" Collinson. • Kamee *Ethel Jones*, Jaadsangkinghliiyas *Ada Yovanovich*, **Chief Gaahlaay** *Watson Pryce* and **Giteewans** *Aldophus "Fussy" Marks* at the fire.

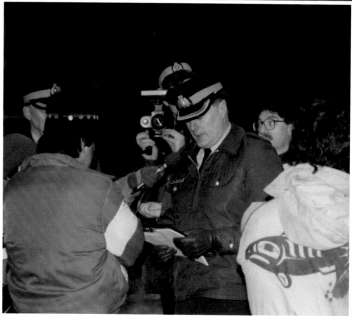

Opposite and clockwise: Dorothy Russ is arrested.
• A Double-headed Eagle blanket. • Tony Greene
• James Young is arrested–Dorothy Russ behind. •
Lawrence Jones is arrested. • RCMP and media on
the line.

Clockwise: Noel White is arrested. • Roy Jones Sr. and
Jackie Hans. • Alfie Setso Jr. is arrested. • John Yeltatzie
is arrested. • Pat Gellerman is arrested.

'3 arrests shameful'

News Services

SANDSPIT — It is a "day of shame for British Columbia."

So said New Democrat MP Svend Robinson after police yesterday broke up a two-week-old blockade by Haida Indians and allowed logging to resume on Lyell Island.

Three Haida riders, one 80 years old, were arrested and charged with mischief.

Some of the 15 protesters had tears in their eyes. Twenty-five RCMP officers had been sent to the island to enforce two B.C. Supreme Court injunctions granted Nov. 8 to Western Forest Products Ltd. and Frank Beban Logging Ltd.

Six officers — including a distressed special Haida constable — approached a barrier the Haidas established Oct. 30 and made the arrests without resistance.

"This is a day of shame for British Columbia when three Haidas are treated as criminals," said Robinson, federal member for Burnaby and a supporter of the Haidas' claim that the logging area is part of their ancestral lands.

After the arrests, other demonstrators pulled back from the barrier and loggers returned to work.

Charged are Watson Price, 80, a hereditary chief, and Ada Yovanovich, 67, both of Skidegate, and Ethel Jones, 65, of Masset.

The three appeared before a justice of the peace in Sandspit and were released. They are to return to court Jan. 29.

Ethel Jones, 65, left, and Ada Yovanovich, 67, are escorted by other Haida following their court appearance on charges of interfering with logging on Lyell Island. —CP photo

Opposite and clockwise: A helicopter brings the arrested Elders from Lyell Island to Sandspit for processing. (L-R) Jaadsangkinghliiyas *Ada Yovanovich*, Kamee *Ethel Jones*, Chief Gaahlaay *Watson Pryce* with Allan Wilson and Diane Brown. • (L-R) Gene Davidson, Jaadsangkinghliiyas *Ada Yovanovich*, Kamee *Ethel Jones*, Lawrence Jones, Allan Wilson with Chief Gaahlaay *Watson Pryce* and Diane Brown.

Clockwise: Chief Skidegate *Dempsey Collinson*; Chief Chee Xial *Miles Richardson Sr.* and Skidegate Band Manager, Willard Wilson. • Jaadsangkinghliiyas *Ada Yovanovich* speaks to the media at Sandspit with Gene Davidson attending. • People gather at the Sandspit Airport to witness the arrival of the Elders from Athlii Gwaii.

Clockwise from top left: Ron Russ, Gene Davidson, Henry Wilson, John Yeltatzie, Colin Richardson, Lawrence Jones, unidentified, Kamee *Ethel Jones*, Jaadsangkinghliiyas *Ada Yovanovich*, Chief Gaahlaay *Watson Pryce* and Giteewans *Adolphus "Fussy" Marks*.

THIS IS WHAT WE CAME FOR
GwaaGanad *Diane Brown*

I AM VERY HAPPY that I stood on the line. As long as I am physically able, I would do it again.

The first time I went down, LaVerne Davies and I were escorts for the Elders. We helicoptered down with them, we landed right on the road: Ada Yovanovich, Watson Pryce, Ethel Jones and Adolphus Marks. Then we were their escorts when they were arrested and shipped back out. I went back again. I went back several times. I was among the first women to get arrested.

I don't know how they did it to this day, the Elders. It was raining and blowing. From the logging road down to the cabins was a really steep incline. There was no trail and it was muddy and slippery. It took us forever to get them down the hill. I wondered about the next day, how the heck are we going to get them up the hill? At this time my dad, Chief Gaahlaay, Watson Pryce, was eighty, and my mom, Ada Yovanovich, was not in the best of health. I was terrified, mainly for Ada. I knew she had a heart condition that was pretty strenuous. It took us ages to get up the hill the next morning. We had to rest a lot.

We got up there, and the loggers and the RCMP came and served us with an injunction. Svend Robinson was there at that time. He interpreted it for us because it was all in legal language. In a nutshell, it meant that if we were there the next day, we would be arrested for breaking the law. We could be in jail for anywhere from six months to two years.

We got calls from the band office in Skidegate through the radiophone. Nathan Young was on the Skidegate side and Ada was down at Sedgwick Bay. They were speaking Haida so the RCMP and loggers couldn't understand what was being said. A group of Elders in Skidegate were asking the Elders in Sedgwick not to be arrested. Adolphus had a heart condition and his heart was acting up, so he had to fly home.

We had been up the whole night before in the cookhouse, all the younger people begging the Elders not to go. It was a real emotional thing for the young men, the young warriors. They were saying, "It's our place to protect the Elders and the children and the women. How do you think it makes us feel to be pushing old people out in front of us?"

I said to my dad, "Dad, did you hear Svend saying we could go to jail for up to two years?" He said, "Yes," and I said, "You are eighty, Dad, what if you don't have two years? Why would you want to spend the last part of your life in jail?" He didn't say anything for a while and then he said, "This is what I came for."

The Elders even arranged which officer would take which Elder once they were arrested. Allan Wilson, he led Ethel Jones. They assigned Bopper (Robert Mills) to Watson. It was very orderly. Watching them, we couldn't find any reason to be upset for how they did it, because they did it with much respect for the Elders. The fact that Allan and Bopper were Haida, it did help.

We tried to stop the Elders but they wouldn't listen. I'm not ashamed to say I cried watching them get led away by the RCMP. After the arrests, we escorted them back to Sandspit where they were fingerprinted. That was fairly painful, the act of watching my father getting fingerprinted, like a criminal, for protecting his land. But they got released quickly, and were able to go to the potlatch that night. Ernie Wilson was taking his chieftainship and the name Niis Wes.

Afterwards, I could see that what they did was amazing. I was extremely proud of their strength and commitment, and the dignity with which they carried themselves. They validated us and gave us strength. They were a huge example to follow; it set the tone for everybody else. None of us wanted it to be a knock-down fight where we were going to force the police to drag us on the ground. The Elders were coaching us nightly to conduct ourselves in a dignified manner.

It changed my dad's life. He went to residential school from age eleven to nineteen. He lost the Haida language in that period. I could ask him any word and he'd know what it was in Haida, but you could not get a sentence out of him, only one word at a time. After Lyell, he started telling me Haida stories, full out in Haida. I started to get my first understanding of our stories and how complex they are. Then he started singing Haida songs. My dad regained pride in his Haida self. That's another thing that I am grateful for. Probably it happened for a lot of people; it certainly happened to me to a degree.

Every Haida person is entrusted with taking care of Haida Gwaii. To have actually done something was quite empowering after a couple hundred years of oppression. •

Chief Gaahlaay *Watson Pryce*, Diane Brown, RCMP Officer, Allan Wilson and Chief Skidegate *Clarence "Dempsey" Collinson* after being processed by the RCMP at Sandspit.

THE LYELL ISLAND DETACHMENT

Kil Naagans *Robert Mills*

FROM January 1984 to January 1986 I was stationed at the Queen Charlotte detachment. At the time I was what they called a "Native Special Constable" with the RCMP. It was difficult being Haida and agreeing with what was going on at Lyell Island, but also being a member of the RCMP and having to enforce the law.

Allan Wilson, who was also a Native Special Constable from the Massett Detachment, and I were asked to take a sergeant from labour relations down to Sedgwick Bay by boat. Being a member of the RCMP, I had a duty to fulfill, so I agreed to it. Before this, I'd never been down to Athlii Gwaii—by water, helicopter or seaplane. I did, however, look at the navigation charts and think, "Okay, I should be able to get there."

As we were launching the boat from Moresby Camp, Colin Richardson was launching his boat. I asked if he was going there, and he said, "Yes."

So I asked, "Do you mind if we follow you? I've never been there." He hesitated, but I think at the same time he knew what it can be like to be on the water and didn't want us to be in any difficulties, so he reluctantly agreed.

RCMP Officer, Robert Mills, at the Lyell Island RCMP Detachment.

We were just heading out on the water when the sergeant asked Allan and me, "Do you guys know where you're going?"

We said, "Yeah, we're going down to Lyell Island."

He asked, "Okay, have you ever been there before?"

I said, "No. Allan, have you been there?"

"No."

So then the sergeant asked, "Well, you did look at the charts, didn't you?"

I thought we'd have a little fun with him. "Well, they're right there. Allan, did you look at the charts?"

"No, but they're right there." So we continue on.

The fellow was looking a little nervous. Colin was awesome. If he got too far ahead, he would throttle back and wait for us. He said we'd be getting into some rough weather just as we rounded the south end of Athlii Gwaii. Sure enough, we hit some really bad weather and couldn't go any farther. There was a guy on fish patrol anchored in a tiny island bay, it was Rob Pettigrew. We tied up next to him for the night. He shared his deer roast dinner with us. We got up the next morning and met up with the RCMP's boat, *MV Pearkes*, coming out of Hotsprings.

Then we headed to Sedgwick Bay. We anchored and went into the Haida camp, where the cabins were being built. A couple were already done; they were making the floors for some others. "We"—as in the RCMP—weren't really sure how to set up at that time. Everybody else was making camp and planning for the long haul, but we weren't ready for that.

At this point, the RCMP was still neutral. We weren't associating with Beban. We weren't associating with the Haidas. Where could we settle to maintain a neutral position? At first we stayed aboard the *MV Pearkes*, anchored out on a log boom. There was myself and Allan, and there was Inspector Harry Wallace from Prince Rupert and a staff sergeant by the name of Len Doyle—two great guys.

Rank has its privileges. The crew stationed on the boat slept in their quarters; Inspector Wallace and Sergeant Doyle got the beds in the aft cabin, and Allan and I slept on the floor in the wheelhouse. There was a shower, there were sleeping bags and pillows, but no foamies to sleep on.

The RCMP realized we were going to be there for a while, so they leased space in Frank Beban's camp. They also barged some police vehicles, some Suburbans, down, as it was quite a walk between the two camps. Beban's was pretty uptown. He had a half-court basketball gym, and a social area with a TV, a pool table and what looked like a small pub in this one building. It was literally a small town. I stayed in the bunkhouse. Inspector Wallace's trailer became like a Lyell Island detachment.

My job at that time was to be a liaison between the Haida down in Sedgewick Bay and the RCMP over in Frank Beban's camp. Every morning, the RCMP would follow the loggers in their crummies and trucks on their way to work. Everyone would stop at what became known as "the line." There'd be cedar boughs across the road, and a line of Haida standing behind that. The Elders sat on makeshift stools, made out of stumps, around a fire in the middle of the road.

The cardboard sign reads, "RCMP Detachment, Lyell Island" and has an outline of the island as a backdrop.

The RCMP was very respectful in that they wouldn't step on, or over, the cedar boughs. I remember Inspector Wallace would say, "Good morning," and speak with whoever was there. Of course, everyone was respectful on the Haida side, too. They would greet the RCMP and say good morning to Frank. At that point, there was no injunction. Frank would say something to the effect of "We want to go to work. You're blocking the road. Please stand aside." He would try that a couple of times; nobody would move.

The loggers made the decision that they were not going to force their way through. They'd just turn around and head back to Frank Beban's camp. There was nothing they could do until they got the injunction, and there was nothing the RCMP could do because it was a peaceful demonstration.

After the injunction was granted, the Elders asked that Allan and I be there to escort them when they were arrested. When I saw Uncle Nathan Young down there, Chief Gid Ḵun, I told Inspector Wallace, "This is part of my Uncle's traditional territory. If he asks the RCMP to leave, I am going to leave. I don't know what the repercussions of that will be, but I need you to know I will have to leave, out of respect for him."

Inspector Wallace, being the gentleman that he is, said, "I understand, Bob, and thank you for telling me that. If that request is made by him, I will make sure that you and Allan can leave."

Inspector Wallace and Staff Sergeant Len Doyle said, "The Haidas are very respectable people, very honourable people. None of them get violent, they don't get verbally abusive." I remember one of them talking to the RCMP's general membership, saying those same words and saying, "We're going to treat the Haidas with respect, because what they're demonstrating to us is respect."

My experience with the loggers was, they just wanted to go to work. I never heard one logger badmouth the Haidas. They were certainly disappointed that they weren't able to go to work. They worried about how long they could stay there; they needed to work. Frank started sending them home to be with their families.

RCMP Officer walking with Chief Gid Ḵun *Nathan Young.*

I didn't really hang out at Beban's camp. We socialized, Allan and I, as much as we could over in Sedgewick Bay, because these were our friends and our relatives. We would sit and visit, have some tea, have a meal. I didn't ever feel tension. Other RCMP would come down once in a while. They'd eat too; the food was way better. Roberta Olson would make them chop wood in exchange. Some evenings, you could tell it was starting to wear on the ones who'd been there for a while. Guujaaw was very good at reading the mood and would start talking about funny situations. Of course, then a song or two would happen and spirits would be lifted.

We were there so long, the RCMP started receiving members from around the Prince Rupert Subdivision to give people breaks. Guys from Terrace, Prince Rupert and Kitimat came over. I don't remember how far east Prince Rupert Subdivision went, but members from all those detachments started cycling through. They'd be brought over for two weeks at a time.

Allan and I didn't rotate much; we were down there a long time. I remember one trip back, I went to a meeting in the old Skidegate Band Office. Some people were uncomfortable with me being there because I was a policeman. I remember someone expressing that, saying, "Look, I feel a little uncomfortable talking about things when we've got one of our own who's a policeman and a part of what's going on down there."

I let them finish and said, "Well, I'd like to say a few words. First and foremost, I'm Haida. I just happen to be a policeman. Law enforcement is what I do for a living. I need you guys to know that I don't tell the RCMP everything. I only tell them enough that they feel comfortable. Whatever is discussed here isn't all reported back."

A couple of others were upset for our roles in the arrests. I said, "Allan and I are down there because our Elders asked for us. They said if they're going to be taken away, they've got to be taken by one of their own." I never arrested anyone and neither did Allan. Inspector Harry Wallace did all the arresting. My and Allan's jobs were to assist with the escort of our Elders and to liaise between the RCMP and our relatives, the Haida.

In January I was sent to Regina for more training because I was promoted from a Native Special Constable to a regular member. Members of our troop went out for dinner and drinks one night, and we caught a cab back to the base. The driver asked where we were from. I told him and he said, "No way! Were you there for Lyell Island?"

I was surprised he was familiar with what was going on. I said, "Yes, I was there before I came here."

He started talking about how awesome the Haida are, how we're going to change things and how he was involved in a fundraiser to help the Haidas out. I thought that was just phenomenal. Here I am in the middle of Canada, in Saskatchewan, and there's a non-Aboriginal raising money for our people to fight what's going on!

I remember one morning on Lyell, we were doing our normal routine —we got up and followed Beban and his crew out to the line. We come around the corner and there was no one there, just the cedar boughs. The loggers get out and they're standing over the line of cedar boughs, but they wouldn't step over it. They look left and right, they look back at us and motion to me. I'm smiling because I think I know what's happened ... the Haidas slept in!

The RCMP were puzzled. "Well, where are they?"

I say, "I'm not sure, maybe they moved the line further up the road. How about I run down and see if there's anybody in camp." I thought I could buy some time for everyone. I went scooting down the path in the dark. There's no light on, so I knock

Michael Nicoll Yahgulanaas and Colin Richardson in conversation with the RCMP.

on the door. Nothing. I knock a little louder and I hear some murmuring inside.

I knock again and I hear "Okay!" Somebody comes to the door. I turn the flashlight on myself so they can see me. "Hey, it's Bopper. Is Guuj here?"

"Uh, yeah, just a minute." Then I hear "Guuj! Guuj! Guuj! It's the cops, it's Bopper."

He opens the door and peeks out with an impish grin. "You caught us sleeping."

I laugh and say, "Oh my God, Guujaaw. They're up there. They're waiting. What do you want me to tell them?"

"Tell them we'll be right up."

I'm laughing and shaking my head while I take my time walking back up the trail. When I get to the top, everyone looks at me. I tell them, "They're coming up, they're right behind me." So everyone's expecting someone to appear within seconds ... which turned into a few minutes. Every once in a while I'd get this look from one of the officers, like "What the heck?"

"Well, they said they were right behind me."

Finally, people started coming up. I got a stern look from an officer because the light went on—he'd figured out what happened.

Athlii Gwaii really brought our Nation together. We stood for something we could no longer tolerate. And I want to commend the people from Old Massett—I was amazed at the amount of Massett people down at Lyell Island. I look at pictures of that time, with people like Lawrence Jones, and I think, "Oh my God, Lawrence, you were just a kid. Look at all these kids!" I was too, I was only 24 at the time.

Vancouver Sun

Athlii Gwaii brought us together and it set the tone for future dealings between our Nation and Canada. It also set the bar for how we, as Haida people, are known for our political will. For me, that's one of the biggest things that came out of Athlii Gwaii—the Haidas' voice in the political world. There are so many things ahead of us. There's so much more we can do if we keep working in that same way together. •

Frank Beban's logging camp at Lyell Island.

THAT'S JUST HOW IT IS

Laadaa *Colin Richardson*

I HAVE A RESPONSIBILITY with the Creator to stand up for Haida
Gwaii and our Nation, to ensure that these Islands are not harmed,
and that activity is done in a sustainable manner consistent with the
laws and values of our people. I was born with that responsibility
and I will die with that responsibility, so I was very focused on why
I was at Athlii Gwaii. I had no concern about breaking Canadian
law. When I stood on the line that morning, I put myself into a
different state. It wasn't just about what was going on at Lyell Island,
it was bigger than that and I had no fear. I was arrested, it was an
emotional day. I didn't like a foreign entity using their authority to
take me against my will.

In 1862, our people were decimated by epidemics, then forced
under colonial rule. By 1985 we were back and we stated it to the
world. It was time to stand up as a Nation and exercise the authority
we have never given up. No one has ever taken this land from us,
no one has ever beat us in a war and we have never signed a treaty.
These islands belong to the Haida Nation and that's just how it is.

There was another reason I went down. My father, Miles Richardson Sr., was Hereditary Raven Chief of T'aanuu and I needed to
support him, front and centre. It was very comforting to have my
father down there, along with my sister Waneeta and my brother,
Miles Jr., our president of the Haida Nation at the time. Having the
Elders and my Haida brothers and sisters down there, and all our
people at home supporting us by sending food, baking, love and
letters—that was crucial to maintain our strength while we did what
we had to do. So now I have a huge extended family called the Haida Nation.

Colin Richardson on the line.

Around 1983 I was hired as the first manager of the Haida Gwaii Watchmen
Program. Back then, my brother Mitch worked in Beban's camp and I used to pop
in to visit, so I knew most of the loggers. During the stand, there was tension on
the loggers' side but it never really got out of hand because the cops were there,
and Frank Beban. I have the greatest respect for Frank Beban. To me, he was a man
of honour. He held a lot of influence over his employees and I believe he instilled
some of that honour in them, that he talked with them, keeping things so they
didn't escalate into violence on their side.

I was willing to do whatever was necessary to be successful in a non-violent
way, but let me tell you, that wasn't my standard operating procedure. It took me
a lot to remain consistent with the direction our leadership, that Athlii Gwaii be a
non-violent stand. It was especially difficult when I'd go up to the road and there
would be 10 or 20 cops with big firearms strapped across their chests. That made
me feel a little rage, but I was able to control it and be gentle and kind, and that
was a new place for me.

I was very encouraged by the presence of the Elders. I felt stronger and more committed. If it was just young people, who knows what the RCMP might have done with all those guns, but when the Elders got there I believe they set a new tone, one that was more of togetherness. We slept in a couple of times and I remember the RCMP would come down and pound on the door, "You better get up, they're coming," meaning the loggers. We became very close with the RCMP and I think that relationship was key to what we were trying to achieve.

Seeing how people came together made this whole event more powerful. But some people couldn't understand what we were trying to do. They couldn't fathom that by shutting down this one logging operation there could be benefits down the road for all Islanders. Things did get ugly with some of these people. There were some nasty, unproductive conversations and terms used that were very harmful. I would suggest racist. I feel a bit different about it today. We've had to work together since then—there's the Gwaii Haanas Agreement, which Guujaaw and I were a part of negotiating, and there's the Gwaii Trust, too. If these Islands are to work well, we need to be inclusive.

One of our biggest opposers during Lyell Island was R.L. Smith, who wrote The Redneck News. But toward the end, before he left us, he'd almost completely changed his mind. He came a long way, he was our friend. There were a lot of people who changed their minds once they understood that what we were doing was not only good for the Haida, but good for everybody else. I was really impressed by the support, it became worldwide. I'd honestly believed other humans just wanted to pave and kill everything in order to bring inner comfort to themselves because they had difficulty dealing with the wilderness. Knowing there were other humans on this Earth that wanted some of what we wanted was very encouraging.

I was a logger back in the day, but I was also very interested in Haida authority over our territory. Not our "traditional" territory, our territory. Athlii Gwaii was a huge win, but that's not to say that we don't want any logging on Haida Gwaii. We want to log in designated areas, using good rules and laws. I stand by the decision I made all those years ago and if called upon, I would do it again. Hopefully we're past that sort of activity now, as we do have agreements and dialogue with Canada, and with British Columbia. A while back I actually worked in concert with the government of BC. That is a huge stretch. I was the Solutions Table Manager for the Council of the Haida Nation and the Natural Resource Manager for BC. It was a great experience to be a part of what these two governments are doing—finding a way to begin an understanding of each other. I think we benefit from this experience, from these two governments labouring through reconciliation. I really support the idea of trying to work together. I'm not talking about ownership, I'm talking about management. Because there is only one owner, and it's the Haida. •

"

I am the youngest Haida warrior here. I speak for my brothers and sisters. We respect the wishes of our Elders to stand first. I stand alone here now, and still there are many more to follow. If the government does not respect our land, we have no choice but to continue our stand.

Ihldiinii *Gene Davidson*

I'M STILL HERE

Ihldiinii *Gene Davidson*

I was walking uptown and they picked me up on the truck saying, "Oh, we're going to protest." They said I'd just be going for one or two days ... I was there for two weeks with one pair of clothes on. It was funny. I had to wear raingear—somebody loaned me their raingear while I washed my clothes.

I think it was John Yeltatzie, Freddy Davis and Lawrence Jones—there was a truck full anyways, and they brought us to Sandspit and we got on the helicopter. We landed right up on the road. I was the escort for the Elders. That's the way they planned it out, they didn't want me to be arrested.

I helped build the sleep shed, because there were so many of us that we couldn't fit in the cookhouse. And we'd march up and down the trail every day to stand on the line.

It was a life-changing thing down there. It just kind of made everybody feel good about each other and what they were doing. I'm hoping that they got funding so they can fix the camp up—it's something to remember—so some people need to go down there and have a look.

I went down on a dive charter a couple of years ago for the CHN. It felt pretty good going back there. My name was on the wall: "Gene Davidson was here." So I put my name under that one: "Gene Davidson still here."

LaVerne Collinson, Gene Davidson and Jaadsangkinghliiyas *Ada Yovanovich* are escorted off the helicopter to be processed by the RCMP after their arrest.

IT WAS ABOUT THE ETHICS OF THE LAND

Xyàhl gùu 'làas *Colleen Williams*

HOW OUR PEOPLE at Lyell Island communicated with the base camp in town was by using our Haida language. Nathan Young would call up to Skidegate from Athlii Gwaii using the VHF radio and speak with Ada Yovanovich. Another Haida speaker was Roy Jones Sr. They did this because everybody could hear what was being said on the radio, so they'd talk in Haida to update on how things were going and to make more plans.

I was down there right from the start, helping build the cabins we were going to live in. We'd always be up late, planning the next day, planning strategy. One time, after they started the arrests, we slept in. The cops and loggers were up on the road waiting for us. Robert Mills, who was a Native Special Constable, came down to check in on us. He asked if we had decided not to blockade that day. We said no, we were going to, but had slept in. He said, "Okay, um, we'll wait for you guys." So, they waited for us. Another time, one of our own was up on the road waiting for us. We'd slept in again and he was waiting so long for us that he fell asleep on a bench. The cops showed up and asked, "What are you doing? Are you the only one here?" Our guy said, "Everybody's still sleeping." So, the cops and loggers waited again. They waited for us twice. We slept in and they woke us up and waited for everybody to go up to the line. That was kind of a cool.

I was arrested in November, but went back and spent many months at Athlii Gwaii, mostly cooking with Roberta Olson. That was the first time I tasted abalone. Fred and Dorothy Russ were there and Fred showed us how to cook it over the fire. We were there until late January; we went home for Christmas then back down to camp. Pat Gellerman and her partner Dave Brock and I were the only ones that stayed down there after a while, keeping camp going just in case.

I think our stand made headlines because we weren't physical about it, we weren't aggressive; and because we were clear what it was about. It wasn't about the loggers, it wasn't about the cops. It wasn't about me, it wasn't about everyone else that got arrested. It was about the ethics of the land and saving it for future generations.

That's what made it so powerful to be there, it was about saving something we believed in. I think it changed almost everyone in one way or another. We became a Nation working together. •

Colleen Williams is arrested.

DETERMINED TO BE THERE

Keenawaii *Roberta Olson*

WE GREW UP always out on the boat with my mom and dad. We used to pull in to Windy Bay quite a bit, and Dad would talk about his best buddy, Clummy (Alfred Moody). Right across the river was Alfred's village site. We'd pick apples at Richardson Inlet in the summertime. It was a pretty island. We'd carry on to Hotsprings, House Island, Pacofi, all those places, gathering food.

I was living at Lyell Island in 1976. My husband, Sam Olson, was the foreman. I remember him coming home complaining about two hippies crawling through the trees to see what the loggers were doing. One of those hippies was Thom Henley, and the other one, I found out, was Guujaaw.

Roberta Olson dances in the camp cookhouse.

I had this favourite beach that I used to get my husband to drop me off at. It was away from the logging, and I would spend all day there with my backpack and food, pick shells up or whatever I was doing. That was my private beach. It was nice, there was a stream with fish in it. I noticed there were no fish in a lot of the streams, mostly logs across them, but that creek was nice. And then one day, all the trees started falling, right near the beach.

My husband was killed before the blockading or any of that started happening. The helicopter went down. So five years later, when I was blockading, a lot of people wondered if I was doing it because of resentment. But that wasn't the case. It was just something that I had to do. I had lived there and I saw what was happening. Sam used to take me for a ride after supper, and he would be marvelling over the big machinery and all the trees gone, and I remember looking out and thinking I just didn't like what I was seeing. It just made sense when everybody decided to shut it down.

There were about fifty people living in that logging camp. They were all my friends, so when I blockaded it was tough. It was like blockading my best friends, but it was something that once you start, you just keep going. Years later they accepted me, finally, but at the beginning it was uncomfortable.

A lot of my family were loggers, so that didn't go too well at first either. Some people couldn't quite understand how we could shut down people's livelihoods, which was huge. But lots of people changed, a whole village changed.

That first morning we blockaded, that's when the loggers realized how serious it was. Frank Beban wanted us to step aside. Nobody said a word and nobody moved. So he walked along, looking at everybody's face. He was quite annoyed. When he came to my face, it was like I stabbed him. His whole face just dropped. You know, I was his best buddy and here I was, one of them, stopping him. But he knew in the end. He said he was sorry, he was in the wrong place, doing the wrong thing at the wrong time.

I was the cook. The villages started sending food. We also gathered food, mussels, clams. Shelley Hageman was always digging clams. That was probably the first time I really realized how important cooking was. When the Elders were arrested, everyone was crying, and I headed back to the cabin and made a big vat of dough and started frying bread. Within half an hour, everybody's laughing, and I realized that it doesn't matter how sad you are—when there's food, people just kind of get happy again.

I didn't really look at it as breaking the law until we started going to court. When the RCMP came to my house, one of my little granddaughters, Erica, heard all this noise outside. She got up and came back with big eyes, saying the police were at my door. I got up and they gave me my summons. I wouldn't take it so they threw it on the floor. There was one at the back door to make sure I didn't run away. While they were standing there, Erica looked at me with her big eyes and said, "Nanaay, are you bad?" So that bothered me more than what a judge would say about me. She was only four and a half. How do you make her understand that I was ... fighting?

I wasn't arrested on the line. I was hand-picked by them. Frank had warned me because he knew there was going to be a select few Haidas, key people, who were going to be charged. The first court case was in Prince Rupert. Buddy (Miles Richardson Jr.) was our spokesperson, he stood up for us. The judge didn't like us one little bit. He sat with his back turned to us through the whole court case, never looked at us once. He's the one that said he was sending us to jail.

We went to Vancouver to be sentenced. When we arrived, there were about a thousand Natives from all over, beating their drums. They shut down the airport to welcome us. That was huge.

I just sort of tuned out the judge. Somebody gave us eagle feathers, and I was fanning myself with the feather, fanning out what he was saying. I guess I was tuned out with the eagle somewhere, because when I came to I realized we weren't going to jail. We were relieved. But if we did go to jail, I had my bottle of cayenne pepper in my purse. That's all I was thinking ... I would spice up jail food.

It was interesting later on because a lot of Haida were afraid of stepping in with Parks Canada, but in the end they realized that's the way it had to go ... working together. But at first, I think it was hard to imagine.

It seems that was the right decision. Memories from Lyell Island bring up a lot of feelings, happy and sad. Yes, I would do it again. •

"

I believe the Haida people should have the opportunity to plan their future before some of the resources that we have claim to are squandered ... I think that Haidas have spoken individually to say that they want their lands to be managed in a better way, and I think that those individuals have also made a clear statement about the trees on Lyell Island, and they have made a decision that they don't want those trees to be cut, and, they have expressed different reasons why they should not be.

You should also consider what the damage would be to us in the event of those trees being lost. How can you compensate us for four-hundred-year-old trees ... we can't get those back in our lifetime.... The damage to Western Forest Products might last over a month ... you can put it in terms of dollars, but those damages will last for our lifetime, so I would say that ours are more important rights.

Russ Jones, testifying at the injunction hearings held at the BC Supreme Court, November 1985.

"

The confrontation between loggers and Haida Indians need never have happened and the courts and the police need never have been dragged into the dispute if only the government faced up to its responsibilities instead of stalling on the issues of wilderness preservation and aboriginal rights.

The Optimist in The Sun, 1985

LOOK AT THAT GUY! HE'S READY TO GO TO JAIL.

Xa'diit Laaygaa *Martin Williams*

WE WERE AT A COUNCIL OF THE HAIDA NATION (CHN) meeting and they were talking about all the logging that was going on at Lyell Island, how bad it was getting. They were looking for volunteers, so a bunch of us decided to go down: Fred Davis, John Yeltatzie, Gene Davidson, Arnie Bellis and a bunch more.

I was down there for the duration. For the first two or three weeks, we were building the cabins at Sedgwick Bay. It was really cold, freezing cold down there. We'd go back to Hotsprings Island every evening. It was nice sitting around in the hot springs. One night it was snowing so hard, everybody was sitting around with snow on top of their heads. Dempsey's (Chief Skidegate, Clarence Collinson) boys, Conrad, Steve, Sugar (Floyd) and Brad Collinson, brought me to all the places they knew to gather food—butter clams, cockles, rock scallops, octopus. Colin Richardson went with us too.

When they started arresting people, there were two RCMP for each person arrested. They took us to the station in Queen Charlotte City. There were eight or nine of us that had been arrested; we wouldn't give them our names. They said they would let us out of jail if we promised not to go back down there, but we wouldn't do that. Eventually they let us go, and we went

Michael Nicoll Yahgulanaas and sister Shelley Hageman sit with Martin Williams in the camp bunkhouse.

to one of the dinners in Skidegate. They were held regularly for us to meet and inform people on what was happening at Lyell Island. During dinner, somebody announced there was another boat heading back down, so three or four of us jumped back on the boat.

Eventually, there were twelve of us charged. I guess they called us the "ringleaders" or something, because we were always in the cop pictures. Court was held in Prince Rupert and everybody else was in there but Arnie Bellis and me—we didn't know we were supposed to be there! Then we got word the judge was going to serve a bench warrant for us if we weren't in court by noon. So, they sent a plane down to Lyell Island and flew us to Queen Charlotte City. We jumped off that plane, got on another plane to Prince Rupert and made it with 10 minutes to spare.

We were found guilty. For sentencing, we had to go to the Supreme Court of BC, in Vancouver. The day of sentencing I didn't know if we were going to jail or not, so I packed my bag right into court with me. Ernie Collison happened to be talking to some reporters just as we were walking in. He said, "See, look at that guy! He's ready to go to jail." We could have got up to two years in jail, that's what they said. But after it was all said and done, they said it would never show up on our records.

I'm glad there is no more logging down there. It's a pretty nice place, and I made good friends with many of our Skidegate brothers and sisters. I knew a lot of them from going to CHN meetings. Even when I was in my teens, I went to CHN meetings. Athlii Gwaii really pulled us together, that whole episode. •

THAT'S WHAT I SAW IN TOWN

Skihl.hlgangaa *Ronald "Rollie" Williams*

When the Athlii Gwaii stand started we went around to every house in Old Massett with trucks to gather food. People would be following us in their cars, bringing things like fresh-baked bread and buns. Some people didn't have anything, but they still gave something. They'd give two jars of fish, saying, "This is I all I have." But when we were done going through the village, we had 19 pallets of food. That's how much the Haida people wanted it to happen.

My brother Martin Williams went down for our family. I was going, but he said, "No, you stay. I'll represent our family." I was just starting off with a young family and he didn't want me getting in trouble yet. I remember when he was going to court he said, "Well, I've got to make sure I have clothes and smokes, and maybe six pairs of underwear." He had it packed all nice, then said, "Agh, I might have to go. So, bro, you take care...." They didn't know what to expect. In those days, they just used to throw you in jail.

Later on, Fussy (Adolphus Marks) used to always come around to our Naanii Marjory Williams' house because they were so close. They'd sit there and have tea and he'd talk about Athlii Gwaii and how well they got treated down there, even by the loggers and RCMP. He said there was nothing bad stated. "We understand what you guys are doing"—that's what he told us the loggers said.

I worked with loggers in Port Clements all my life. I liked them even 30 years ago, when I worked for the Marie Lake Hatchery (aka, King Creek Hatchery). I didn't experience any conflict, they just said, "That's your guys' right." There was lots of support from the non-Native community. They helped gather food and did other things too, like loading gear on the *Haida Warrior* and the other boats. They'd bring cakes and cookies. It was happy going; everyone worked together. That's what I saw in town. •

Supplies arrive from Old Massett and Skidegate via floatplanes, skiffs, and fishing boats: Chief Skidegate *Clarence "Dempsey" Collinson's Haida Warrior* and *Haida Raider* and Roy Jones Jr.'s *Haida Spirit*.

WANTING TO CRY, TOO
Daphne White

EVERYBODY WAS ALWAYS TALKING about the over-logging, seeing those barges going out all the time. When we were staying at Fussy's (Adolphus Marks) house, one of the barges was going out. Ralph Stocker, he jumped onto ... I think it was a little dugout or something. He jumped on and he was challenging the barge while it was heading out. I went running down the beach. I had a camera and I got pictures of him challenging the barge. I think that was the first action against all that logging.

They finally had a meeting and decided to go and shut down the logging. After that I went to a million meetings. The day they first went down to Lyell Island, we went to Charlotte. Their guys were loading up the boats, getting everything ready. Sandra Dan, Bobby Collison and I, we volunteered to go shopping. We made up a list and we separated it into three parts, went into City Centre Store and started doing the shopping. There were boxes and boxes of things. It was going on Hallowe'en, so we threw in a whole bunch of candy for the guys. We almost forgot the slanjaaw. We were already outside when all of a sudden I remembered, "We didn't get slanjaaw!" We had to run back in, we were still right by the store, luckily.

Later on, I would just give what I could. I would bake stuff and send it down, like bread or pies. I'd send them down in boxes. People had grocery drives. We gave cans of food, jarred foods, whatever we had; everybody pitched in. It was a pretty emotional time.

There was lots of news on the TV about it, so we'd all watch the news. I

remember I was up at my sister Rosie's. My mom, Rita White, was there when the news came on. Someone said, "There's Noel!" We saw my brother Noel on the news. I think he was getting arrested. My mom was pretty proud of him, but we were all standing around in the room wanting to cry, too.

They were planning to go down—my mom, Rosie and one of my other sisters, Nora. They were going to head down but that's when Eugene Samuels passed away, my sister Nora's husband. He had been really excited to go down. He was a logger and had some time off, so he was going to go down with them. They were all just waiting for him to get home. He was on his way home. •

Eugene Samuels belonged to the Kwii Un-glis Yahgu Laanaas Raven clan, the son of Reuben and Lillian Samuels. His siblings were Archie, Russell, Thomas, Audrey, Rosita, Gladys and Johnny. He passed away on November 18, 1985, survived by his wife, Nora; their four children, Steve, Ross, Lloyd and Cynthia; and his two toddler granddaughters, Beverly and Tarah, whom he doted on.

Eugene was always involved in Old Massett and Haida Nation business. He was a fisherman, logger, Chief Council-lor, Village Councillor, Band Manager, Council of the Haida Nation (CHN) representative and alternate. He believed in the CHN and knew that talking to his children about it was important, that they knew their history and what needed to be done. Eugene was deeply involved in strategizing and planning for the blockade with many others, and was looking forward to getting down to Athlii Gwaii. His son Steve helped set up camp.

Opposite: There were many public meetings to organize, inform, and receive direction from citizens of the Haida Nation.

Top: Skidegate Band Manager, Willard Wilson speaking.

Bottom: Ernie Collison speaking, with Tom Greene Sr. on the right.

THE LOGGERS' FEAST
Kuuyaa *Jeffrey Gibbs*

THE HAIDA DECIDED to use all their stockpiles of food on a feast for the loggers and their families on Athlii Gwaii. Before dawn the next morning, everyone made their way to the logging road. Ethel Jones, Diane Brown and Tom Greene Sr. stood close together in the middle of the road, blocking it, facing where the logging trucks would soon appear. The rest of us stood on the sides of the road and sang Haida songs as Guujaaw drummed. Soon the rumble of the approaching convoy of logging trucks could be heard.

The logging trucks came to a halt in front of the blockade, and what must have been the foreman walked up to the line. The look on his face seemed to express the sentiment of "Oh my gosh, here we go again—round two of the Haida blockade." Diane, Ethel and Tom stepped forward and said to him, "We would like to invite you and your men and their families to this feast we are having tonight at our camp." The foreman seemed completely taken aback and genuinely moved by the invitation. He said, "Yeah, thank you, we will be there!" So Ethel, Diane and Tom cleared off the road and the loggers continued on to work.

We spent the entire day preparing the feast. In the late afternoon there was a long line of logging company trucks parked at the trailhead leading to the Haidas' camp. A tremendous feast began. Miles Richardson Jr., President of the Haida Nation, welcomed the loggers and told them that the conflict was not with them personally, but with the governments. He said that the feast was to bid them

Top left: Logging company pickups parked at the trail head.

Above: Marianne Jones leads a procession of ladies dancing the food to be shared at the loggers' feast.

Opposite left: Chief tlajang nang kingaas *Claude Davidson* with a guest at the feast.

Opposite right: A large table was constructed and set with a feast of food sent down from Skidegate as well as foods collected from around Athlii Gwaii.

All photos: Jeffrey Gibbs

"

I felt for the loggers. We weren't fighting them, we were fighting the government—that was the enemy. Caught in between were these normal, everyday people just like us. Just trying to make a living for their family, but caught in this huge event that changed a lot of things. So I can't say we all jumped up and danced for joy when they turned back and went away from the line. I believe we were respectful to them, and they were to us, too.

GwaaGanad *Diane Brown*, 2011.

farewell from Athlii Gwaii. After everyone started eating, the tension dissipated and the button blankets and logging jackets were all intermingling—the loggers and the Haidas were actually having a meal together and talking! I thought this was the most enlightened thing ever. It was a real gesture of compassion, diplomacy and reconciliation. •

PASSION TO BE HAIDA
Adiitsii Jaad *Marni York*

I'M FROM OLD MASSETT AND WAS 22 when the Lyell Island blockade went on. Uncle Paul Pearson came through the door, saying, "They need people. They're arresting Haidas." We looked at each other and started packing; we were down at the seaplane base in an hour.

There were seven of us cousins in Prince Rupert that responded to the call to support Athlii Gwaii that day. We flew directly from Rupert to Athlii Gwaii. That evening there was drumming and singing in the cookhouse; all this laughter, all of this sense of camaraderie. It was such strong emotion. It was just so powerful, the sense of community that happened!

They were asking for volunteers to get arrested the next day, but because we'd just arrived from Prince Rupert, we wanted to stick around a bit longer and share some more of the goodness that was happening in camp, so none of us put our hands up. The next morning we stood on the protest line. The strategy was to slow the RCMP down as they started their arrests. My cousins were lined up in front of me and then—what the heck—they were getting arrested! So I thought, if they're getting arrested, then I'm getting arrested, too!

There was media there, and the cameras came right in front. They were so close, like, a foot away from me. And the cop was right in front of me ... all I remember hearing is the legal stuff. "Step aside or you will be arrested." The RCMP brought us to the bun wagon, but they didn't put any handcuffs on us. Then they brought us to this big garage, it must have been where they repaired the logging equipment. I felt like a real sitting duck there. I felt very vulnerable because we didn't know what was next. But then I remembered the night before: we were all very emotional because we were defending our Island, defending our way. The Elders said we have to conduct ourselves as Haidas, to hold our head up and walk strong and walk proud. We could not be physical or violent. We were going to conduct ourselves as Haidas.

The RCMP flew us out with the Sikorsky Coast Guard helicopter to the Queen Charlotte City jail. When we landed, Uncle Paul came bounding over and gave us all a hug. That was pretty emotional, too, because my cousins and I were arrested together. We stuck together, our family. We might have been in the jail an hour or so. Not too long, just for processing.

Athlii Gwaii united a lot of people. It took a lot; it was a major undertaking. It was the first call, right? It was the first time in modern history anybody had an opportunity to defend our place. The war cry was made. And responding was so emotional. Defending our homeland. Defending our place. It could have easily turned into violence. So when the Elders said how to conduct ourselves, it was much appreciated.

There was so much support from the people in the community that didn't go down to Athlii Gwaii. If you asked people to stand up in our community hall– anybody that baked a loaf of bread, sent a case of orange juice or food, lent a skiff

The solitary figure of Marni York stands on the line.

or any other gear—if you asked people to stand up if they contributed, that would be a good visual. And I'm sure the Old Massett Church Army was praying for us, sending prayers.

There were quite a few non-Haidas that supported us. I remember the South Moresby Caravan, the train raising awareness and getting our plight out onto the news hour—that was much appreciated. And there are still a lot of people that don't appreciate the practice of logging that continues. People want to keep our Island pristine—they appreciate it like we do. The former Mayor of Port Clements, Gerry Johnson, he was a logger. He was quite a figure. When I saw him working with the Haida Nation years later, that was a good example of the movement coming full circle.

I had an opportunity to meet some loggers through tree planting. They were falling trees right alongside me planting trees. They're just people trying to earn a living. We have loggers in our own communities, too. We have the resources here; we just have to do it in a less destructive manner. It's the actual practice of logging that's the challenge. Now our Nation has Taan Forest, but it's still a challenge. We're still exporting our logs raw, we're still clear-cutting, maybe in smaller patches, but that needs to change. The irony is definitely there. So we still have a lot of work to do, which is okay. It's non-stop, as a thriving culture should be.

We all feel grateful for Athlii Gwaii. I feel lucky that I was able to contribute. I've been feeling pretty fortunate to have heard the call and been able to respond. Since then, I've been to almost all the CHN meetings on policy, our Constitution and the formation of what we have today. Being part of that, I feel pretty fortunate. It's influenced me to have that passion and emotion to be a Haida, and to help other people find that passion and that emotion. •

The media was in full attendance and followed the story over many months.

YOU ARE A STRONG HAIDA WOMAN

Gidadguudsliiyas *Kim Goetzinger*

THERE WERE MEETINGS about the logging, and people started getting arrested on Athlii Gwaii; I remember a newsletter going out, and some bumper stickers that said, "The Haidas Are Coming." They were neon. I just loved them, everything we wore was neon back then. I stuck mine on my bedroom wall and looked at it every day. One day I woke up, looked at my sticker, and decided I wanted to go.

My mom, Ada Yovanovich, had gone down and been arrested. She said to me, "You shouldn't go because of your job, you are young, don't get arrested." I'd grown up with my mom always fighting for women's rights, for First Nations' Rights and environmental rights, so there was no question I was going to Athlii Gwaii. I won't say how old I was then, because Percy Crosby will find out how old I am now, but I was underage, I will tell you that much.

I didn't get arrested right away; I hung around to help around camp—I didn't really know what I was doing, I'd just felt that urgency to go. Every night there was singing; Guujaaw would go several songs with the group. I didn't sing, it was just not something I did. But the day I got arrested all those songs came to me and I sang away. It was quite nerve-racking, standing on the line. I was a kid and I didn't know what was going to happen to me, but I knew in my heart that what I was doing was the right thing.

We were flown out on the Sikorsky to Sandspit, then trucked over to the police station in Queen Charlotte. I'd never spent time in jail. They put all the women in one cell. Rose Russ thought we should carve our names in the bunk; I'm so sorry now that I didn't do it. My sister Diane Brown was demanding a meal. Apparently, you are supposed to get a meal when you're in jail, so she was putting her order in for Chinese food and coffee. It was a bit of a gong show, just hilarious. We were laughing so hard in there, but it was so emotional that we were crying, too. I can't imagine being in jail with a better group of women. Whether it's language, culture or environment, when you get a bunch of us women together and we all feel the same, you feel like you can move mountains. That's what we were going to do.

There was an RCMP officer who was a good friend of mine. He was very upset to see me in jail, visibly upset. It was hard on everyone—we're such a small community. An example of how the police were back then is, one time I wanted a convertible, so a bunch of us girls cut the roof off my Pontiac Prism four-door with a chainsaw. There were all these jagged edges, but we were just so thrilled to have a convertible! Somehow the police got wind of it. One came down and said, "You aren't driving that." We argued with him, "Well, we just spent eight hours doing this, you can't take our coolness away." He said, "Okay, I'll let you girls drive around once, but I have to lead you through town." So, we drove around town in my new convertible, but nobody was out! Nobody saw the work we put into my car. But the officer had let us drive it around, at least. That's how it was back then, so it was tough for them, too. It was tough on everyone, there were a lot of tears.

But there was no question as to why we were there. Nobody was blaming

Kim Goetzinger performs a cartwheel on the beach near camp.

anybody. No one wanted anything bad to happen to Frank Beban or to anyone. I don't think some people realized that until later. There was tension for a few years afterward. I'd become a truck driver, picking up and delivering freight to different places on-Island, including logging camps close to town. Sometimes people would say, "You guys killed logging," or say stupid things about Haidas, or call us "environmentalists." I would just do my job and leave. You knew you had to leave; you knew you weren't going to stay overnight in Port Clements for Loggers Day anymore. We all used to go to Loggers Day.

There's still some of that left over, but mostly, everybody pulled together and survived. Nobody that wants to be here is going to go anywhere else. If you talk to a non-Haida about any threat to these Islands they will jump right on board, where before it was a bit of a kafuffle.

My family, we were "Bill-C31 Indians"—my mom lost her Status because she married my dad, Bill Yovanovich Sr., who was non-Status. We couldn't live in Skidegate because "non-Status Indians" couldn't live on Reserve. We couldn't have our traditional foods. Every year Diane would bring my mom k'aaw, and we'd be so happy. Mom would hang it out to dry so we could save some for winter. As soon as she hung it, Department of Fisheries and Oceans (DFO) would show up to confiscate it. We would see this pain every

(L-R) Diane Brown and Barbara "Babs" Stevens leave the RCMP Queen Charlotte Detachment after being proccessed for their arrest. Babs, Diane, and Willard Wilson oversaw the administration and organization of the Athlii Gwaii stand out of the Skidegate Band Council office.

k'aaw season—she'd be fighting DFO on the porch, saying her daughter gave it to her. It was like Monday night movies for us! We would sit there and watch her go to town on the officers. She would blast them, saying, "This is Haida territory," and that they were visitors, they should be working with us. They'd go skittering off, down the hill, scared shitless of her. Nothing ever came of it; I don't remember her ever getting charged.

All the non-Status stuff didn't really bother us because Mom always drilled it in that we were strong Haida people, that it didn't matter if we had a Status number or not. Sometimes we were treated badly by people, not often. My mom was so strong that if you tried to complain about things, she would just say, "Ahh, don't even listen to that crap." We were lucky that we didn't feel too broken by the ridiculousness of "Status/non-Status Indians," but were always very conscious about that sort of stuff.

I feel Athlii Gwaii solidified where I belong. I will never, ever forget Skilay, Ernie Collison. I felt so connected to him, like he was my very own blood. Ernie, Guujaaw, Michael Nicoll Yahgulanaas, Buddy (Miles Richardson Jr.), they all had that ability to bring people together ... they just had this wonderful way of making you feel included down there, that everything that you did helped.

"It's so easy to make someone's day," is one of my favourite sayings. Skilay was like that, Guujaaw is like that, Michael Nicoll … it was so easy for them to make your day, whether they stood there with the drum, or hugged you, or just empowered you with Haida Gwaii love, regardless of what your "numbers" or "blood tests" were.

I clung on to the experience of Athlii Gwaii for a long time, I still do when shit hits the fan in my life. That's the one thing I'm just so proud of, not that I was arrested and acquitted (the courts thought I was too young, they thought I'd been influenced). That wasn't the big hoopla for me. It was that I went, and that I was made to feel so comfortable. No one saw me as a "non-Status Indian." You felt Haida, you were Haida. We were included; that was Ernie and the others' doing. They made everyone so welcome that you couldn't help but feel powerful. There were people who just sobbed with connection.

Keeping the memory of that time alive is key. We cannot forget the fight that people did for us—for myself, for the Bill C-31 people; for Haida women in particular; and, for Gwaii Haanas. We can't forget any fights that have come up. We have to keep it going; keep protecting Haida Gwaii on every level. Not just the trees, not just the air, not just the ocean. We have to protect our culture, our language and the people that want to be here. We've got lots to do, lots to protect. Lots to stand up for. We have to hold each other together. That's the magic of staying in one place forever: nobody forgets a damn thing.

I try to go down there every year now. When you go by the village sites and see the monumental poles and longhouse pits left untouched, that is a legacy to me. Athlii Gwaii created a sense of belonging on all levels. I still draw strength from that experience no matter what I am doing, whether giving birth to my daughter or trying to bike up a steep hill, or whatever. That phrase, "You are a strong Haida woman," keeps me going.

All humans are like that—you can forget dates and times, details, but you never forget how someone made you feel. •

Rose Russ leaves the RCMP office followed by Merle Williams.

BE CAREFUL AND DON'T SWEAR

Yaahl Kuunang *Christopher Collison*

Christopher Collison on the road with an eagle given to the Haida Nation by the Nuu-chah-nulth people.

I'M THINKING THAT there are a few events in my life that have defined me as a Haida person. Making a stand for Athlii Gwaii, that's one of those times. Making a stand for your Island, making a stand for your people, making a stand for something you believe in.

I was 22 at the time. It was then and there that I truly began my journey as a Haida person, in understanding that this is what I need to do. At the time, there were some offshore oil panels going on in Skidegate, it was a pretty big deal. We had a break in the afternoon, so I went up to Charlotte. There was a lot of activity at the government dock, so I went down to see what was going on. A bunch of our people were loading a seine boat with lumber and all kinds of supplics, so I asked them what they were doing. One of them said, "Well, we're going to go pick a fight. You want to come with us?" I said yes, and went home to pack up my camping gear. I told my mom, Jocelyn Allen, what was going on. I told her, "I don't know how long I'm going to be gone, but I'm going to be down in South Moresby protesting logging." She said, "Just be careful and don't swear."

When we first started getting arrested, you wouldn't believe how many cops were down there, and, there were about seven or eight paddy wagons. The RCMP were thinking we were going to start a fight; that we weren't going to go peacefully. They'd come up to us and hand us papers—we had our arms folded and would let them fall to the ground. We had a fire in the middle of the road, so after the RCMP took a couple of steps back, we picked the papers up and threw them in the fire. One of the most emotional days we had was when our Naaniis and Tsiniis were arrested. It was pretty hard to watch my Naanii Ethel Jones, and yet I knew she was strong enough to handle anything. After that, our emotions were set aside and we were prepared to go to jail. We weren't prepared to take anything less. We had no idea if anything was going to be okay, but the Elders' reassurance, and their presence, made everything cool. It gave us this assurance that we were doing the right thing.

When I got arrested, they sent me over to Prince Rupert to stand in front of a judge for my civil disobedience. I introduced myself and he introduced the charges against me. A minute later he said, "The charges are stayed, you're free to go, Mr. Collison." So that was it—no jail time, no nothing.

Our president, Miles Richardson Jr., told us that each and every one of us would make our own decision as to whether or not we were going to get arrested; that we should do what was right for each of us. One night, we were all speaking to the idea of losing our property and assets. We stayed up until five or six in the morning talking about what would happen if we lost this, if we lost that.... We slept in! Everybody slept in! At about eight o'clock in the morning we heard a knock on the door. One of the RCMP came down and said, "They're waiting for you!" So we all hopped into our clothes, ran up to the road and stood on the line like we were there all morning. No one had crossed the line while they were waiting for us. The RCMP, the loggers, they didn't try to cross the line until we stood there, so, we stepped aside and let them pass. They symbolically didn't cross the line and we symbolically stepped aside.

My sons, when they were young, we were going for a walk and they kept asking, "Where are we going, Dad? Where are we going, Dad?" I told them, "It's not where we're going, it's our journey there." And it's the same thing with our Nation—the lead up to Lyell Island, then getting down there, building our cabins, getting ourselves set up for our stand, going to court, that's our journey. Even the aftermath, Gwaii Haanas, Gwaii Trust, and the work that's going on today that's not our destination, it's a part of our journey. We're still battling for Haida Gwaii. We always will. •

(L-R) Martin Williams, Henry Wilson and Christopher Collison hold the line. Kilsli Kaji Sting *Miles Richardson Jr.* and Arnie Bellis in the back speaking with loggers.

BE WHO YOU ARE
S<u>G</u>aa-nn Kida Leeyga *Reg Wesley*

ATHLII GWAII WAS LIKE FATE FOR ME. I was born in Skidegate, but the system took me away when I was little. When I was old enough, I started coming back home. I didn't know anybody, I was there to figure out who my family was. Then Lyell Island started up. I listened to what our Elders were saying and jumped right in with both feet. There were so many of us down there, I think almost every family in Skidegate and Old Massett was represented. Everyone bonded instantly. My father, Si (Simon) Wesley was from Cumshewa and that is my tie to being Haida. I'm not from the Cumshewa clan, but I was representing my father and the Wesley side of my family; I was being Haida. If I represent my mother's side, I'm being Gitxsan. We need to be who we are and be proud of it. Be Haida. Be Tsimshian. Be Gitxsan. Be Nisga'a. Be who you are.

Reg Wesley (bottom right) took part in paddling the *Loo Taas* home to Haida Gwaii from Vancouver in 1987. Seen here with Guujaaw.

Before Athlii Gwaii, religion was a tough subject for me because of what our people went through with residential school and the church. It's a real struggle—the world might know about what happened to us, but they also might not understand it. Our people live with the impacts of this history every day. I think making up for what was done is going to take a century or more. People were hurt; we almost lost our language; most of our culture was shut down. I was struggling back then because I believe in God, but also know what was done to our people. You can't justify what the church did, what Canada did. The ones that bring us out of these situations are people like Ada Yovanovich. I asked her, "Didn't our people believe in God?" and she told me that when she says "Haawa Sah 'Laana," she's saying, "Thank you Creator." And that stuck with me. We say "Creator," the church says "God." We're saying the same thing. She taught us a lot of things. She wasn't afraid to say what she thought and she didn't say it behind closed doors. That's a transparency few can copy, but Ada had that from day one. I hold my hat up to Ada.

When I got arrested they tried to make me sign some papers, but I wasn't going to sign anything just because they told me to. I said, "You arrested me, you can sign those papers." I felt great satisfaction in saying that. Our stand was so embedded in me that I felt like a solid rock. The choice to say "yes" or "no" was mine. Their choice was to keep me or let me go. I think it was the justice of the peace who signed the papers so they could kick me out of their jail.

I paddled on *Loo Taas* when she travelled up the coast from Vancouver to Haida

Gwaii in 1987. I'd been living in Vancouver and had gone to visit Bill Reid's studio. People there knew me because of the time I was at Lyell Island. Someone said, "Reg, we need you to paddle this canoe back to Haida Gwaii." I'd just left there, but they said they needed me. I thought, "Okay, let's do this." During our trip, some of the seas were four- or five-foot chops, even six-footers or more—these big waves were coming at our bow and we'd battle it out. It was amazing, the canoe held up beautifully.

We all talked about whether we were going to head home to Skidegate or down to Lyell Island. We had a lot of time to think because the trip was 21 days—we got to stop at lots of other Nations' villages along the way. We decided if Canada didn't stop their logging, we'd beeline it to Windy Bay. There was big media coverage on our canoe trip almost every day, so we planned to take the media there with us. But in the end, Canada and BC decided to agree with us on the logging. So we paddled into Skidegate and *Loo Taas'* homecoming feast became an even bigger celebration.

I went from the extreme experience of Athlii Gwaii to the extreme experience of *Loo Taas*. Both brought me back home—my bond with my father's side was forever ingrained and everybody knew who I was. I was Reg Wesley, son to Si Wesley. My father was proud of me. I knew I loved home, that Haida Gwaii is the greatest place in the world. Sah 'Laana was part of that, bringing me to that point. I've since been brought into the St'langng 7laanaas, so I have a clan on Haida Gwaii, too. My name is SGaa-nn Kida Leeyga, it means Killer Whale Carver.

Nothing pleases me more than knowing the next generation is going to have a better time moving forward than we did. But what's on my mind now is, why is Canada attacking our salmon? Things are changing, but liquid natural gas, pipelines and tankers are still a threat to our whole coast. I feel Canada is targeting our food source. Why else would they put those fish farms everywhere, attacking native salmon populations with Atlantic salmon? They could farm them out of the water, but they don't. Canada probably understands that. I can see what's going on.

I can live on all that Haida Gwaii offers. Without it, I am nothing. Just like my art—it's nothing without the culture. Our culture comes from Haida Gwaii. We've always been a Nation but Athlii Gwaii made us stronger. We've come a long way from having been pushed so far down. The heroes of today will be the ones that will stop the disruption of our food source. Our Nation is not going to go lay down and let this happen. That's not how we do it. •

I FOLLOWED MY CHIEF

id taawgan *Mervin Dunn*

PEOPLE IN SKIDEGATE, where I'm from, they call me Chop-Chop. It's a nickname meaning "unruly one," or "unruly hair." I was adopted in 1958 by a family from Quesnel, BC, and went back to Haida Gwaii as an adult, wanting to know my background as a Haida.

I was down in Athlii Gwaii from Day One. My main influence was Chief Dempsey (Clarence) Collinson—he told me what was going on, where he was going. I remember saying, "Well, I guess I'm going with you." He smiled and said, "Ho-ho, houy-houy, Chop-Chop." I followed my gut and my Chief. That's how much respect I had for him, and my birthplace. I loved him and I love Haida Gwaii. It was the best decision I ever made.

Getting prepared was really exciting, I could feel everyone's adrenaline. My great-uncle Nathan Young, Hereditary Chief of the T'aanuu Eagle Clan, once told me never forget where I come from. "Your people are from SGang Gwaay," he told me. That made me realize this roadblock was more than just a roadblock. These two Chiefs inspired my commitment to being a Haida Gwaii Watchmen Warrior. People like Miles Richardson Jr. and Guujaaw also influenced me. Listening to them, and others, made it easy for me to join in. Fantastic leadership.

Mervin Dunn in the bunk house at Athlii Gwaii.

One time everyone wanted a well-deserved break to Hotsprings. There was a request for someone to watch the camp, so I volunteered. It was totally dark by four o'clock. By eleven o'clock, I was hearing noises. Not having been on Haida Gwaii that often, being alone on Athlii Gwaii was kind of a spooky thing. I went to investigate and lo and behold, two huge sea lions were fighting. They fought all night, I didn't sleep.

Early in the morning, I went up to the road. Frank Beban showed up with his loggers and asked if he could go by. Our people had agreed that when we were on the line we would say nothing. I found that interesting, because for me it connected us as one. So I stood my ground and said nothing. Beban talked about the weather for a while, but he knew I was standing firm. He turned around and said, "Let's go boys." I got back to camp just as everyone got back from Hotsprings and told them what had happened.

Another time, we were told the RCMP were looking for us, so a few of us went into the forest. The cops were out of their element, so it was kind of fun playing hide-and-seek with them.

The first time I was arrested, a Massett Haida and I had locked arms. His name was Joey Parnell. It took several cops to separate us. We were put on the Sikorsky Coast Guard helicopter, flown to Queen Charlotte City and then taken to jail for processing. When we landed, a large group of Haida Elders were waiting for us. Behind them, more Haidas were welcoming us, cheering us. That was overwhelming. Remembering that brings a lump to my throat.

While we were getting processed, I had to promise to not go back to Athlii Gwaii. When I got out, we went to Skidegate to stock up on supplies and found some more Haidas to go back down with us. That's when I got arrested a second time. I was advised not to, but being a stubborn Haida, I did.

All those involved felt a bond. We were there for the same reason, and that commitment made us all who and what we are today. Haida. Watchmen. Warriors. Protecting our homeland showed there's no rivalry in our villages. Standing side by side, this made us stronger. We felt kinship with our crew, and with people around the country. The world was watching over our battle in Athlii Gwaii—I think that put many of us in awe.

When we went to court, my great-uncle Nathan lent me his button blanket; it was very old and it made me more at ease. For me, it represented our connection, bonding us as one with each other, and with the other Haida Watchmen. The proceedings were peculiar. They showed a video of Noel White and said it was me. To the dismay of their lawyers, I stood up with my ID and said, "Kilslaay, I'm Mervin Dunn." I wasn't surprised when my case and Noel's were automatically dismissed, because I was a court worker for three years. I knew that because they mixed up our names, we would be dismissed.

The legacy of Athlii Gwaii is thriving and strong. Many are gone now, but will be remembered as Watchmen—our battle was won with their commitment and dedication. Now, over 30 years later, our people have other challenges. But Athlii Gwaii will always remind me that our Nation is very strong and resilient. We not only stopped logging in Gwaii Haanas, we know that this stand will always be important to our people, that this work has been instilled in our young Haida, our future leaders, who will protect our beloved Haida Gwaii.

I feel blessed with my name, id taawgan. It means "stand beside/with us." I will love and cherish the memories of Athlii Gwaii, instilled so long ago. I was and will always be id taawgan. •

THAT'S WHAT WE'RE BROUGHT INTO THIS WORLD FOR

Yahldaajii *Gary Russ Sr.*

I went to Athlii Gwaii with Chief Skidegate (Clarence Collinson) on the first trip down. I brought a power saw I'd found on a logging road to make a clearing for the cabins to be built and to cut firewood. On our first day, October 30, we went and did a cursory road-block; Buddy (Miles Richardson Jr.), myself, Guujaaw; there was a handful of us.

I spent a few days falling trees and helping build cabins. We needed someone to drive people back and forth from Skidegate to the Moresby Camp, that's where people would catch a boat down to Athlii Gwaii. I had a chauffer's license so they shipped me back into town to do the driving. I kept a record of every crew that went down.

Athlii Gwaii was my first political action as a Haida. I'd lived away, I went to Residential school. After that I lived in Prince Rupert. I was one of the fortunate ones, because I was in grade ten when I was sent away. I was old enough to fend for myself, but it was still an interesting

Supplies were rowed ashore throughout the stand.

three years of my life. I can't imagine being pulled away from your parents at four or five years of age and pushed into one of those establishments. The first thing they'd do was shave your head. It was demeaning. Our children were abused physically, mentally and sexually. When they were deemed old enough to be responsible for themselves, they'd be pushed back out into the world and be told to go act like real people. Cultural genocide, that's what they call the Residential school now. The problem is, most of Canada's general population are still not aware of the history between Natives and non-Natives. Most don't know that Aboriginal people owned and occupied 100% of what's called Canada; that Canada moved in and pushed us aside. So why should we be silent?

Athlii Gwaii made me conscious of my Haida heritage and everything I'd been taught by my grandmother and parents when I was young. Before our stand, I didn't give much thought to being Haida or Canadian. In my mind I was a Canadian, and somewhere in that Canadian-ness I was a Haida. But after I moved home and began getting politically involved, I changed my mind. I decided I was a Haida and somewhere, lurking in the background, was my Canadian-ness. After the blockade, nine of us renounced our Canadian citizenship. I wrote to the Canadian government. Their response to me was that I had to pay…I think it was $35, and I had to move away. How the hell could I move "away?" This is our land. So that was the end of that, and I've been involved in politics ever since, including the formation of the Gwaii Trust and later sitting as a board member; and serving on the Council of the Haida Nation and Skidegate Band Council.

Athlii Gwaii was one of the most important, interesting and profound things that I have done in my life. That, and being a part of the *Loo Taas* journey. She was paddled from Vancouver, up the coast and over to Haida Gwaii in summer of 1987. There were paddlers from Skidegate, Old Massett and Hydaburg. I joined in on the paddling at Port Hardy. From Bella Bella on I was a steersman. When we left Bella Bella, our support boat, the *Ivanhoe*, broke down. We kept paddling and it was midnight when they caught up to us. We were about an hour from Klemtu, so we continued paddling. It was about 13 hours in total. Three of those paddlers were women—Nathalie Stevens, Nika Collison and a lady from Masset, Audra Collison.

When we were in Hartley Bay, ready to cross the Hecate Strait, we didn't know if we were going to Skidegate or down to Lyell Island. It depended on what Canada was going to decide about the logging. We paddled across and waited it out for a night in Grey Bay. As it turned out, Canada decided to agree with us about protecting Gwaii Haanas. We paddled up to Skidegate and had a big feast at the George Brown Rec. Centre, celebrating *Loo Taas'* homecoming. Tom McMillan, Canada's Minister of the Environment, helicoptered in to make their announcement at the feast.

A lot of media were following both *Loo Taas* and our battle over Gwaii Haanas. The blockade was over, but we kept our presence down there, ready for another stand if needed. I think that moment of everyone wondering where *Loo Taas* would go strengthened our Nation's stance. If we weren't threatening to end up at Lyell Island, it might have been a different scenario. I think *Loo Taas* helped Canada and BC become a little more amenable and receptive to what we wanted.

What our Nation was shooting for was cessation of all logging in Gwaii Haanas, and that's what was accomplished. On paper the Gwaii Haanas Agreement looks okay, it's a step in the right direction. But I don't think it goes far enough. At the end of the day, Haida Gwaii is Haida territory. I guess you can say we won the skirmish, that Canada's attitude changed briefly enough that it was willing to compromise its position on "ownership," but we're still at battle. There's a lot more that needs to be addressed.

I am glad I moved home and re-connected with being Haida. I love being here, I enjoy my life. I have my grandchildren—a grandchild is the most beautiful thing in this whole world. I think that's what we are brought into this world for: to have our grandchildren, to appreciate and love them. To protect them. •

WE'RE THINKING OF BOTH SIDES

Giteewans *Adolphus "Fussy" Marks*: I'm here to support my younger generation that's here now, and we have good reason to be here because we're thinking of our new generation to come....And it's not only for us, it's for the White man's new generation to come, too. What are they going to make money on when they strip the Island ... could you answer that question?

Reporter: What do you think the answer is?

Giteewans: The answer is, we're thinking of the both sides ...We're protecting this, our Island, so the future generations [can] live off it too ...We were here thousands and thousands of years before anybody stepped on this Island besides the Haidas. From Cape St. James right to North Island and Rose Spit, there were villages right clean around this whole Island. That's why I'm here. The government didn't make this Island. No way.

Reporter: Can you tell us, what is your name?

Giteewans: My name is Adolphus Marks .... But the people know me here as Fussy Marks. I'm not fussy, but I'm fussy today.

Reporter: Why are you fussy today?

Giteewans: Well, we're trying to protect our Island, that's why.

Giteewans *Adolphus "Fussy" Marks* in *Athlii Gwaii: The Line at Lyell*, Ravens and Eagles Productions, 2003.

WE ARE DOING IT
Captain Gold

I GREW UP WITH MY DAD'S GENERATION, they were my buddies. I fished all over Haida Gwaii with my dad, listening to his stories. When we'd get storm-bound, the fishermen would fleet up—tie their boats together like a raft and set several anchors in a sheltered bay. Then they'd start telling stories. I grew up with this, so these oral histories have a very strong presence in my life.

Then I went logging. It was 1959 and I was 16. I worked in different camps until around 1971, but was dissatisfied with how logging was being done—I saw all kinds of crap. I quit and went seining instead. During that time, I lost a good friend of mine—Pat McGuire—so I was pretty unhappy. I went to Alaska for work but didn't like it so I came back home and went into the logging industry again. I wound up working 20-hour days. I lasted just over five weeks then I jumped on a plane to Vancouver. I was drinking and partying, but finally said "to heck with it" and quit. I never went to a bar or nightclub again. I started hiking around Vancouver to get to know it a little better and ran into my childhood sweetheart, Bernice Dixon. She was also from Haida Gwaii. She caught my eye as she stepped off the bus while I was walking around Vancouver. It was a nice surprise. We wound up having a cup of coffee together. Even though she had to go to work, we sat together for a long time. We wound up meeting each other again years later and getting married at SGang Gwaay, in front of the poles. As we walked toward the preacher and my mother-in-law Louisa Dixon, we could feel the Ancestors walking with us.

When I was still hiking around Vancouver I started thinking, "What the heck am I doing logging?" I quit for good and ordered a canoe; I think that was in 1973. I paddled all the way down to SGang Gwaay, that's about 100 miles one way. My only next-door neighbour was the lighthouse keeper at Cape St. James. I was 15 miles away, so I had a good time down there all by myself. I lived off the land. I had rice, coffee, drink mixes like Freshie, different things like that, but otherwise I fished and harvested shellfish. I packed a gun with me too, to hunt deer.

Leading up to the Athlii Gwaii stand, Huck (Thom Henley) asked what I'd do to save Gwaii Haanas. I was as concerned with our old village sites as I was with the logging because some off-Island people were taking our Ancestors' remains as the burials became exposed from the elements. I was worried about the poles, long-houses and other cultural remnants, too. I said we need to create a series of camps manned by our people, to regulate and manage the tourist traffic, to look after the old villages and answer questions on our history and culture. Huck really enjoyed that idea. He'd worked with some people to find money to start the Haida Gwaii Rediscovery Program in Lepas Bay, so he knew how to find monies. Skidegate Band Council was on board—they administered the monies and managed the program. And that's how the Haida Gwaii Watchmen program (HGW) got going. It wasn't a lot of money, but there was some to help start it up. People volunteered to live down there; volunteered their boats, too.

Before that, Wesley Pearson would ask for details about my summers in SGang Gwaay. I'd tell him everything I could, then he'd tease me, "I was just about to get a group together, to go down and capture you and bring you back home." When the HGW got going, Wes signed up right away. At end of season I turned the tables on him and said, "I was just about to get a group together, to go down and capture you and bring you back home." He just said, "My babe and I sure love it down there."

He and his wife Bubby (Marjorie Pearson) lived their summers at Windy Bay for years. They made a real reputation for the place—tourists loved visiting them. Whenever I present on the history of the program I always honour them and the other Elders too. Quite a few spent their summers down there for years: Caroline and Charles Wesley lived at Skedans; Chief Git Kun (Johnny Williams), the Eagle Chief of T'aanuu (who succeeded Nathan Young), lived there and at Windy Bay. I also honour Dempsey (Clarence) Collison, his wife Irene and their kids for taking care of Hotsprings for years before and after the HGW started. Bernice and I spent our years at SGang Gwaay. I honour these people because they're the ones who created the reputation of the HGW, who made it such a

Standing aside to let the loggers go to work.

success in those early years. In a lot of ways, the HGW has become a model for other programs across Canada and other parts of the world, just like the Council of the Haida Nation is a model for many, and how Gwaii Haanas is managed. People like to come and learn how we do it.

I was involved in the start of a lot of things during those early years, at the foundation of many programs and initiatives: the designation of SGang Gwaay as a UNESCO World Heritage Site; the Haida Gwaii Watchmen program; I was part of the archaeology program that Simon Fraser University (SFU) got going; and later made conservation and archaeology training programs for our people down in Gwaii Haanas. I don't know how many took part in them, but I bet you it's well over a hundred. I enjoyed it all, it was an exciting time.

It was in 1974 that I got involved in archaeology. Pearle Pearson was Skidegate Band Council's (SBC) chief councillor at the time. She called me up because the

SFU field school came to her wanting someone interested in archaeology to be their guide in South Moresby, as it was called then. Pearle knew I'd been canoeing in the region and knew I was interested in archaeology. I ended up going all over the east coast of Gwaii Haanas with SFU, recording hundreds of old sites. One of the best memories out of that trip was finding a village Solomon Wilson had talked about. He was chief of the K̲aay'ahl Laanas group. He said, "No matter how hard the wind blows in this village, the smoke goes straight up." I wondered how that could be. When I was down there with SFU I came across the village! It's real close to Cape St. James, exposed to the southeast wind. There were about eight houses that used to stand there and a big bluff behind. Having the bluff there means when the wind blows in, it can't go through the village. A back-pressure is created and the smoke goes straight up. When I got back home I visited Sol and pulled out a map, describing the location and explaining what happened with the smoke. He was very happy.

I brought this information to Joe Tulip, an old fisherman. He was so interested I couldn't get over it. He had a high interest in archaeology so I got him on the next SFU trip. He was so happy to be going out to the west coast, visiting all these different places and doing all this archaeology recording. He loved the whole experience and talked about it for years. We shared lots of our stories with the group. Our oral histories and the archaeology information started coming together in my head and a germ of an idea began. I started producing a report for myself, combining archaeology with some of our oral histories to see how old these stories could be. The earliest one I could think of would be the moving of Tow Hill because there's a detailed account in the old stories told by an earlier Captain Gold to James Deans. I went on to match more of our stories with archaeological findings and made a report for the Haida Gwaii Museum named The Golden Years. I later published it as a book.

There've been a lot more discoveries since that SFU trip. One was when our SFU team came across a couple of ancient village sites located above sea level, but we didn't have the funding to expand our program so we stuck to the "above high tide line" areas and found a lot of amazing things there: lithic scatter, old fish posts and so on. Parks Canada archaeologist Daryl Fedje started coming up in the '90s. He did a lot of work in areas above the shore line and he also found more villages located higher than our current sea level. In later years, Parks wanted to install a gas cache in a certain place, but I had remembered surveying the area. Bernice and I went there to do some looking around and it was just rich with lithic scatter and middens. I called up Daryl and we excavated a few places. We came up with all kinds of exciting tools and different things. Some date back eleven thousand or thirteen thousand years. It turned out to be one of the oldest sites at the time.

I started thinking, if the water was once higher, it might also have been once lower than sea level. A really exciting discovery was in 1980, when I wanted to compare sea level changes over millennia with our oral histories. I mapped out the lower sea levels using a marine chart and our oral histories, connecting the dots every 10 fathoms. Sure enough it showed that at one point there was no Hecate Strait—the waters were so low there was only a river going between us and the mainland. Daryl looked at the map and listened. We figured we knew where some of the villages must have been given the lay of the land ... and he was able to pull up a 12,000-year-old tool from the middle of the Hecate Strait. We were lucky there was a lot of oral history knowledge and growing access to archaeological information. All of us piecing it together—all of us working together.

When Athlii Gwaii started up I was designated the official recorder, so I was down there the whole time. I even had my birthday down there. Willard Wilson was Skidegate Band manager at the time, he gave me 12 rolls of film to take photos and I did some tape recording too. There was high activity going on—clearing the land and building houses. There was the cook house; the Honeymoon Shack, a bunkhouse for couples; and the Snake Pit, which was the main bunkhouse. We had all these things ready when the injunction against our blockade was granted by the courts. I went up on the line with some others the next day, but the loggers never showed up. A few hours later a chopper landed right in front of us on the logging road and four Elders stepped out—Ethel Jones, Ada Yovanovich, Watson Pryce and Fussy (Adolphus Marks).

Everybody cheered and in no time we had a little shelter built, a fire going and a place for them to sit. We all sat there sharing stories. We spent the evening trying our best to talk the Elders out of getting arrested the next day. We wanted them to be our advisors, but they wanted to get arrested first. They said the world would see what was going on and that it would create a big stir. Diane Brown's words for her father Watson Pryce, who was set on going, were, "I'm letting him go with much love." It helped us understand.

We had a lot of great times down there even though our people were facing two years in jail. There'd be lots of talk about having to leave families behind; how old the kids would be when the jail sentences were over; the criminal records and all of that. But we were all ready to go. That was our commitment.

In the end, it turned out in our favour. I always say that Lyell Island taught us how to stand up again. After that, we had to re-learn how to walk and even run—meaning managing our lands and waters in modern times. And we are doing it: managing forestry, fisheries, Gwaii Haanas, the Watchmen, all of that. We are doing it. •

IT MAKES IT ALL WORTHWHILE

Gwaay guu anhlaans *Arnie Bellis*

THE STORY OF ATHLII GWAII is not just about the blockade, or even Gwaii Haanas. The story is also about the commitment and sacrifice that the people made to bring us to where we are now. A huge amount of energy, cooperation and resources were required; all the people who went down there, all the organizers in town, all the food and money donated.

A big part of the success of Lyell Island was the relationship between our Haida men and women. Our functions from the past still play a role today—when there's a potlatch, people know what to do; when there's a death, people know what to do. This was along the same lines. What made it so strong was the cooperation between our people.

I was a Council of the Haida Nation regional representative when Athlii Gwaii began, and part of the first group that went down to build the camp. I stayed down there the whole time, helping oversee the building of the camp and maintaining it. Quite a few carpenters went down to get that camp set up. It was a hard-working crew. The women down there—Shelley Hageman, Waneeta Richardson, Colleen Williams, Roberta Olson—they were very determined; everyone had to work hard to keep up to them.

All the material we collected to build the cabins at Lyell Island, it was by donation from the people. Dempsey (Chief Skidegate, Clarence Collinson) and Roy Jones Jr. donated the use of their fishing boats. I was on Roy Jones Jr.'s boat when we went down to get camp ready. It was very rough out, like rough rough. He lost a brand new herring punt—never did recover it.

If you went to Lyell Island, it was made very clear to everybody that nobody was to pressure you to go up to the line. That was a choice only you made. If you didn't decide to go up to the line, people would never question you. Working in the camp was just as important. Chopping firewood, food gathering, getting water, keeping the camp clean, making sure people were fed and kept warm. People had to do all those things. There was lots of hard work to do.

Sometimes we were feeding about 70 people down there. People sent all their food down to Lyell Island, emptied their cupboards. By Christmas there was no food in Old Massett or Skidegate, period. Haidas from Prince Rupert and Vancouver were sending stuff over, too.

The other thing that sticks out is that everything else had to keep going on, too. During that time there were some big losses. Alfred and Rose Davidson passed on, and Eugene Samuels. The Native Brotherhood held a convention in Old Massett for about a week, and there was Ernie Wilson's chieftainship potlatch in Skidegate. All this while we were down there. Our villages kept everything going; people didn't let off for a minute. And somebody had to pay the bills at home. While we were all running around, somebody had to look after the kids and look after the home front. Those people were our spouses. I think about that, it wasn't just three or four months, it was months.

Our first day on the blockade was a pretty challenging moment. We didn't have anything personal against the loggers—it was the methodology of logging that was the problem. They're family men, they've got kids, Christmas was just around the corner. We also have a lot of fellas that log, so we made it very clear that we weren't against them personally. We didn't want it perceived that way, and we didn't want to have any trouble, either. Frank Beban himself was a pretty good guy that way. He didn't want to have violence or anything that like.

When we went to Prince Rupert for court, the judge said if we apologize and say we're not going down to Lyell Island again, he'd let us free. We came back home and had a public meeting in Old Massett. My dad, Charlie Bellis, got up and said, "Somebody's gotta go to jail," so that was it. None of us were going to apologize for going anywhere on Haida Gwaii. It's our Island. So away we went to Vancouver to be sentenced. We were packed up and ready to go to jail for two years. The determination had been made to represent ourselves, because nobody else could tell our story but us. He was a real hard old judge, Judge McEachern. But in the end he said, "I don't know what made you guys think you're going to jail."

Travelling from Gaw *Old Massett* to Moresby Camp prior to heading for Athlii Gwaii From left: Frank Parnell, Arnie Bellis, NDP MP Svend Robinson, Gene Davidson, Oliver Bell and Henry Wilson.

My dad had taken us out for supper the night before, because we thought we were going to jail: $850 for supper! So now, no jail—he wanted his money back. We had a good laugh.

But I guess my story wouldn't be finished if I didn't tell one about Ernie Collison. He was my best friend. His task was to organize up in the Massett end, organize rides and get food down, handle the logistics—Ernie, Frank Collison and May Russ. We couldn't function without people doing those things, too. One time, Ernie came down to Athlii Gwaii. There's a road about three or four miles long, and at the end is a pretty steep hill, where the landslide went into Landrick Creek. Ernie finally gets to the top, and he's looking down at it when a reporter asks him, "So are you telling me that loggers put these big logs in this salmon-bearing stream?" Ernie looks at him, puffing away, and there just so happened to be a big cut in this one spruce—a big, white-faced spruce stump. Ernie looks at it, and he says, "You see that one there. Does it look like a beaver did that?" So we called Ernie "Leave it to Beaver" after that.

Years later, I went back down to Gwaii Haanas. There was Cindy Boyko and myself, I can't remember who else. There were thousands of porpoises around; it was just beautiful. This was the first time I went down after the blockade. Over thirty years later ... I mean, goodness, where did the time go? But when you see it, it makes it all worthwhile, all that sacrifice. You know, we were a small part of making that happen, and I feel good about that. You know, not to get all mushy about it, but it feels good, eh. •

CHAPTER FOUR

WITH HELP FROM OUR FRIENDS

WHERE PEOPLE STAND AND SUPPORT A JUST CAUSE

PETE
SEEGER
SINGS FOR
ATHŁII GWAI (LYELL ISLAND)
WITH THE RAINBOW CREEK DANCERS

A BENEFIT EVENT SPONSORED BY
THE COUNCIL OF THE HAIDA NATION

ALL PROCEEDS TO THE LYELL ISLAND FUND
TICKETS AVAILABLE AT ALL VTC/CBO OUTLETS

ORPHEUM THEATRE
MARCH 21 1986   8:00 P.M.

ILLUSTRATION: CHILDREN OF THE GOOD PEOPLE   ROBERT DAVIDSON

POSTER DESIGN: NOLA JOHNSTON

THE ISLANDS PROTECTION SOCIETY, ed.

In 1974, TFL 24 licensee ITT Rayonier had finished wreaking havoc on Talunkwan Island and was now proposing to the province a five-year logging plan for Burnaby Island. Dead set against the proposal, the Skidegate Band Council's Chief Councillor, Percy Williams, set off to reason with the province and to keep the logging off Burnaby Island. At the same time, Guujaaw and Thom Henley, an adventurer who'd found his home in Haida Gwaii, drew a line on a map—the same one that exists today—identifying the region that would come to be known as Gwaii Haanas. Along with Captain Gold, John Yeltatzie and a few others, they also formed the Islands Protection Committee, a grassroots group of concerned citizens who came together to address the onslaught of industrial threats facing Haida Gwaii—wholescale industrial logging, supertankers bringing oil into Kitimat, and the heavy use of herbicides at the time.

President of the Council of the Haida Nation Vancouver Region, Robert Davidson, with musician Pete Seeger.

The group quickly grew to include many from across the Islands. Central to their work was supporting the Skidegate Band Council with the creation of the South Moresby Wilderness Proposal, which was submitted to the Provincial Government with signatures of 500 locals petitioning for the deferral of logging until an environmental review could be done.

The committee soon formalized to became the Islands Protection Society (IPS) and joined Chief Gid Kun (Nathan Young), Guujaaw and Glenn Naylor in filing a joint petition against the pending renewal of TFL 24. The IPS wasn't granted standing in the courts but continued on in other ways, gathering thousands of photos and scientific information about the forests, ocean, seabirds, raptors and other spectacular life forms of Gwaii Haanas.

The IPS also focused heavily on communications and gathering support on and off-Island by working with the media and by lobbying organizations, big business and government. One of the highlights was the South Moresby Caravan. Envisioned by Thom Henley, Haida Elders and supporters from all walks of life travelled by train across Canada, reaching thousands of people along the way and focusing the public's attention on Athlii Gwaii. They held countless presentations and slide shows for the public and published All Alone Stone, a magazine which brought to light the environmental threats facing Haida Gwaii. Following All Alone Stone, John Broadhead worked with a dedicated group to put together Islands at the Edge, a publication whose purpose was to ingrain the beauty and importance of Gwaii Haanas into the minds of people far and wide. Published by the IPS in 1984, it went on to sell over 15,000 copies.

Over the next few years, as the Council of the Haida Nation organized the stand on Lyell Island and negotiated to protect Gwaii Haanas once and for all, the IPS continued their support via bridge building, lobbying and education. The IPS was there right from the beginning—Islanders from all backgrounds, all walks of life coming together because at the end of the day we really are all in the same canoe. •

Opposite: Poster advertising a benefit concert for the Council of the Haida Nation with all proceeds going to the Lyell Island Fund.

Paul George   Guujaaw   Thom Henley

ALL ALONE STONE
Taaxiit *John Broadhead*

AN ISOLATED ISLET in a remote archipelago, All Alone Stone is small as islands go. On maps it's a little dot in Juan Perez Sound near the middle of the place we called South Moresby. But up close, with your hands wet jigging for cod, it's a substantial chunk of rock skirted in seaweed, draped in moss, grass and salal and capped by windblown spruce. An eagle perches in a snag, the breeze ruffling its feathers; another rides a thermal, watching. Below the waves ....

An insignificant dot at first glance, but profoundly beautiful up close, guus-dagang hlGaa—literally, all alone stone—is a fitting symbol for one of the most contentious environmental issues in Canadian history. Haida Gwaii was known by another name in 1974—the Queen Charlotte Islands—if it was known at all. And yet slowly but surely the Islands came to attract the attention of regional, national and global audiences, until the issue reached a climax in the Canadian House of Commons and the British Columbia Provincial Legislature.

Ultimately, thousands of people across the country had something to say about protecting Gwaii Haanas and respecting the rightful place of the Haida. They came from labour unions, churches, fish industry associations, political parties, First Nations, airlines, wildlife and environmental groups, human rights organizations and tourism industry associations. More than a million people who were members of local, provincial, national and global organizations advocated for an end to the logging. Prominent politicians, celebrities and even several heads of foreign states weighed in.

It was also arguably the highest-priced protected area issue. Participants spent a million dollars on meetings, newsletters, raffles, rallies, posters, legal affairs, travel, magazines, books, groceries, gear and fuel. And because it involved the greatest reduction ever to a BC Tree Farm Licence, the value of the BC–Canada South Moresby Agreement to stop the logging came to $126 million—worth over $238 million today.

It's hard today to grasp how many of the Islands' forests and streams in the 1950s, '60s and '70s had been torn apart by logging-induced landslides, clogged with boulders and silt, and scoured by flood waters. In some places, roads were built with gravel dug from creek beds even while salmon were actively spawning in them. There were 37 times as many landslides found on logged-over slopes as there were on natural, unlogged slopes. Several dozen salmon populations were exterminated, and today only half as many salmon spawn in Haida Gwaii waters as did sixty years ago.

It was this relentless destruction that led to a late, moonless night in the autumn of 1974, when, in the green house by the Tlell River bridge, Guujaaw and Thom Henley (Huck) sat at the kitchen table with a map of Moresby Island. ITT Rayonier Canada Ltd, a multinational logging company that controlled Tree Farm Licence 24 on Moresby Island, was planning to move its contractor operations off Talunkwan Island, which had been heavily damaged by logging, down to Burnaby

"

We know we didn't pull it off all by ourselves, we had help from all over the world. Knowing that people throughout the world, like in Europe and England, were supporting us felt pretty amazing. So many people agreed that the logging had to stop.

Letters came from all over the world, pulling for us, wishing us luck. Some would have money or cheques. One of the most touching letters that I saw come through was from Mae Moody, an Elder from Skidegate. She wrote the most supportive, beautiful letter and gave a donation. Everybody helped in any way that they could. Some of the return addresses were from Switzerland, Germany and all over the United States. There were hundreds of phone calls.

The Hopi sent an amethyst and a quartz crystal, and they wanted them buried in a certain direction, so I went and did that ... They said they watched very closely what was going on in our Nation, and with Haida Gwaii, because that would set the trend for the rest of the Earth, how it would make out.

The fact that the logging was stopped and Gwaii Haanas was preserved, they said that it showed there was hope. They wanted us to know that the fact that the logging had stopped and Gwaii Haanas was preserved sent a message and good energy all over — that it created an awareness of exactly what we were all doing to the Earth.

GwaaGanad, *Diane Brown*

Bruce Fraser presenting at the first
South Moresby Symposium.

Island, which remained untouched by modern industry.

By the light of an oil lamp, Guujaaw and Huck drew a line separating the active logging blocks in TFL 24 from the undisturbed area to the south, including Lyell and Burnaby Islands. It was the original South Moresby Wilderness Proposal, the same line eventually established in Haida law in 1985 and in Crown law in 1987.

Witnessing the damage was also what moved me to get involved with a small group of people in Masset called the Islands Protection Committee, formed by Huck, Guujaaw, Captain Gold, John Yeltatzie and a few others shortly after the line on the map was drawn. The Committee quickly grew to include many people across the Islands.

We were a loose affiliation of Haida and hippies, fishermen, housewives, teachers, carpenters, poets, farmers, engineers, artists, truck drivers, writers, photographers and musicians. We wrote letters and circulated petitions.

We worked with the Skidegate Band Council on the South Moresby Wilderness Proposal, which was hand-delivered to the Parliament Buildings in Victoria by Huck, Viola Wood and Trudy Carson. It contained a map with the line drawn on it and more than five hundred local signatures supporting and calling for an immediate moratorium on all cutting in the area until full environmental impact studies were completed.

We held benefit dances and raffles, organized scientific research projects and field trips and photography expeditions. Eventually the Islands Protection gang formalized into the Islands Protection Society (IPS)—the first registered environmental group in the Islands' history—effectively combining the voices of Indigenous and Western folk in a land-use issue for the first time in Canadian history. We lobbied the provincial government and occasionally tried to sue it.

Four volumes of All Alone Stone magazine were produced, named after the island in the centre of South Moresby. The first was printed in 1975 on a Gestetner mimeograph machine and stapled. By the time we produced the fourth volume in 1978, we had colour printing and proper book binding. As the dedication page said, "This magazine and our efforts are dedicated to protecting the Islands and the Earth, the little ones and the unborn."

In 1984, the coffee-table book Islands at the Edge was published, containing 130 of the best of over 3000 photographs we'd collected from several dozen experienced photographers. With a foreword by Jacques Cousteau, speaking to the fragility of small island ecosystems; with chapters written by Bill Reid (about hope in the face of environmental and cultural loss), Bristol Foster (ecology and evolution), Wayne Campbell (bird life), David Denning (sea life), Jim Pojar (forest and plants), myself (the political story) and Thom Henley (the ethics and hazards of protecting natural areas); with paintings by Takao Tanabe, Toni Onley, Robert Bateman, Donald Curley and Jim Willer; and with a cover logo of an iconic "fat bear in the nest" designed by Bill and me, Islands at the Edge was an award-winning, best-selling book—16,000 copies—and it became a highly effective brief about the issues at hand. It was both a calling card and a gift that made the rounds in government and business offices and diplomatic circles across the land and overseas.

Fat Bear In The Nest designed by Bill Reid and John Broadhead for the publication Islands at the Edge.

The acknowledgements on pages 156 and 157 list over a hundred people who played a part in those early days and the events that followed. A few names ought to be mentioned here though, for the record, only because in my experience they made extra special efforts that are not commonly understood or acknowledged.

Paul George and Richard Krieger came to Masset around 1977 with an idea for a coffee-table book about the Islands, the Haida and the logging. Paul was a wily, strategic thinker and a prolific pioneering publisher of books, posters and pamphlets about South Moresby and a great many other environmental issues. Richard took a thousand exceptionally beautiful large-format photographs in Gwaii Haanas and other parts of Haida Gwaii, and they were instrumental in the success of many slide shows and posters that were key communication pieces. IPS produced the book about Haida Gwaii, but Paul went on to publish a series of outstanding books that gave voice to all the big battles through the Western Canada Wilderness Committee.

The three thousand photographs we'd collected were sorted into a slide show that was scripted, duplicated and taken on the road for presentations in small community halls and churches, to hundreds of people in auditoriums, to politicians in offices—from the municipal to the federal level—to impromptu talks on railway platforms, in corporate boardrooms, high school classrooms, newspaper offices, public theatres and private living rooms.

Colleen McCrory was an outstanding campaigner with the Valhalla Wilderness Society in New Denver in the Slocan Valley. She worked tirelessly, briefing reporters and lobbying civil servants and politicians from Victoria to Ottawa and back again, many times.

Vicky Husband was and is one of BC's most respected environmental advocates, a keen and capable spokesperson for whom the doors and op-ed pages are usually open. Like Colleen, she was tireless in briefing media, lobbying government and public speaking, and she was a force in convincing Ottawa that there was only one right thing to do.

And so when the Haida took a rightful stand on Athlii Gwaii, many people from across Canada and beyond who tuned in to the evening news had been learning about the issue for several years, and were ready and willing to mobilize public opinion to the cause. They wrote letters to editors and their elected representatives, and they gave generously of cash and kind to support the Haida and stop the logging.

It was around then that I stayed with Bill and Martine Reid quite often. I would drive Bill to his studio on Granville Island, where he was creating his seminal bronze sculpture, The Black Canoe, for the Canadian embassy in Washington DC. Bill was angry that the Haida were not being respected, and for a while he stopped working on the sculpture in protest. He also mused in public about bringing a logging crew to the tree-lined streets of Vancouver's Shaughnessy Village so that people there would understand what a clear-cut was and what the Haida meant when they said their place in the world was at risk. It got the attention of some people around there for sure, because they donated tens of thousands of dollars to the Skidegate Band Office to help pay for gas and groceries on Athlii Gwaii.

Dan Culver, a friend of Bill's and an owner of the sailboat Island Roamer, laid down a $10,000 personal challenge to his fellow tour-company owners, who responded in kind as they could. Jeff Gibbs and his classmates in the BC Quest Program had explored Gwaii Haanas first-hand, and they helped to arrange slide shows with their friends and parents (the people with the chequebooks), and injected youthful energy into the South Moresby Caravan parade.

One of the most generous and effective friends was Monte Hummel, at the helm of World Wildlife Fund Canada (WWF), who brought Prince Philip of England and Prince Bernhard of the Netherlands into the fray to express their support. WWF Canada members contributed over $80,000 to help Haida and environmentalists who'd paid some significant costs of involvement, and to the Skidegate Band Council. Glen Davis, a WWF Canada director and wealthy businessperson, and without a doubt the least known and most generous conservation patron in Canada, was a keen supporter of protecting Gwaii Haanas and establishing the Gwaii Haanas Agreement.

As the South Moresby wheel turned in Ottawa, Elizabeth May was at the hub. Senior Policy Advisor to federal Environment Minister Tom McMillan, she was and is an irrepressible and tireless networker, activist, political analyst, communicator extraordinaire and angel advocate.

Jim Fulton, Member of Parliament for Skeena, was the voice of Haida Gwaii in Ottawa—a big voice—and he was never far from political intrigue and mischief. One of his great oratorical accomplishments was a unanimous, all-party resolution from

the Canadian House of Commons to end the logging in Gwaii Haanas.

The Honourable John Fraser was the Speaker of the House of Commons at the time of that unanimous resolution. In earlier years, as the Minister of Fisheries, he had visited Athlii Gwaii and brought national attention to the destruction of salmon habitat by logging. Later, he was quietly instrumental in bringing Canada to see the wisdom in the Gwaii Haanas Agreement with the Haida.

One day I had a phone call from Hanne Strong, wife of Maurice Strong, a supporter of Islands at the Edge and an articulate advocate for Athlii Gwaii on national television. Hanne said that Hopi Elders in Arizona were very interested in what was happening and felt that the outcome would have global consequences. They had some crystals they wanted delivered to the Haida, with the stipulation that they could not go by air and no money could be paid, and could I please arrange that.

A few weeks later, in an office across the street from Bill Reid's studio, I opened a hand-delivered box. Inside were two large crystals of amethyst and quartz. I picked them up, one in each hand, and immediately, strangely, there was a spot

Left to right: Thom Henley, Jeffrey Gibbs, Kevin McNamee, Vicki Husband, John Fraser, John Broadhead, Colleen McCrory, Tara Cullis, Elizabeth May, David Suzuki, Greg Sheehy, Terry Husband.

of bright pink light in the middle of the window. The spot of light grew bigger and bigger until it enveloped me, and I started to feel so light-hearted it was silly. Someone else in the office—Jeff Gibbs—was repeating my name and saying I had a phone call. I put the crystals back in the box, told him everything was going to be all right and walked out into the sun and down the street to the Kitsilano Marine store, where the owner, a proud redneck, retired from falling, liked to tease me about being an environmentalist.

I mentioned the crystals to him and wondered how a person could get them to Haida Gwaii without flying or paying. He grinned the way he did when he was thinking up a new tease; then he pointed toward the dock where a high-speed, hard-bottom Zodiac boat with a self-righting tower was tied up. He handed me a set of keys, saying, "Would you just bring it back in one piece, please."

I took the crystals by bus to Victoria and walked over to the lawn in front of the Legislature Building, where Premier Bill Vander Zalm had just arrived by limousine for the opening of a new government session. A rally for Athlii Gwaii was in progress on the plaza just below the front door. Four guys with chainsaws played the opening bars of "O Canada." Ten blue herons appeared in a V-formation in the sky, soaring over the Legislature Building with the statue of Captain George Vancouver clad in gold at the top—the herons and the captain both pointing north toward Haida Gwaii.

A few days later the Zodiac left the dock in False Creek, loaded with totes of groceries and gear, and manned by Alex Gryzbowski, Captain Gold and Geoff Greene. They headed across the Salish Sea to Quadra Island, then north to Bella Bella and over to Haida Gwaii. There, Diane Brown took the crystals and put them in the ground at Windy Bay. Given how the Hopi felt about things, I think the crystals were a way for them to log in and lend their support, pre-internet.

Some of this sounds a bit far out, I know, but that's how it was. Ask anyone who was there. And from start to finish, Guujaaw and Huck were in the thick of it, two ravens tumbling through time and space and meaning. They were responsible for all kinds of bright ideas and brilliant tactics, and they inspired a nation or two along the way. Maybe one day they'll write a book.

The Haida went to the line on Athlii Gwaii, and a new national anthem was born. The boat got back in one piece (a year later), and the rest is history. •

"

The success of our stand for Gwaii Haanas depended upon the support of people around the world, it was important that we had our neighbours with us.

Guujaaw, 2010

"

I guess I just decided that it was time for me to stand up and say something. I suppose to the largest degree, I spoke in favour of the South Moresby Park Reserve. At the time, I could see the merits; there was certainly a lot of good timber there. It was a very difficult time.

Local logger, Terry Husband, in *How and Why Non-Violence Works*, CBC Radio Ideas, 1991

THE NATURE OF THINGS
GyaaGang *David Suzuki*

"SOOZOOK," BEGAN THE HANDWRITTEN NOTE from typically cheeky Jim Fulton, Skeena Member of Parliament. He was suggesting that a good story for The Nature of Things would be the showdown between Haida and loggers at Windy Bay in what was then known as the Queen Charlotte Islands. I knew Jim and I knew his riding, but I didn't know where Windy Bay was or much about the Haida. I soon found out.

I sent his letter to Jim Murray, executive producer of The Nature of Things, and suggested it might make a good program. He, in turn, assigned Al Bailey to research the story, and when Al recommended that we do it, Nancy Archibald was assigned to produce the show.

Over a period of several weeks, I interviewed people with different perspectives on the issue: Dr. Bristol Foster, government biologist, made a passionate plea to preserve an "ecological jewel" of a kind fast disappearing around the world. Forester Keith Moore pointed out that Windy Bay represented a fraction of one percent of the total forest tenures in British Columbia. Bill Dumont of Western Forests Product emphasized the economic value of Windy Bay, stating that logging fuelled half of the BC economy, so Windy Bay had to be logged for the good of all British Columbians. I also talked to Nick Gessler of the Haida Gwaii Museum, environmentalist Thom (Huck) Henley and Haida leaders like Diane Brown, Miles Richardson Jr. and Guujaaw.

This was my first encounter with the Haida. I felt like a total ignoramus as Diane informed me of the importance of the forest and ocean for Haida people and their culture, while Miles gave me

Gud Bald eagle sits on a spruce snag.

Gwaii Haanas/Stef O'cen

Taan *Haida Gwaii Black bear.*

the insight that the line to be drawn at Windy Bay was a demonstration of Haida sovereignty over the entire archipelago. I learned that while billions in revenue from resources had flowed out of Haida Gwaii, little of it trickled down to the Haida.

But it was Guujaaw who made a huge impact on my thinking. I knew that like all First Nations, the Haida suffered chronically high levels of unemployment and needed community economic development. Logging provided jobs to the Haida, but nevertheless Guujaaw told me, "Our people have determined that Windy Bay and other places on the Islands must be left in their natural conditions so that we can keep our identity and pass it on to following generations. A forest like that, and the ocean, are what keep us as Haida people today."

"And if they're logged off?" I asked him.

He replied, "If they're logged off, we'll probably end up the same as everyone else, I guess."

I suddenly realized this simple answer opened a radically new way of seeing our place in the world. His answer informed me that Guujaaw and, by inference, all Haida don't see themselves ending at their fingertips or skin. To be Haida means being inextricably bound to the land, the oceans and the air. Haida history and culture, and the reasons they are in this place, are informed by that connection to the land. Sever that and they become "the same as everyone else."

That insight forced me to reassess everything about the way I see the world and our place in it. I had perceived the problem as humans taking too much from, and putting too much waste back into, the environment. But now I could see this was the wrong way to frame the issue. There is no separation between us and the "environment." We are embedded in and utterly intermeshed with our surroundings.

I became a student and learned that this perspective is held by most traditional people around the world. They call Earth our "Mother" because we are literally created out of the sacred elements of Earth, Air, Fire and Water. They call all life our "biological kin," not "resources."

The Nature of Things program on Windy Bay was first broadcast in 1982. Afterwards, we were overwhelmed with phone calls and mail from people supporting the protection of Windy Bay. It was the greatest response The Nature of Things ever elicited in the 25 years of the series.

The story of Lyell Island has achieved legendary status in Haida lore, a great battle and a great victory. It is also instructive for those opposing the continuing assault on Mother Earth. The struggle must be led by the perspective of those with a deep sense of connection to the land, the Indigenous people. It is not an issue of money or power, but an understanding that we are utterly dependent on the biosphere for our well-being and happiness. For me, the past 30-plus years have been a marvellous period of surprise and learning as I've bonded with the Haida and their bounteous land and waters. And now, with two Haida grandsons, I am truly blessed. •

"

Tonight we take a look at a special issue that affects all Canadians and that asks us to redefine the very notion of progress ... We often hear of "harvesting" trees, but in areas like this, you can't farm a forest the way you do corn or tomatoes ... It took thousands of years, and countless seeds and seedlings, before giant trees like those in Windy Bay took root and survived. Some of these trees are over 600 years old. Once it took two men weeks to cut one of them down. Today one man can do it in minutes. Is this progress?

Wilderness preserves are more than just museums for relics of the past. They're a hedge against our ignorance, a tiny reserve from which we might learn how to use our powerful technologies more wisely. But in the end, our sense of awe and wonder in places like this changes us, and our perspective of time, and our place in the nature of things.

David Suzuki on *Windy Bay,*
The Nature of Things, 1982

EVERYTHING DEPENDED ON GWAII HAANAS

Kuuyaa *Jeffrey Gibbs*

IN THE SUMMER OF 1984, I spent two weeks travelling through Gwaii Haanas with about ten other teenagers. That journey changed my life. Up until then I had lived in the urban environment of Vancouver, where everything was right angles and created by humans. What a contrast to Gwaii Haanas, where I experienced seas teeming with life and forests of trees over a thousand years old. It was an epiphany when I realized that there was a web of life on the Earth that was so much grander than me, yet included me.

On the last day of the trip we travelled past parts of Athlii Gwaii where the trees had been clear-cut. My mind was not prepared to process the sight. The place was so devastated that at first I thought it must be a bomb test site for the military. The loss of the nature I had come to love felt very personal and viscerally painful. I had to do something. On that day, helping to protect Gwaii Haanas became the number one goal in my life.

Immediately upon returning home to Vancouver, I created a group called Teenagers' Response to Endangered Ecosystems Club—the T.R.E.E. Club—with 40 high school students focused mainly on trying to protect Gwaii Haanas. Our first action was to contact politicians directly by writing to every Member of Parliament in Canada and all the Members of the Legislative Assembly of British Columbia (over 400 handwritten letters), citing our first-hand knowledge of Gwaii Haanas, and imploring the politicians to prevent its destruction. Next we created an elaborate musical slideshow about the place and toured it to packed theatres in Vancouver and Victoria. I then organized my friends to go door-to-door in neighbourhoods across Vancouver in order to engage citizens in conversations about the value of Gwaii Haanas and, most importantly, how to influence politicians to protect it. We reached over 5000 households! During this time, I met with the premier of British Columbia, the Minister of Environment and the Leader of the Official Opposition in the House of Commons.

I returned to Haida Gwaii often and sought out key Haidas, many of whom became my mentors, including Guujaaw, Diane Brown, Golie (Kathleen Hans), Colin Richardson, Miles Richardson Jr., Watson Pryce, Ada Yovanovich and Ethel Jones—as well as Haida allies John Broadhead and Thom Henley. Listening to them was my introductory education about Indigenous societies, human rights and colonialism. I began to learn how clear-cutting the ancient forests was just the latest of many assaults on Haida society and culture. Then, with even more determination, I spearheaded a large public rally for Gwaii Haanas in downtown Vancouver around the time of the Athlii Gwaii blockade. David Suzuki, Bill Reid and Robert Davidson spoke at the event, along with a few of us teenagers. Hundreds of people came out, and it was a top news story. A lot of people in Haida Gwaii saw the TV newscasts and thought, "Look at this community of young people in Vancouver! We've got allies down there who are just teenagers!"

Jeffery Gibbs

I felt (with a teenager's passionate intensity) that the fate of the entire world depended on the fate of Gwaii Haanas. Because it was so tiny compared to the world, yet so beautiful and important, I convinced myself that there was no hope for saving the rest of the planet if Gwaii Haanas couldn't be saved. On July 11, 1987, the provincial and federal governments finally signed an agreement that saw them join the Haida in stopping the logging (which then led to the Government of Canada and the Haida Nation negotiating the historic co-management accord for Gwaii Haanas). This was the same day that *Loo Taas* arrived in Skidegate from her historic voyage up the northwest coast of BC. I was there on that magnificent day and wept for joy when she came ashore. I realized there was hope for the world after all! •

Looking Around Blinking House, named by Chief Gid Kun *Nathan Young*. House designed by Guujaaw and built by Mark Yaroschuk with help from people onsite. The house front design is by Robert Davidson. It was painted by Reg Davidson and assistants, including dentist Dean Nomura, who painted the teeth at the insistence of Jaadsangkinghliiyas *Ada Yovanovich*. Reg Davidson dances the Eagle.

THERE WERE PEOPLE IN VICTORIA

Kihlguulaans *Christian White*

When I heard Athlii Gwaii was going to be saved from logging, it made me really happy. I'd grown up watching all the logs leave our Island. I grew up in Old Massett, and on any given week I'd see log barges coming out of our inlet fully loaded with old-growth cedar, spruce, you name it. Every week there'd be two, three or even four barges coming out of our inlet, and very little wealth staying here on Haida Gwaii.

When the stand started, I was living in Victoria. There was quite a group of Haidas that lived there and we'd get together every so often. Once we heard about the blockade at Lyell Island, we gathered together even more, trying to figure out what we could do. One of the things we did was to make a presence at the BC legislature, we protested. We gathered all our people together. We made signs to stop logging on Lyell Island. We wanted to gather support from other people in the city, too. There were people in Victoria, such as John Broadhead and Vicky Husband, and I remember seeing Thom Henley there, too. We held rallies on a number of occasions.

In particular, I remember Grace Wilson-DeWitt and her husband, Forrest DeWitt. Their daughter and grand-daughters were also there. It felt good to have Elders there with us. And we felt proud that they were there with us. It felt like we were doing the right thing.

WHEN CANADA CAME TO ATHLII GWAII

Taaxiit *John Broadhead*

THE SOUTH MORESBY CARAVAN was a transnational tour of heroic proportions. At whistle-stop gatherings from St. John's, Newfoundland, to Vancouver, the caravan brought media attention across the country to events at Athlii Gwaii. It inspired an instant grassroots network of the kinds of people who wrote letters, organized public speaking events, attended rallies and hounded elected officials and industry to stop the logging, to stop the arrests, to do the right thing.

Like some other parts of the Save South Moresby campaign, the caravan was dreamt up by Thom "Huck" Henley, and so it ran on optimism and serendipity, from the Atlantic to the Pacific. A huge eagle puppet with a 20-foot wingspan emerged from the train at every station.

The doors of St. Paul's Anglican Church on Bloor Street opened for a crowd of 1700 people to hear the preeminent Canadian historian Pierre Berton call the logging "a national disgrace" and to welcome Elders Ethel Jones, Ada Yovanovich and Watson Pryce with a standing ovation as they walked down the central aisle of the cathedral to speak at the podium.

Greg Sheehy at the Canadian Nature Federation provided logistical and moral support for the cross-Canada South Moresby Caravan. Along with Kevin McNamee at the National and Provincial Parks Association of Canada, they mobilized hundreds of members across Canada to lobby the government and donate to the cause.

There was a large official button with the image of a CN train barrelling south down the coast of Lyell Island, symbolically bringing Canada to Gwaii Haanas and the blockades, under the watchful eye of Raven and a full moon. It became a collector's item to be worn on Via Rail caps and suit lapels.

By the time the caravan arrived at the CN station in Vancouver, the media were waiting along with a crowd of several thousand people who marched with Haida Elders, singers and drummers through the streets of Vancouver to Canada Place, escorted all the way under the watchful eye of the huge eagle puppet; Huck in the lead as ever. •

A selection of buttons that were produced to bring awareness to the Athlli Gwaii stand.

Opposite: The movement to protect South Moresby was supported by a cross-section of people throughout Canada and the world.

This page: Thousands of people came out in Vancouver to support the protection of Gwaii Haanas.

Opposite top: Haida from across the country came to Vancouver to support the cross-coungtry caravan. Emma Matthews and Dan Helmer, on right.

Opposite bottom: (L-R) Svend Robinson, Jaadsangkinghliiyas *Ada Yovanovich*, Chief Gaahlaay *Watson Pryce*, Kamee *Ethel Jones* and Grace Wilson-DeWitt with Forest DeWitt standing behind.

Chief Gaahlaay *Watson Pryce*, Jaadsangkinghliiyas *Ada Yovanovich*, Grace Wilson-DeWitt and Kamee *Ethel Jones*.

Impressario and Master Abstractor, David Phillips.

Young Donnie Edenshaw sings after a cedar tree is planted during the Vancouver rally.

Grace Wilson-DeWitt
and Forest DeWitt at the
Caravan gathering in Vancouver.

THE DEAL

WHERE THE IMPORTANCE OF HOLDING UP GWAII HAANAS IS RECOGNIZED BY ALL PARTIES

THE SOUTH MORESBY AGREEMENT, ed.

On July 11, 1987—almost two years after the stand at Athlii Gwaii and over ten years after actions against unsustainable logging in Gwaii Haanas began—Canada and the Province of British Columbia (BC) signed the South Moresby Memorandum of Understanding, committing themselves to stop logging in Gwaii Haanas.

One year later, the two Crowns formalized the deal through the South Moresby Agreement (SMA), which outlined how logging would be halted and how Gwaii Haanas would be turned into a "national park." Colonial mindset dictated that Canada had to "buy out" BC. In return, BC would transfer to Canada its "administration, control and benefit" to any "fee simple estates" and any forest and marine interests that they "owned" in the region.

The buyout cost Canada $106 million. This money, along with $20 million from the province, was earmarked for:

"third party compensation and an eight-year program of local economic diversification and start-up operations by Parks Canada. All federal funding [was] charged to the Western Diversification Fund, a $2 billion federal regional economic development program. In particular, the SMA allocated funds as follows:

- $23 million in federal funds and $8 million in provincial funds for compensation of forestry interests directly affected by the agreement to stop logging in Gwaii Haanas;

- $1 million in compensation to other third party interests;

- $20 million in capital costs and $12 million in operating costs for the proposed park and marine park reserves, including park administration, visitor reception and information centres;

- $38 million to the QCI Regional Economic Development Initiative (REDI) for tourism infrastructure, local economic diversification and support of small business development; and

- $12 million in federal funds and $12 million in provincial funds to create the South Moresby Forest Replacement Account (SMFRA) for enhancing regional timber supplies through intensive silviculture projects."[1]

The Haida Nation was not party to this arrangement and let it be known that a "park" was not acceptable as it was, and neither was the proposed management of the SMA monies; we would not relinquish our ownership of Gwaii Haanas, and an agreement would be needed with our people. The parties entered into over five years of negotiations.

The resulting Gwaii Haanas Agreement, the Gwaii Trust and Gwaii Haanas itself are now widely recognized as leading the way in respectful and sustainable co-existence. Certainly there is much more work to do, but where we are today is a wonderful example of "how non-violence works."[2]

[1] Broadhead, John. Gwaii Haanas Transition Study: social & economic trends in communities on Haida Gwaii (the Queen Charlotte Islands) affected by the creation of a Haida Heritage Site and National Park Reserve in Gwaii Haanas (South Moresby). Queen Charlotte Islands Museum Press, Skidegate, Haida Gwaii, 1995.
[2] The phrase "how non-violence works" was borrowed from the CBC Ideas program of the same name. Hosted by Lister Sinclair, aired in 1991.

THE POSSIBLE
Guujaaw

Mary Collins, Minister of State, Canada and Kilsli Kaji Sting *Miles Richardson Jr.*, President of the Haida Nation at the signing of the Gwaii Haanas Agreement in G̲aw *Old Massett*.

ON THE EASTERN SEABOARD, contact between the original peoples and Europeans might have begun amiably enough, but goodwill gave way to treachery. Over the next 500 years, colonial powers employed devices and strategies (mostly killing people) that would leave Indigenous lifeways in ruins.

For our people, contact came almost 300 years later, but settlement in the midst of thousands of Haidas was not happening. By the early 1900s, however, foreign epidemics had left only 600 people holding our lineages together while settlement and industrial exploitation took hold.

Logging started at the beginning of the 20th century and steadily increased over the years, reaching its height in the mid-1900s when the Province of British Columbia (BC) began handing out "Tree Farm" licences. The Haida Nation was without influence as the wheels of industry ravished our lands. Our people were witness to entire salmon streams being laid waste, while expansive clear-cuts replaced 10,000-year-old forests.

Where disease and cultural oppression had failed, the wholesale industrial assault on the land had the capacity to put an end to our way of life.

In the early 1970s, Canada attempted to sever the ties of our people to the land through the "regulation of Indian hunting and fishing." It was becoming the norm

I

Top: Hereditary Leaders enter the hall, from front: Chief Iljuuwas *Reynold Russ*; Chief Skidegate *Clarence "Dempsey Collinson"*, Chief Cumshewa *Charles Wesley*, Chief Gid Kun *Nathan Young*, Chief Chee Xial *Miles Richardson Sr.* and Chief Gya awhlans *Alex Jones*.

Bottom: Chief Niis Wes *Ernie Wilson* signs the Gwaii Haanas Agreement. From left: Chief Gid Kun *Nathan Young*, Chief Cumshewa *Charles Wesley*, Minister of State, Mary Collins and Miles Richardson Jr., President of the Haida Nation.

Top: The Hereditary Leaders are drummed into the hall by Guujaaw, from front: Chief Niis Wes *Ernie Wilson*, Chief Gya awhlans *Alex Jones,* Chief Giteewans *Vern Brown*.

Bottom: Iljuuwas *Reynold Russ* signs the Gwaii Haanas Agreement with Miles Richardson Jr., President of the Haida Nation with Minister of State, Mary Collins looking on.

for our people to stand before the courts for feeding our families. Meanwhile, as the lands and rivers were being spoiled by logging, our oceans were being depleted by a highly mechanized fishing fleet. This was the awakening.

When Tree Farm Licence 24 came up for renewal in Gwaii Haanas, we challenged the province in its own court. While this effort didn't stop the logging, it did put the spotlight on Gwaii Haanas, contributing to its evolution as a cause célèbre.

In 1985 the Haida Nation designated the southern 15 percent of Haida Gwaii as the Gwaii Haanas Haida Heritage Site and stood on Athlii Gwaii to uphold that decision. The media treated the world to a spectacle of Mounties escorting loggers to work while people were arrested for defending their lands. In the following months, support grew as images of the heavy hand of the logging industry were brought to light. As time went on, provincial cabinet ministers were exposed for having shares in the same logging company.

As our people defended their actions in the courts, the intrigue grew as the showdown became an international embarrassment for Canada. Two years later the Government of Canada relented and signed a Memorandum of Understanding with the Province of BC—no more logging permits would be issued.

Within a few months, Canada and BC worked out a bilateral deal, and in 1988 they signed the South Moresby Agreement, whereby BC would stand aside while Canada designated Gwaii Haanas as "South Moresby National Park." With unanimous support of the Canadian Parliament, the designation carried with it a $126-million package that included payouts for the logging companies, "Park" monies and a multi-million-dollar package, of which $38 million was to be spent over a number of years with "advice" from the Islands' community on the spending decisions of federal bureaucrats. The remaining $24-million South Moresby Forest Replacement Account (SMFRA) would be spent under the auspices of the Canadian and BC governments.

The Haida Nation was not involved in, and did not agree to, the deal or the spending processes for any monies associated with Gwaii Haanas. More than five years of negotiations and wrangling were to follow.

In 1993 the Government of Canada and the Council of the Haida Nation finally signed the Gwaii Haanas Agreement. Both parties came in under their own authorities with an agreed process of management. We now have a joint management system in Gwaii Haanas that has been celebrated by National Geographic's Traveller Magazine as the best-managed protected area in North America. Indigenous people from across the continent, as well as from Australia, New Zealand and China, have come to look at the Gwaii Haanas model up close. As for the associated funds, REDI and SMFRA have become the Gwaii Trust and Athlii Gwaii Legacy Trust — important parts of the function of the "Islands Community."

Why, then, did it take so long to get an agreement? The casual observer sees the Gwaii Haanas Agreement as a model of cooperation and reconciliation, yet stopping the logging was only the first of the obstacles in coming to terms.

Canada initially believed that the South Moresby Agreement with BC was enough to formalize its involvement in Gwaii Haanas. To our people, a "park" was

"

The Gwaii Haanas Agreement is not a treaty, our Rights are intact, we didn't compromise our Title, there is shared management and the sky didn't fall. Gwaii Haanas remains as our Ancestors knew it, and our traditional use of the lands and waters are seen as a natural function of the environment.

Guujaaw

just another kind of nuisance, set up for tourists and managed by foreign governments, while hunting, fishing, trapping and living in natural ways were outlawed.

The parks we knew were "Naikoon Provincial Park," which had already alienated our people for 40 years, and "Anthony Island Provincial Park," where our people had to chase out a park warden (that's another story). We had already sacrificed too much to be expected to turn this precious piece of the Earth over to strangers.

The Haida Nation advised Canada that Gwaii Haanas wasn't BC's to give.

There were very real issues on both sides, and neither side was willing to compromise its legal or political positions. Canada cited concerns of being challenged by its own citizenry on matters of constitutional duties and administrative laws if it were to enter an agreement with a "third party." The Haida Nation had to protect not only its Title, but also its Rights to a way of life and culture that were already imperilled by the abuse of our lands and waters.

Any rejoicing at the end to logging was a long way from the negotiation tables. While Environment Canada dearly wanted an agreement, it was held up by Canada's Department of Justice and an unwritten doctrine that would rather keep its "subjects" in their place. It seemed the deeper the negotiations with the Crown, the more elusive any possibility of an agreement.

Since European contact, and throughout the era of colonialism, our people have never given up our Title. Canada's claim to Haida Gwaii is based on finding "vacant lands" (terra nullius), i.e., these were lands "void of people." In other words, it is theirs because they came here. We called BS on them.

At that time, Canada would not agree to any language that would acknowledge a "Title dispute," as that would trigger the need to resolve conflicting claims. Furthermore, the Crown wouldn't admit that the Haida Nation had any kind of interests affecting Title, nor would it concede that there were any Rights to be exercised unless proven in court.

So how do you create an agreement without settling the matter of Title? How do you create an agreement where everyone gets what they need without compromising the position of the other party, and come through this intact?

While the Haida designation of a Heritage Site predated Canada's designation of a National Park Reserve, Canada would not recognize a designation made by the Haida Nation in any agreement. Canada would not agree to any language suggesting that this is the Ancestral home of the Haida Nation, and would not even admit that our people had protected Gwaii Haanas.

Canada expected us to accept the Minister of Environment as the "ultimate authority" and wanted Haida participation limited to an "advisory role." Our response was, "We have kids in our villages who have more authority in Gwaii Haanas than the Minister."

In regard to the REDI fund, Canada's position was that it could spend its money however it saw fit. As Canada saw it, the spending process had been established in the South Moresby Agreement. Our position was that any monies associated with Gwaii Haanas must be part of an agreement with the Haida Nation, and "not one nickel" was to be spent until a deal was made. The notion of a perpetual fund

HOW NON-VIOLENCE WORKS

Unity, commitment, and determination—they're necessary, but they aren't always enough. Groups with the same strengths have failed in their campaigns. The Haida also got people, supplies, and money where they needed to go. They had a positive, trusted leadership. They picked a strategy and tactics that suited the goal. They were clear about the limitations of the strategy they had chose. They maintained control of the agenda. They quit when it was time to quit, and they compromised when it was time to compromise. They were disciplined enough to keep themselves under control. They didn't burn out, and they maintained excellent relations with all the key groups, with their supporters and the media, of course, but they also maintained good relations with the police, the courts, and their opponents. Every one of these elements is important in a successful campaign.

If the Haida had [responded with violence], they would have lost a great deal of their advantage. In order to win, the Haida had to do more than convince people that they were right; their victory depended on appearing to the world as the upright underdog in a David and Goliath struggle. They would have lost that moral position if they had succumbed to violence. Without the moral position, they probably would have lost the campaign. If the governments or the loggers had resorted to violence, but the Haida continued to be perceived by the public as both non-violent and right, the Haida probably would have won and their opponents would have lost a great deal more than the logs....

CBC Radio Ideas host, Lister Sinclair, in *How and Why Non-Violence Works*, 1991.

Rolf Bettner

(L-R) Sandra Davies, Director-General Western Region, Parks Canada; Minister of State, Mary Collins; Kilsli Kaji Sting *Miles Richardson Jr.*, President of the Haida Nation; Tom Greene Sr., Skidegate Band Council; Ernie Collison, Council of the Haida Nation; and Oliver Bell at the signing of the Gwaii Haanas Agreement in Gaw *Old Massett*.

in what would become the Gwaii Trust was now gaining traction in the Islands' community.

Finally, Canada did not want to set a precedent for a fair arrangement with the Haida Nation, as other "natives" would expect the same.

With positions this far apart, it seemed that a renewed showdown was imminent, this time with the Government of Canada. We were not going to give in or let them take charge. Without an agreement, we would not let them set up as much as an outhouse.

We were outgunned for sure, but our people were firmly in control of Gwaii Haanas, having cabins and Watchmen in all key sites, and we had the cooperation of the visitors.

In October 1988, our Nation's negotiators withdrew from the process, and we sent out a press release announcing "Haidas Go It Alone." Since we could not come to terms with Canada, we would manage Gwaii Haanas by ourselves. The Haida Nation continued issuing unilateral permits for visitors to the area.

A flurry of meetings followed, and several envoys were sent in from Ottawa. By this time, we were dealing with the third Environment Minister since the stand

at Athlii Gwaii. Tenacity, diplomacy, some fancy formatting and a lot of change in attitude eventually solved the problems. Finally, we had come to terms....

The Gwaii Haanas Agreement is not a treaty, our Rights are intact, we didn't compromise our Title, there is shared management and the sky didn't fall. Gwaii Haanas will remain as our Ancestors knew it, and our traditional use of the lands and waters will be seen as a natural function of the environment.

This change of standard has had far-reaching effects, making possible the protection of vast areas without conflict with the original people in many places around the world.

When all of this started, there was not a chance that Canada was going to hand over the loot from the REDI and SMFRA funds to the people of these Islands. But now the notion of a "six-year spending spree" has been supplanted by the perpetual Gwaii Trust, which, after almost 30 years of spending, has more than tripled in size.

The Gwaii Haanas Agreement has also provided a template for the Gwaii Haanas Marine Agreement and the management of SGaan Kinghlas, the Bowie Seamount. And it set the format for the Kunst'aa Guu—Kunst'aayah Reconciliation Protocol with the BC Provincial Crown; protected area agreements with BC for another 35 percent of Haida Gwaii, which includes Naikoon and adjacent marine areas; protection for cedar, medicinal plants, fish and bird habitats; and shared decision-making on what happens with the rest of our Islands. This is in stark contrast to the British Columbia Treaty Process, which calls for the surrender of most of our lands in exchange for a "treaty."

When decision-making includes the people who will continue to live with the consequences of those decisions, the predictable outcome is ... better management.

When our people stood on Athlii Gwaii, it was said that there was little chance of stopping the industrial juggernaut. To some, it might have seemed that the only future for Gwaii Haanas was to accept Canada's rule.

Today, Gwaii Haanas is celebrated worldwide as a model of reconciliation and idealistic land management. Gwaii Haanas remains integral to our lives while providing career opportunities in the stewardship of our lands.

Gwaii Haanas now boasts some of the finest outhouses a person can find, accommodating and quiet sentinels to remind us of ... the possible. •

Opposite: Mary Collins, Minister of State, Canada with Kilsli Kaji Sting *Miles Richardson Jr*, President of the Haida Nation and Tom Greene Sr., Skidegate Band Council.

Opposite: Mary Collins, Minister of State, Canada with (from left): Chief Skidegate *Clarence "Dempsey" Collinson*, Chief Cumshewa *Charles Wesley*, Chief Iljuwaas *Reynold Russ*, Chief Niis Wes *Ernie Wilson* and Chief Gid Kun *Nathan Young*.

GWAII HAANAS AGREEMENT

BETWEEN THE GOVERNMENT OF CANADA, represented by the Minister of Environment

AND: THE COUNCIL OF THE HAIDA NATION, for and on behalf of the Haida Nation and herein as "the Archipelago" (described in section 2 below). The parties agree as follows:

1.0   REASONS FOR AGREEMENT

1.1   The parties maintain viewpoints regarding the Archipelago that converge with respect to objectives concerning the care, protection and enjoyment of the Archipelago, as set out in Section 1.2 below, and diverge with respect to sovereignty, title or ownership, as follows:

The Haida Nation sees the Archipelago as Haida Lands, subject to the collective and individual rights of the Haida citizens, the sovereignty of the Hereditary Chiefs, and jurisdiction of the Council of the Haida Nation. The Haida Nation owns these lands and waters by virtue of heredity, subject to the laws of the Constitution of the Haida Nation, and the legislative jurisdiction of the Haida House of Assembly.

The Haida have designated and managed the Archipelago as the "Gwaii Haanas Heritage Site", and thereby will maintain the area in its natural state while continuing their traditional way of life as they have for countless generations. In this way the Haida Nation will sustain the continuity of their culture while allowing for the enjoyment of visitors.

"Haida" means all people of Haida ancestry.

The Government of Canada views the Archipelago as Crown land, subject to certain private rights or interests, and subject to the sovereignty of her Majesty the Queen and the legislative jurisdiction of the Parliament of Canada and the Legislature of the Province of British Columbia.

By virture of the above, the Constitution Acts and, more particularly, by an agreement between the Governments of Canada and the Province of British Columbia dated July 12, 1988, the Crown in right of Canada is or will become the owner of the Archipelago and an area within the Archipelago Marine Park Area in order that these lands may constituted as a reserve for a National Park of Canada and a reserve for a National Marine Park of Canada respectively, to which the National Parks Act will apply. The Government of Canada intends to establish the park reserves pending the disposition of any Haida claim to any right, title or interest in or to the lands comprised therein.

For the purposes of the Government of Canada's authorization and implementation of this agreement "Haida" refers to the aboriginal people of Haida Gwaii with respect to whom sub-section 33 (1) of the Constitution Act, 1982 applies.

1.2   Both parties agree that long-term protection measures are essential to safeguard the Archipelago as one of the world's great natural and cultural treasures, and the highest standards of protection and preservation should be applied.

MY LIFE HAS BEEN SHAPED BY GWAII HAANAS
Nang Kaa Klaagans *Ernie Gladstone*, Gwaii Haanas Superintendent

Gwaii Haanas

Laana DaaGang.nga *Swan Bay*, Gwaii Haanas

GWAII HAANAS, WHICH MEANS "ISLANDS OF BEAUTY" in the Haida language, is a place equally renowned for its spectacular natural environment and vibrant culture. Designated a Haida Heritage Site, a National Park Reserve and a National Marine Conservation Area Reserve, it is the only place in the world protected from the tops of the mountains to the depths of the ocean.

Gwaii Haanas is home to temperate rainforests, rich and abundant sea life and hundreds of ancient village sites, including SGang Gwaay, a UNESCO World Heritage Site. It continues to be a home for our people, with families travelling into the region to food-gather and explore, while Haida Gwaii Watchmen live in the area and youth attend Swan Bay Rediscovery.[1] It is a place enjoyed by other Islanders and by visitors from away. Gwaii Haanas has come to represent the strong relationship built between the Haida Nation and the Government of Canada. While born out of conflict, the relationship that exists in Gwaii Haanas today is regarded internationally as an outstanding example of cooperative management.

WORKING TOGETHER–THE GWAII HAANAS ARCHIPELAGO MANAGEMENT BOARD

Suudahl *Cindy Boyko*, Archipelago Management Board

Born from the Gwaii Haanas Agreement, the Gwaii Haanas Archipelago Management Board (AMB) governs all aspects of planning, operations and management of Gwaii Haanas, from the tops of the mountains to the depths of the ocean. Made up of equal representation from the Council of the Haida Nation and the Government of Canada, the AMB operates under a consensus-based decision-making process, using the Gwaii Haanas Agreement and the Gwaii Haanas Marine Agreement as its guiding documents.

I've been a member of the AMB for over 17 years. Previous to that I managed the Haida Gwaii Watchmen Program, a cultural program in Gwaii Haanas, for 12 years. The importance of the Gwaii Haanas Agreement and the AMB became obvious to me early on. Working together in cooperation to protect the cultural and natural aspects of Gwaii Haanas has proven to be very effective. Before a decision is made, all sides of an issue are covered and board members understand all concerns ahead of time.

Cooperative management is not something I have taken lightly. It's our bridge—to each other and to a better future. It's the way forward. It's challenging sometimes, but getting through the differences, and coming out with a solid decision together, is rewarding. Each decision made in this way builds a stronger foundation. We all need each other, and these types of management arrangements are the way of the future.

Gwaii Haanas is a world in itself. Part of our Ancestral homeland, it is a touchstone to the past and our sense of belonging in the present. It is the future for our children. Its natural beauty and ecological diversity provide a glimpse into the past and also an opportunity to teach about connection—that we don't exist in a vacuum and that all our actions have a consequence.

We have an opportunity here to "do it right," to set an example for others to follow regarding management. Haida are people of the sea. Our lives are surrounded by the ocean, we are sustained by the bounty of the ocean, the land we're on is affected every day by the patterns of the ocean. We are intertwined inextricably with the land, sea and tides. It is our sacred responsibility to protect these places on Earth, places that provide us with history, with plenty and with peace. Without them, we will lose our identities. If we forget who we are, we'll forget how to take care of ourselves, each other and these places that nurture us as human beings. I believe if we continue to do it together, we are the most effective we can be and will bring forward the best solutions for everyone.

Personally, Gwaii Haanas is my sense of belonging, my peace with the world. There is no question of where I come from or where I belong. The future must offer this to our coming generations. We have the privilege of protecting this beautiful place for them, and for the world, in the best and most respectful way we can, together. •

My own life has been shaped by Gwaii Haanas. When I was 12 years old, I travelled in the area on a small inflatable boat, camping on a different beach every night. We sat among the ancient house pits and poles in the villages, listened to the tide rise over thousands of colourful bat stars and witnessed clams squirting in all directions. We rested on spongy layers of moss and gazed up at monumental cedar trees. We hiked surf-pounded beaches in search of Japanese glass balls and bathed in the steaming pools at G̲andll K'in Gwaay.yaay. We didn't bring much food. Instead we dug clams, gathered scallops and sea urchins, and caught cod and halibut to feed ourselves. This experience connected me to Gwaii Haanas and is the reason I've returned to visit this special place every year.

Gwaii Haanas has sustained livelihoods for millennia. We know this first from the stories that have been passed down through oral histories, and more recently from archaeological surveys. The entire Gwaii Haanas area has been completely mapped with Haida place names,[2] and over seven hundred archaeological sites have been located. The more recent sites are found near almost every accessible shoreline, while those dating back to 13,000 years before present are elevated in the forest on raised beach sites, or submerged in tidal areas. These older sites correspond with Haida stories about floods and lower sea levels, as well as with the most recent ice ages on the Pacific coast. Along with ancient sites, remnants of industrial activity from the 1900s can be found—logging operations, mining operations, fish camps, canneries and a former whaling station.

Efforts to protect Gwaii Haanas were set in motion as I was heading into kindergarten. In 1974 the Skidegate Band Council, Hereditary Leader Nathan Young, Guujaaw, Glenn Naylor, and the Islands Protection Society joined together to oppose the planned logging of Burnaby Island in what was then called South Moresby.

By the time I entered high school, visitors had already begun to learn about and travel to Gwaii Haanas. In 1981 the Skidegate Band Council established the Haida Gwaii Watchmen Program, where community members live several months of the year in key cultural sites, serving as guardians of the area. Protection, education and visitor experience are the three elements at the heart of Parks Canada's mandate. While the Watchmen got started well before Parks Canada became involved, it is difficult to imagine a program that delivers this mandate more effectively. The primary role of the Haida Gwaii Watchmen is to protect the sites at which they are located. They do this by educating visitors, who in return say the time they spend with the Watchmen is one of the most memorable experiences they have in the area.

Also in the 1980s, concerns about unsustainable logging activity in the Gwaii Haanas area began gaining momentum. In 1985 the Haida Nation designated the lands and waters of Gwaii Haanas a Haida Heritage Site to ensure they'd be protected for future generations. Plans were then made to prevent the Windy Bay watershed on Athlii Gwaii from being clear-cut. Volunteers built a small camp in Sedgwick Bay and blockaded the road that logging crews used to get to work. There were seventy-two arrests, including Elders. These efforts to protect Gwaii

Haanas quickly gained local, national and international support and attention. Finally the logging was stopped, and along came a new beginning—a fundamental change in how the people of Haida Gwaii would live and work together to care for the Islands.

In 1988 the Governments of Canada and British Columbia signed the South Moresby Agreement, in which both agreed to take the necessary steps to ensure the lands and waters of Gwaii Haanas would be set aside as a protected area. The agreement included commitments to create new economic opportunities and set aside funds to compensate for the reduction in forestry activities in the Gwaii Haanas region. These funds, managed locally by the Gwaii Trust Society, support programs and infrastructure on the Islands.

I graduated from high school in 1988, and my passion for Gwaii Haanas continued to grow. I spent some of that summer in the area, this time as an assistant guide operating tours on *Looplex*, a fibreglass replica of Bill Reid's famous canoe *Loo Taas*. We visited and camped in many spectacular places and gathered seafood to feed our guests. It was amazing to watch the first monumental canoe in over a hundred years enter the bay of SGang Gwaay.

At the end of this summer I decided that working in Gwaii Haanas was my future. I planned to start a tour business and went off to school with this in mind. I returned home during the summer months and back into Gwaii Haanas for work. I spent much of the next two summers on Athlii Gwaii, planting trees and helping with a slope stability assessment to determine what post-logging rehabilitation work was required. We used the blockade camp at Sedgwick Bay as our base. It was a privilege to have lived there for a time. In the fall of 1985, when the blockade was underway, I had been in high school watching the events take place on TV. I had saved many of the same news clippings that were still posted on the walls of the bunkhouse. Each day we walked the same trail and used the same road as those who stood on the line only a few years before.

I joined Parks Canada in 1992, planning to stay there only until I had my tour business underway. I began working as a deckhand for the late Tucker (Robert) Brown, captain of *MV Gwaii Haanas*. Tucker inspired me every day. He brought me to—and taught me something different in—every bay and inlet, and he encouraged me to continue my career at Gwaii Haanas.

A year later, in 1993, the Haida Nation and the Government of Canada signed the unprecedented Gwaii Haanas Agreement. Twenty-five years after its signing, it is still rcfcrrcd to as an agreement before its time. At its core is the agreement to disagree. Both the Haida Nation and the Government of Canada assert ownership over Gwaii Haanas. However, both parties respect the other's views and maintain their respective authorities under Haida and Canadian laws.

Canada and the Haida had different reasons for wanting the area protected, but the end result is the same. The Haida are committed to maintaining the area in its natural state while continuing their traditional way of life as they have for countless generations. In this way the Haida Nation will sustain the continuity of their culture while allowing for the enjoyment of visitors. The Government of

Robert "Tucker" Brown aboard the *MV Gwaii Haanas*, circa 1990s.

Section Cove, Gwaii Haanas

Canada has protected Gwaii Haanas as one of Canada's representative natural and cultural areas, and as a place that present and future generations can appreciate and learn from.

The Gwaii Haanas Agreement created a structure to manage Gwaii Haanas, called the Archipelago Management Board. This board is made up of equal representation from the Haida Nation and the Government of Canada and is responsible for all issues related to planning, management and operations in Gwaii Haanas. This Agreement is unique in that it provides a process for two different governments to come together and make shared decisions under two completely different authorities.

After playing a number of different roles within the Gwaii Haanas organization, I became the Superintendent. Being Haida and representing the Government of Canada on Haida Gwaii is sometimes a difficult position to be in. But I believe in this partnership and I've been honoured to experience all the opportunities and challenges that go along with the incredible role I have in this special place.

Another groundbreaking milestone occurred in 2010. Government of Canada and Haida Nation representatives came together once again to sign the Gwaii Haanas Marine Agreement. The Marine Agreement provides an opportunity for

Parks Canada and Fisheries and Oceans Canada (DFO) to work with the Haida Nation to cooperatively manage the surrounding waters. From the shores of Gwaii Haanas to the deep seas below, this remote wilderness is home to over 3500 marine species. Haida traditional harvesting will continue, and sites of special spiritual-cultural significance will be protected. Sustainable use activities, including commercial fishing and tourism, will continue to support local and coastal communities and will be managed to ensure healthy and productive ecosystems exist in the future, just as they do today. To help support this added responsibility, the Archipelago Management Board has recently been expanded from four to six members and now includes a representative from DFO and another from the Haida Nation.

As the years go by, the intergenerational benefits of the Athlii Gwaii stand, and the resulting Gwaii Haanas Agreement, continue to grow. Along with the Haida Gwaii Watchmen Program, the Skidegate Band Council implemented the Swan Bay Rediscovery Program in the 1990s, providing youth with the opportunity to learn about the environment, Haida culture and life skills. Haida citizens still carry out traditional activities, including food gathering and accessing cedar for poles or canoes. Islanders and visitors experience all that Gwaii Haanas has to offer, and the area continues to serve as a unique benchmark for science, a place where researchers have the opportunity to study and learn.

I am one whose life has been shaped by these Islands of Beauty. Today, Gwaii Haanas supports me and my family and the livelihoods of many others who benefit from, or provide necessary services that support, activities in this region. Our children's lives are also shaped by the cooperation that exists in Gwaii Haanas. The times of conflict that resulted in the protection of Gwaii Haanas are now a story that they may be told or read about in a book like this. Many individuals, communities and governments have made sacrifices and investments to establish and manage Gwaii Haanas, and it's important that everyone understands what has happened in the past and why Gwaii Haanas exists today. Gwaii Haanas is a place of opportunity. It is important that youth today and our future generations understand this and take full advantage of these many opportunities. •

---

[1] Laana DaaGang.nga, the Swan Bay Rediscovery Program, is a seasonal cultural camp based out of the ancient village of Laana DaaGang.nga which is located in Gwaii Haanas. It's programming is based on Haida values and our knowledge of and relationship to the land and waters, and is open to all youth both on- and off-Island. Inspired by the Haida Gwaii Rediscovery Program, which began operating in the North end of Haida Gwaii in the 1980s, Swan Bay Rediscovery was created in the 1990s by the Skidegate Band Council, and is now run through an independent not-for-profit organization.

[2] The Haida Place Name Project is a partnership between the Gwaii Haanas organization and the Skidegate Haida Immersion Program to identify and map locations in Gwaii Haanas.

THE GWAII TRUST SOCIETY
Sk'aal Ts'iid *James Cowpar*, Gwaii Trust Chair

BORN OUT OF CONTROVERSY, the Gwaii Trust Society is now a model of cooperation that has made meaningful contributions to the environment, people and economy of Haida Gwaii for over twenty years, and will continue to do so for generations down the line. Overseen by a consensus-driven board made up of equal representation from the Haida Nation and our neighbours on Haida Gwaii, our vision is to "advocate and support an Islands community characterized by respect for cultural diversity, the environment and a sustainable and increasingly self-sufficient economy."

The society is responsible for two different funds that came out of the Athlii Gwaii stand: the Gwaii Trust and the Athlii Gwaii Legacy Trust. Before these monies became what they are today, they existed in the South Moresby Agreement as the Regional Economic Development Initiative (REDI) and the South Moresby Forest Replacement Account (SMFRA), to be used as compensation towards any forest-related loss of income or employment associated with the end of logging in Gwaii Haanas. After years of negotiations with Canada, these monies were transferred to the people of Haida Gwaii. In 1994, the $38-million REDI fund became the Gwaii Trust.[1] In 2007, the SMFRA monies, originally worth $24 million, became the Athlii Gwaii Legacy Trust.[2] Today these funds combined are worth over $127-million, and to date they've contributed over $58 million to the education, language, arts, culture, health and infrastructure of Haida Gwaii.

I was 14 years old when the Gwaii Trust was under development by a savvy group of forward-thinking Islanders—a complex story that's been eloquently recounted by Norman Dale. Today it's an honour and privilege to have served on the Gwaii Trust board of directors for several years, most recently as Chair. I enjoy witnessing and being a part of all that the Gwaii Trust brings, particularly building synergies between communities and building a legacy of working together for the benefit of everyone.

"

The biggest legacy, by far, of the Gwaii Trust is that it has brought our communities and cultures together, to work cooperatively for the Islands community as a whole. We're distinct, we're different cultures, but we're one community. It's because of the forward thinking of the Haida and the "redneck loggers," who put aside their staunch positions and had a discussion, that we found a solution. Maybe it's because we're so isolated from the rest of the world that we may not know what "we can't do" ... we don't know the norms. So, we come up with solutions and we figure it out our way.

Warren Foster, Gwaii Trust Director

"

We found a way to create a far better place, not a perfect place, not a place without challenges, but a place where every person counted and no one would be left behind. And when we asked for friends to join with us in a new relationship, they were there. Settlers, who lived in a world where Indigenous peoples were always described in the worst way possible, overcame systemic propaganda and saw someone else. Someone that looked a lot like themselves.

Michael Nicoll Yahgulanaas

[1] The name Gwaii Trust contains both Haida and English words, honouring the two Nations that have come together for the economic, environmental and social health of Haida Gwaii.
[2] Originally named the Gwaii Forest Charitable Trust when handed over to Haida Gwaii, the fund was renamed in 2014 as the Athlii Gwaii Legacy Trust in honour of its birthplace.

FINDING (THE) TRUST
Norman Dale

THE CREATION OF THE GWAII TRUST is the most fascinating project I've worked on in my life. It was certainly an education. I became involved following Canada's formation of the Planning and Coordination Committee, which was tasked with overseeing the spending of the South Moresby Agreement's (SMA) Regional Economic Development Initiative (REDI) fund. I was hired as the Community Liaison Officer, a member of a technical team that would draft a plan to spend the monies. I moved to Haida Gwaii in early 1990.

As part of REDI, a Residents' Planning Advisory Committee (RPAC) had been formed on the Islands. The notion was that community leaders would feed ideas into the "bigger" planning process. It did not, by any means, give Islanders the authority to actually make the plan or spend the money. Basically, I felt that I had been sent to "babysit the kids in the sandbox" while the "adults" on the mainland did the "grown-up stuff" of making spending decisions. Initially I worked as both chair and secretary of RPAC, which was made up of two representatives each from New Masset, Port Clements, Queen Charlotte City, and Sandspit. My mandate at first was narrow: to seek local advice and guidance on a plan for spending $38 million. Commitments had already been made for these funds to go toward a small-craft harbour in Sandspit and visitor information centres in Sandspit and Queen Charlotte.[1] The rest was to be spent within eight years of the SMA's signing in 1988 ... and it was already 1990.

There was one Haida observer, G̱iitsx̱aa (Ron Wilson), who the Council of the Haida Nation (CHN) appointed to attend meetings as an observer. The original intent was to have two Haida representatives on the committee, but the Haida boycotted RPAC because of its advisory nature. This was a jurisdictional issue, as put to me very clearly by Miles Richardson Jr., president of the CHN. He said something along the lines of "We're not a stakeholder; we're a government. We don't sit on committees that merely advise the province and the feds. That's not the way it works."

Formalizing a nation-to-nation process was really tricky. In RPAC's meetings, G̱iitsx̱aa absorbed a lot of stuff that I'd call unintentionally racist—but it was still racist. Sometimes he spoke vigorously in defense of his people: they were not a colony of Great Britain, but a sovereign people. He educated RPAC a great deal, and it was at some emotional expense because of the very difficult history of colonialism. I remember in particular him explaining very forcefully that in pre-contact times, and still today, there was an effective Haida governance system: "It works!" He was a wonderful educator.

I worked closely with G̱iitsx̱aa to find ways to talk with the Haida leadership, principally Miles, and also Frank Collison, CHN Vice President at the time; Michael Nicoll Yahgulanaas, Chief Councillor for Old Massett; and Paul Pearson, Chief Councillor for Skidegate. It was in the course of those discussions with them, with RPAC and with individual locals, that it became very clear—people didn't want "a

six-year spending spree of the $38 million." They wanted to see these funds under permanent local control.

The priority of a locally managed perpetual trust arose as I performed a kind of "shuttle diplomacy." Since I wasn't able to convene a meeting of all community leaders under the RPAC umbrella, I basically carried messages back and forth for months, trying out ideas for alternative strategies. Eventually an agreement came about: the CHN and band councils agreed to sit down with RPAC, but only under a very strict understanding that it was unbinding and not to be construed as legal consultation. It was simply an airing of views.

Fortunately, the meeting went well. We continued to meet through the fall with the common goal of turning REDI into a community fund. "The Group of Eight,"

Clockwise from top left: Fran Fowler, Michael Nicoll Yahgulanaas, Giitsxaa, Frank Collison, Gerry Johnson, Warren Foster, Terry Carty, David Wilson, Marcia Crosby, Norman Dale, unidentified and Mary Morris.

as they came to be called, was made up of equal representation by Haida and other Islanders: Miles and Frank from the CHN; Michael and Paul for the band councils; Dave Penna, the mayor of New Masset; David Wilson, mayor of Port Clements; and Mary Morris for Skeena–Queen Charlotte Electoral Area D, which at the time included Queen Charlotte City and rural Graham Island. Fran Fowler acted as Mary's alternate. Duane Gould, Area E Representative for Sandspit, appointed Warren Foster.

I was the facilitator, draft-maker and researcher for "The Group." The feds and the province still saw me as their operative, but as things turned out, my role became much more than that—I was working for those eight people, not for the provincial or federal government. It took several months to draft an accord, whereby the Haida and RPAC affirmed their commitment to work together for a permanent, community-run development trust using REDI funds. Completed in February 1991, significant features of the accord included a commitment to create a society to receive funds to plan for the eventual Gwaii Trust, and agreement that the Haida would pick the chair for both the interim and permanent board.

Much of the remainder of 1991 was spent putting together a plan and proposal. This time also included a visit to Prince Edward Island to attend a national rural development conference, "Innovative Rural Communities." We'd originally contacted the conference organizers for advice, but once they heard our story, they invited us to give a paper describing the proposed Gwaii Trust and how it all came about.

Once we were in PEI, we all met for a lobster dinner on my father's deck to prepare for the conference. As we put together a presentation, what surfaced were some very different perspectives on what we'd been doing, and on the relationship of Haida and other people on the Islands. Through this, the group came to understand each other much better, seeing each other's different senses of history in a way that they never had before.

The audience was amazed by our presentation. When we asked what they would do in these circumstances, they replied, "We'd probably try to do what you're doing, but we really don't know how. You inspire us!" What came out of that conference, then, was our group being forced to come together and share a story. The work we did with each other, and the spirit of cooperation in the face of divisive colonial history, was far more significant than the presentation itself.

During this time, Michael Nicoll Yahgulanaas, Warren Foster and Terry Carty (Dave Penna's alternate) were also on the phone, trying to reason with the Deputy Minister of Western Diversification. Things weren't going well, so Michael threatened to call Brian Mulroney, then prime minister. Terry didn't want the group to be making idle threats, so they actually did call his office. They reached the Chief of Staff and arranged a meeting in Ottawa to make the case for the Gwaii Trust. Michael and Warren were delegated to head off for several days of hard lobbying, where they initially encountered several strongly opposed politicians and bureaucrats—but such opposition was surmounted because of the solidarity of our group. Over the next few months, the concept of a locally controlled perpetual trust was gradually agreed to by Canada, which committed around $750,000 of REDI funds to the development of a plan for what would become the Gwaii Trust.

In November 1991, the Group of Eight incorporated and became the Gwaii Trust Interim Planning Society (GTIPS). The planning monies were received in January 1992, and GTIPS began developing the institutional design and legal drafting of the Gwaii Trust, as well as a financial plan. Frank Parnell, a Haida with extensive experience in managing economic development programs, was appointed chair of GTIPS.

As the year wore on, Islanders became more and more worried about the erosion of the remaining REDI funds, still in the hands of the Canadian government. While Canada's compensation monies for the forest industry sector were sitting in interest-bearing accounts, the Island's $38 million existed only on paper—inflation alone was making the sum, allocated in 1988, worth less and less. And, of course, there was a lot of federal agency opposition to handing over the monies, as the original vision had been clear: federal and provincial agencies would receive increments for their day-to-day spending programs from REDI funds. Locals imagined agencies like BC Highways seizing the opportunity of getting a few more dollars to fill in potholes!

Analytical and political work was done through the fall of 1992, pushing for an "interim trust," whereby the REDI money would be placed in an interest-bearing account until a plan for the Gwaii Trust was approved. As the work progressed, relationships between Haida and non-Haida individuals changed dramatically; from adversarial negotiators they became friends working in common cause.

Giitsxaa continued to be involved, this time as a liaison between GTIPS and Haida Hereditary Leaders and Elders. He'd update them on progress made, including the building of trust between people, making it easier for everyone to proceed with cross-cultural planning. As you might imagine, there were some strong feelings among people in all communities, worried about finding trust in people with whom there had been such dramatic battles so recently.

In November 1992, I went with several GTIPS representatives, as well as David Zirnhelt, the lead provincial minister on this file, to Ottawa and lobbied key cabinet ministers with the help of our local MP, James Fulton. Probably one of the most significant moments in all of this happened by chance: we'd gone to the parliamentary restaurant for lunch. Miles Richardson spotted Brian Mulroney, whom he knew from the Athlii Gwaii stand several years back. They talked for a few minutes, and after that we had a much easier time getting receptive meetings at the highest cabinet level.

In early 1993, both Canada and BC endorsed the idea of the Gwaii Trust. In September 1994, the Gwaii Trust Society was formalized and received the $38.2 million, which has been locally managed ever since.

Why did Canada finally sit down with the Haida Nation? I think Parks Canada wanted very badly to have an agreement between the two nations for the management of Gwaii Haanas. Canada eventually gave in, in part because of the political leverage that the Haida had: no Gwaii Trust deal, no Gwaii Haanas deal. I think the idea of a cross-cultural, Native/non-Native cooperative institution was also irresistible. I was told later, by a person high up in Treasury Board, that his agency had fought the community trust idea tooth and nail, as Parliament had to change some regulations governing Treasury Board in order to create the Gwaii Trust. This had never been done before, and—as far as I have heard—hasn't been done again since.

The promise of the harbour in Sandspit had always been a potential deal-breaker during negotiations. There was a perspective among the Haida, and among other Islanders, that it was like a reward for the people most opposed to protecting Gwaii Haanas. During the 1980s, Bill Vander Zalm, the premier of BC, had asked Sandspit's leaders what it would take for them to stop fighting the cessation of logging in Gwaii Haanas. Their answer was a harbour. So the project was written into REDI.

The harbour was estimated to cost at least $6 million. As you can imagine, not only the Haida, but also other Islanders, thought, "What the hell? Of the $38 million, six million is going to come right off the top for the harbour?" Eventually, negotiations with Ottawa led to separate funding for the harbour through Canada's Western Diversification Program. Yet even with this major change, concern remained over "unfair funding" of the harbour. In time, the solution was to create a special Haida Parity Fund with monies equal to the cost of the harbour, which was to be used specifically for Haida-led projects.

Great things have come out of the Gwaii Trust—arts, culture and infrastructure support, scholarships for students, many important initiatives. The Islands' communities came together to protect these funds, which otherwise would have been squandered by bureaucrats. It has left something tangible and permanent for Haida Gwaii, and has brought people together in an unprecedented way. I'm not going to say that the many cooperative initiatives that have occurred since wouldn't have happened without the Gwaii Trust, but I really do think it helped clear the path. It helped people realize that when you have different perspectives, the solution is not to make inflammatory statements but to sit down with people who you might think you don't like, and then discover, through collaboration, that perhaps they're not that bad after all.

I am so impressed by the abilities of the people who worked on this. It was a real privilege to work with them all. There were a lot of local heroes in this story, some well-known, and many who just put their shoulder to the wheel to get this challenging but exemplary trust up and running. •

---

[1] Instead of being funded out of the $38-million REDI fund the Haida Nation and RPAC negotiated with Canada to have the two visitor information centres built by Parks Canada, Sandspit's harbour was funded with separate monies from Canada's Western Diversification Program.

REFLECTING

WHERE A MOMENT IS TAKEN TO CONSIDER RESULTS

THE POWER WE HAVE
Taaw.ga Halaa' Leeyga *May Russ*

Injunction papers burn.

MY MAIN INVOLVEMENT was being told by Ernie Collison that I was in charge as he was racing out the door to go down to Athlii Gwaii. I took over the administration of the Old Massett Village Office in his absence and helped to support the camp—coordinating donations and moving people back and forth. We just tried to provide everything needed to keep camp operational. People went door to door, everyone was very generous.

Lyell Island was one of the first big ... I wouldn't say "fight," but first big political action in modern times. Everyone supported what the Council of the Haida Nation (CHN) was doing. Both Band Councils supported it with funding, with logistics and with food. Up until then the CHN was "just another organization." It didn't have a lot of clout. Taking this action definitely increased the presence of our government, especially out in the greater world. We became recognized a lot more, even here.

The outcome has also definitely helped with Haida Title. It formed the ground-work for the protected areas we have today. We have them in the north and the south, it's been good. Athlii Gwaii set the table for the CHN's nation-to-nation position—we're not talking band councils or tribal councils; we're talking Nation to Nation. It established that we're not just here to negotiate the little things, we are looking for the big things.

It was an exciting time. Our Nation as a whole felt the power we have when we decide to work together. The standard was set at Athlii Gwaii. •

WATCHING OVER VILLAGE SITES—THE HAIDA GWAII WATCHMEN PROGRAM
Suudahl *Cindy Boyko*

ON THE TOPS OF MONUMENTAL POLES one will often find "Watchmen," human figures that can see for miles, watching over a specific house or village and ensuring the safety of their people.

In the 1970s, Captain Gold spent several summers travelling from Skidegate all the way down to SGang Gwaay in his 16-foot fibreglass canoe, looking after the village and inspiring the birth of the Haida Gwaii Watchmen Program (HGW). When the program was formalized in 1981 by the Skidegate Band Council, people began volunteering their summers to live at village sites throughout Gwaii Haanas, protecting their cultural heritage and maintaining a Haida presence in the Gwaii Haanas region. To offset costs such as transportation, watchmen began collecting visitor fees onsite. Eventually, growing resources allowed the Watchmen to be compensated for their time.

While our people have been present in Gwaii Haanas for countless generations—gathering food and medicine, trapping, fishing and harvesting materials for artistic practice—it was important to us, after the ravages of colonial regimes, that the world knew we still exist and that our culture was alive and well. It was important that we firmly assert our Rights and Title and uphold our responsibilities to Haida Gwaii.

From spring through fall, watchmen live at K̲'uuna Llnagaay, T'aanuu Llnagaay, Hlk'yah GawG̲a, G̲andll K'in Gwaay.yaay and SGang Gwaay, caring for the villages and welcoming visitors. Although there are many, many old village sites in Gwaii Haanas, these particular ones were chosen as the primary Watchmen sites because they were the last major villages to be inhabited before the survivors of smallpox migrated north to Skidegate in the late 1800s. These villages also have the most visible cultural remains, which need protecting.

Being at these sites brings a sense of belonging and pride to all who have the opportunity to work there. Watchmen also enjoy interacting with visitors from around the globe, many making lifelong friends. For many visitors, meeting the watchmen is their favourite part of a memorable trip in the southern reaches of Haida Gwaii.

The Haida Gwaii Watchmen Program is a touchstone to our past and promises protection of this place for future generations. Time spent in these areas helps us to remember who we are. There are few places left on the planet where one can go to feel that sense of being a part of all things. Gwaii Haanas is one of those places.

The goals and aspirations are simple. We must protect these sacred places so we can connect to the Earth. When we are connected it reminds us of equality and peace; and when we feel equal and peaceful, we can join together with others to do great things for the world. •

Gwaii Haanas/Barbara Wilson

Captain Gold at SGang Gwaay.

HAAWA. HAAWA. IT'S BEAUTIFUL OUT THERE.

G̱uut 'iiwaans *David Dixon*

MY COUSIN DOLL (Darlene Squires) said I should try being a Watchman. Growing up in Old Massett with my grandparents, we used to go out and get seafood all the time, so I thought, "This would be cool to go out and do that again." I went out for two weeks and ended up staying longer because I enjoyed it so much. I've worked there over 10 years now.

The first time I went there was in the '80s, before the Athlii Gwaii stand. I was 17 years old and I went with the Haida Gwaii Rediscovery group, kayaking from SG̱ang Gwaay all the way up to Moresby Camp. There was Thom Henley, Guujaaw, Mugsy (Jerry) Brown, Alex White, Guy Edgars, a whole bunch of us, all Massett people. When we were going to SG̱ang Gwaay, we could hear people drumming and singing. Guujaaw was just smiling. "Can you guys hear it? They are welcoming us." We camped everywhere, Ikeda Cove, Hotsprings, T'aanuu. I think that's what made me want to be a Watchman.

On the low tide, you can go out and get your mussels and little black chitons—I just love those in soy sauce! Those mussels about the size of your thumb, I steam them open and make a cream curry sauce. At Hotsprings, when we have free time, we'll go out on the boat and get a halibut. We get those huge mussels and sG̱yuu, and there are clam beds ... clam fritters and clam chowder, it's so good! And guud-ing.ngaay all over the place.

We can get lots of naw, we just go out on the beach and grab them. My grand-ma, Louise Dixon, used to make this for me all the time, and no one can make it like her: she would pound the naw and chop it up in flour, take a big frying pan and pour water in it, cover it and throw it in the oven for an hour. Then she would make rice, and she would chop up little vegetables and onions and everything. Naw Fried Rice.

One year I was at SG̱ang Gwaay with Chuck Jones and Steven Yeltatzie, and we got stormed in for nine days. Our groceries couldn't come in. We had to live solely off the land, and it was pretty crazy. I never want to eat another lingcod. Holy, it was cod this, cod that ... I could write you a cookbook: 101 Ways to Cook Cod. We went over to Rose Harbour, and Susan Cohen, one of the residents, said, "Come over and get some vegetables," and she also gave us powdered milk. It was fun. It was an experience that made you think, "Okay, this is how it was in the old days. The grocery store is not around the corner."

At Hotsprings, if you see herring in the Beach Pool, that's the river otters. We found a naw in the Big Pool, up the hill, too. The otters are cooking their food in the hot water. They are pretty smart, crafty little critters. They make noises at you, scare the heck out of you. The nerve of them, too! They stop on the trail, turn around and glare at you, like, "What are you doing out here?" My granny told me stories about them: "Whenever you see them you scare them away. They are transformers, they are not good."

Gwaii Haanas

David Dixon hangs halibut to dry at SG_ang Gwaay.

The martens at Skedans are so cute. I was having my curried chicken and one popped up right beside my head, beside the window screen. I was like, "Awaayah! Go on, you aren't getting any of this." Goox (Laura Beaton) was busy with her camera, "click, click, click." We named him Ricky Marten. We radioed into town, "Oh, Ricky had lunch with us, Ricky Marten." So the gossip went around that Ricky Martin was in Skedans. It was hilarious! There were quite a few, so we named them. There was Ricky Marten, Dean Marten and Steve Marten. They look like weasels, almost. They are reddish-brown and have that little black tip on their tail.

And there are bears all the time, black bears. You sit in the living room looking out, watching the water, and the bear will walk right past the house. They go dig around in the kelp looking for food. When you go out, you have to bang your pot and make noise. Then they will run off. If you see them in Windy Bay, they are pulling rocks over and eating those tiny crabs underneath.

I love Windy Bay. The trees are amazing, and another reason is my grandmother Louise was on the blockade with Ethel Jones; Nora Bellis, my other grandmother; and all of them. There's a videotape of them sitting there, waiting for the plane to come take them home. Naanii Nora and my grandmother Louise, sitting there singing Haida songs. Naanii Nora is poking around at the spruce roots and says, "Gee, the thing's taking so long, we should just make a hat." I laughed so hard.

When I am cutting the grass around the poles in Skedans I'm like, "Look at this beautiful artwork! Somebody did this and I am here looking after it." I wish I could go back in time. I want to see what it would look like in a longhouse, and I want to go out on a big canoe and go fish.

Haawa. Haawa. It's beautiful out there. I am so fortunate with what I have. It reenergizes me; it detoxifies my brain and my soul. Then I come back to the city and I am like, "Look out, World, here I come." •

TO SEE THIS PLACE LIKE THEY HAD
Niisii Guujaaw

TALL CEDAR TREES hundreds of years old, small bubbling barnacles on wave-beaten rocks, burrowed nests of delicate seabirds, forests of bull kelp and fields of guuding.ngaay. Watchmen stand guard on SGang Gwaay's poles, a whale sprays on the horizon, a sea lion king roars to show his territory, songbirds invite the sunrise.

Gwaii Haanas has been a big part of my life, embedded in my history and rooted in my soul. Spending every summer down there, whether travelling in my dad's speedboat or paddling the *Looplex* with Swan Bay Rediscovery, this area has highlighted my childhood. By following our Ancestors' footsteps so clearly— sleeping in a longhouse pit or landing on ancient canoe runs—I feel a sense of peace and belonging like no other, a feeling shared with many others.

I've been blessed to spend that time learning from many people: my parents, always; Golie (Kathleen Hans) at Hotsprings, always willing to share her knowledge; and Captain Gold, leading our canoe. I have memories of being at SGang Gwaay when I was very little, catching a halibut with chiefs Niis Wes (Ernie Wilson) and Gid Kun (Nathan Young). I remember walking along the beach with Nanaay Mabel Williams, looking for shells. I remember shyly dancing with my brother for the Elders during a House Naming ceremony at Hotsprings.

My time at Swan Bay Rediscovery has been my biggest growing experience—expanding my comfort zone as did my first solo night on the Bolkus Islands, exploring everywhere, pushing *Looplex* through Burnaby Narrows and learning our culture and history. Today, the most rewarding part of Swan Bay for me is watching that growth in other kids. Youth that would rather be playing video games change into thoughtful, compassionate people who are completely aware

The *Looplex* canoe at Swan Bay.

of themselves, their history and their surroundings. To paddle in sync amongst small islands while singing a paddle song is one of the best ways any child can reconnect with their culture and themselves.

Gwaii Haanas is home to a UNESCO World Heritage Site, and Burnaby Narrows holds the largest intertidal biomass in the world. Along with these internationally recognized treasures, there are countless special and unique places and moments of amazement here, and many more to discover.

There are very few places in the world where a child like me could have grown up in a place like Gwaii Haanas. I've always been conscious of how lucky we are to have this place—an invaluable group of islands, so culturally and ecologically rich, connecting us to our past and teaching us to be stewards of our land and waters.

In my last year of high school, my class chose to spend our grad trip in Gwaii Haanas. We went to many areas, but for me the highlight was going to Sedgwick Bay, where the Lyell Island blockade took place. It was such a powerful moment to

stand on that road, now being reclaimed by the forest, and take a minute to think about that time when my dad (Guujaaw), aunties and uncles, nanaays and chinaays, stood on the line because they wanted me and my children to be able to see this place like they had.

Today I work for Gwaii Haanas as a resource conservation technician. I work on many different ecosystem monitoring and restoration projects and travel throughout the area, through sea and forest, all summer with a great team. We live and work alongside the seabirds, whales, salmon, eagles and monumental cedars. I am constantly learning, experiencing once-in-a-lifetime moments, and fascinated by the diversity of this area and all that it gives. Because of those that came together and fought with the determination that it would be here for future generations, we're able to explore, learn from, work in and cherish these Islands of Beauty: Gwaii Haanas. •

THE SPACE BETWEEN OURSELVES

Michael Nicoll Yahgulanaas

Photo: Martin Roland/John Broadhead Collection

(L-R) Jaadsangkinghliiyas *Ada Yovanovich* with grandson Len Arens; Chief Gaahlaay *Watson Pryce*; Chief tlajang nang kingas *Claude Davidson*; Kamee *Ethel Jones*; Chief Gid K̲un *Nathan Young*; Ida Smith; Lilly Brown, Chief Gya awhlans *Alex Jones*; RCMP officers in ceremonial red serge at the opening of Looking Around Blinking House, Windy Bay.

THERE ARE A LOT OF PEOPLE who don't quite understand how the Indians and the cowboys can be on the same team. The reasons for that reluctance, I think, are attached to a worldview that has us all separated into little boxes with spaces, tidy little spaces between us, isolating us.

Compartments are not only about who is on the outside; they are also about what is on the outside. The spaces in between are patrolled by security guards, such as overly invested thought-leaders well-armed with myth and generalizations. Like living human batteries in the Matrix movies, some people welcome the security of the box and its promise of a safe life. Moderated by untested assumptions, such boxes become caskets. If we are brave enough to look outside, we will see that the space around is neither empty nor isolating.

Take, for example, November 1985. The sky is tarnished silver, anxious to rain. It's cold, and the dark trees loom over two lines of people on the road below. One dressed in dark blue with yellow-banded hats, and the other, a line of Haidas with arms interlocked; we are standing between the police and the trees. Two groups, two boxes, and an extremely intense space in between. I know, I was there. When the police came to arrest my friend Ada Yovanovich, she pulled out a bible and said, "Lord forgive them for they know not what they do," and in that moment, Ada walked out of the box and into the space.

Ada Yovanovich, Ethel Jones, Watson Pryce and the many others who were arrested rejected the threat of assault; we rejected the idea of violence against the land. And when that RCMP officer cried, he too moved into the space. Millions of you also entered that space. This is a victory for us all. •

Adapted from the talk *Art Opens Windows to the Space Between Ourselves* at TEDxVancouver, November 14, 2015.

EPILOGUE

EPILOGUE
gid7ahl-gudsllaay *G.L. Terri-Lynn Williams-Davidson, B.Sc, LL.B, Counsel for the Haida Nation*

THIS EPILOGUE WILL CONCLUDE WITH exploring the context and significance of the stand at Athlii Gwaii and the exercise of Haida laws in the development of Aboriginal law in Canada and the development of the Haida Nation.

Haida laws are woven throughout our oral traditions—both narratives and songs—and into our written language of the arts. They are also woven into the land and sea, manifesting in the form of Creek Women, Low Tide Woman, the One-in-the-Sea and many other Supernatural Beings. They guide our conduct, both consciously and unconsciously. One can visualize the Supernatural Beings standing up and calling out to the Haida Nation, and others who might hear their call, to remind us of our responsibilities as human beings to take care of Haida Gwaii.

Our Ancestors heard the call of the Supernatural Beings: our historical record is replete with our Ancestors' voices speaking up for Haida Gwaii. It is against this backdrop that in 1981 the Haida Nation stood with the Supernatural Beings to protect Haida Gwaii. Much like Kuuya GyaaGandal *Sacred-One-Standing-And-Moving*, the Haida Nation stepped forward to accept and extend the challenge of supporting and upholding the Islands and people of Haida Gwaii.

The actions of the Haida Nation were exciting and bold. It was a time of two nations exercising their laws. Until then, the Haida Nation had exercised our laws internally, regulating Haida conduct. The excitement of Athlii Gwaii was that of a Nation awakening to its own power, and also that of people in distant places realizing their power to help affect change. Support from people throughout the world helped to broaden the Haida Nation's jurisdiction, to guide conduct of people external to the Haida Nation

There was boldness in the declarations creating the Duu Guusd Tribal Park and the Gwaii Haanas Haida Heritage Site. The former predated constitutional recognition of Aboriginal Rights under section 35 of the Constitution Act, 1982. The boldness was not that of defiance, or blatantly breaking Canadian law. Rather, the boldness was upholding Haida laws flowing from the land and sea and manifesting physically as Supernatural Beings.

The most profound exercise of Haida laws was the noble gesture of the Haida Nation to feast the loggers, signalling to the world that the Haida Nation was willing to begin along the path of reconciliation. Noble, because of the colonial history of the "taking" of "resources," discriminatory laws, the history and pain of residential schools, and all that comes with colonization. Especially noble because Canada was not ready for reconciliation: Parks Canada correspondence during the negotiation and initial implementation of the Gwaii Haanas Agreement, both with the Haida Nation and within its own department, documented Canada's fear of sharing jurisdiction through co-management, as well as Canada's resistance and denial of Haida laws. Yet, both the Haida Nation and Canada persevered.

A large part of the success at Athlii Gwaii was the willingness of the young leaders to listen to, and take direction from Elders, rather than indulging in the tendency of youth to charge forth on their own initiative. This conduct is also a reflection of a Natural Law voiced by the land and sea of Haida Gwaii over millennia: each species decays and returns back to the earth and sea to foster the next generation, thereby reminding the next generation to draw upon the strength and wisdom of those who have come and gone before.

Like the boldness of Raven re-creating the world, the Haida Nation's reconciliation progress has profoundly marked and changed the course of history, weaving a path that we're still persevering to finish over three decades years later. The art of weaving can help to illustrate and explain both the progress since Athlii Gwaii, and future actions to protect Haida Gwaii:

UNIQUE/IDENTIFIABLE FIRST STEPS

Weavers "sign" and leave their mark in their weavings. For instance, master spruce root weavers begin their woven objects with a pattern unique to them.[1] Athlii Gwaii was the start of the Haida Nation's weaving together co-existence, first with Canada for Gwaii Haanas and then later with British Columbia through the Kunst'aa Guu–Kunst'aayah Reconciliation Protocol. These are the earliest on-the-ground examples of reconciliation found in the often troubled history with Aboriginal Peoples in Canada. These governance and operational structures are as identifiable as weavers' signatures.

MODEL FOR CO-EXISTENCE

A template for reconciliation is found within Naaxiin, or Chilkat blankets. Naaxiin contain parallel borders around a central design element. The borders and design elements are individual segments joined together with techniques that physically interlock the segments into one weaving, thereby creating structural strength. The interlocking nature of these borders is hidden by braids that weave over and through the segments. Naaxiin demonstrates that it is possible for each nation's traditions to continue intact, but in a manner that allows for the interaction needed for co-existence in contemporary society.[2] The Gwaii Haanas model echoes this template, facilitating both the maintenance of Haida legal traditions, institutions and land designations within our own jurisdiction, but also the interactions and governance institutions needed for collaborative management.

PATH OF RECONCILIATION

Our path and progress with implementing reconciliation since the events at Athlii Gwaii has twisted back and forth, at times seemingly not moving forward, but yet creating an identifiable path—much like that of the st'aalaa pattern in spruce root hats and baskets. Each "crook" in the path has marked either the exercise of Haida laws or litigation—both encouraging movement in negotiations.[3]

Our present challenge is to find ways to apply and exercise our laws, and our Ancestors' teachings, in the face of even larger challenges than that of Athlii Gwaii: energy

and shipping projects that are national in scope with the potential for enduring or permanent impacts upon our oceans. Collectively we are at another crossroads. For many coastal First Nations, marine spaces are the last frontier—both in terms of third party use and future litigation.[4] The unwillingness to recognize that Aboriginal Title includes marine spaces has perpetuated a corresponding *terra nullius—mare nullius*, or empty sea, that facilitates further exploitation of fisheries and marine transportation. The parallel to the rampant logging and lack of legal recognition of Haida Title that led to the Line at Athlii Gwaii is clear. However, the difference lies in the potential for an enlightened path towards reconciliation. Canada has ostensibly entered a new era, if the report of the Truth and Reconciliation Commission (and its recommendations to repudiate the Doctrine of Discovery and the related concept of terra nullius, and to recognize Aboriginal Title),[5] and Canada's adoption of the United Nations Declaration of the Rights of Indigenous Peoples is any indication.[6]

A weaver might make their individual mark at the start of a weaving, but a weaver also creates her or his Nation's mark at the end of a weaving—such as with the six-strand "ending" in spruce root weaving.[7] When we complete the weaving of the fabric of reconciliation, blanketing not only the land but the sea, will we finesse it with a beautiful and skilled ending that surpasses the success of Gwaii Haanas? Our collective challenge, now and for the future, is to find ways for lasting, respectful co-existence. •

Pictured here is the first South Moresby Symposium, circa 1977.

I For instance, see the concentric circles in the work, and interviews, of master weaver Isabel Rorick, or the four-pointed star with bi-coloured points in the work of Isabella Edenshaw. Both exhibited in the "Signed Without Signature: Works by Isabella and Charles Edenshaw" at the UBC Museum of Anthropology. Also, see the tie-off in the side-braids of Naaxiin robes as explained by Cheryl Samuel in The Chilkat Dancing Blanket (USA: University of Oklahoma Press, 1990).

2 Similar to the representation of treaties in two-row wampum belts. The significance of these belts is well-documented; see for instance the Final Report of the Truth and Reconciliation Commission (TRC Final Report), Volume 6, p. 39, quoting legal scholar, Dr. John Borrows.

3 Some of the Haida litigation includes: IPS et al. v. The Queen; Edenshaw and Naylor [1979] (Aboriginal Rights over TFL 24); Western Forest Products Limited v. Dempsey Collinson et al. [1985] B.C.W.L.D. 4340 (S.C.) (Protection of the South Moresby area from logging); R. v. Fred Davis [1988] 3 C.N.L.R. 116 (BC Prov. Court) (Aboriginal Rights to Coho and the DFO's allocation policies); Massett Band et al. v. Stejack Logging (1990, Victoria Registry No. 901244) (Protection of "Culturally Modified Trees"); R. v. Richardson and Wilson, 1990 BCPC, No. 1793C (Aboriginal Rights to herring, DFO's licencing requirements and the Crown's infringement of Haida Aboriginal Rights); Moresby Explorers Ltd v. Canada (Attorney General), 2001 FCT 780 (Intervention in litigation unsuccessfully challenging the Gwaii Haanas Agreement); Haida Nation and Guujaaw et al. v. British Columbia (Minister of Forests), [2004] 3 S.C.R. 511 (Judicial Review of the Minister of Forests replacement and transfer of a tree farm licence); Council of the Haida Nation and Peter Lantin et al. v. Canada (Fisheries and Oceans), 2015 FC 290 (Injunction overturning the Minister of Fisheries and Oceans opening a commercial roe herring fishery in Haida Gwaii); Tsilhqot'in Nation v. British Columbia, 2014 SCC 44 (Intervention in litigation, providing submissions about the territorial nature of Aboriginal Title); and Gitxaala Nation, Gitga'at First Nation, Haisla Nation, the Council of the Haida Nation et al. v. Canada, 2016 FCA 187 (Judicial review of the Governor in Council's decision approving the Northern Gateway Pipeline Project).

The Haida have also provided many submissions regarding Haida laws and Haida Title, including the following formal submissions: the Joint Committee on Indian Reserves (1876-1908); British Columbia's Commissioners for Indian Affairs and Indian Agents (1872-1916); submissions through the Indian Rights Association (1909-1916); meeting with Richard McBride in 1911; the McKenna-McBride Commission (1913-1916); the Royal Commission on Indian Affairs; submissions through the Allied Indian Tribes (one of the leaders was Peter Kelly, a Haida) (1916-1927); the Special Joint Committees of the Senate and the House of Commons (1926); through the Native Brotherhood of British Columbia (1931 1966); the Indian Claims Commission; the West Coast Oil Ports Inquiry; the Priddle Panel; and the Cohen Commission.

Events upholding Haida laws in addition to Athlii Gwaii include joining with the population of Haida Gwaii to file a vote of non-confidence of the Ministry of Forests in 2005, and an Islands-wide peaceful action in 2005, entitled Islands Spirit Rising.

4 Future litigation may be necessary to protect various marine species from exploitation, or to prevent increased tanker traffic through Haida territorial waters, and of course, the Haida Title case (Haida Nation v. British Columbia and Canada, SCBC Action No. L020662, Vancouver Registry, filed 6 March, 2002).

5 TRC Final Report, supra, Vol. 6, at pp. 32-33.

6 Declaration on the Rights of Indigenous Peoples, GA Res 611295, UNGAOR, 61st Sess, Supp No 49, UN Doc A/61/L67 (2007).

7 For example, see the knowledge that Delores Churchill revealed in the hat of the "Long Ago Person Found", which contained a six-strand ending. See: https://www.newday.com/film/tracing-roots

END MATTER

HEARINGS, ARRESTS, CRIMINAL CONTEMPT OF COURT CHARGES

INJUNCTION HEARINGS

Vancouver Registry No. C854987

Plaintiff: Western Forest Products Limited

Defendants: Dempsey Collinson, Chief of the Skidegate Indian Band, on behalf of himself and all other members of the Skidegate Indian Band; Miles Richardson, Administrator of the Haida Tribal Council, on behalf of himself and all other members of the Haida Tribal Council; Gary Russ, Gary Edenshaw [Guujaaw], John Doe, Jane Doe and Persons Unknown

And:

Vancouver Registry No. C854988

Plaintiff: Frank Beban Logging Ltd.

Defendants: Dempsey Collinson, Gary Russ, Miles Richardson and Gary Edenshaw [Guujaaw] and Persons Unknown

From November 5–8, 1985, hearings for an interlocutory injunction regarding the Lyell Island blockade were held at the Supreme Court of BC in Vancouver, and were heard by the Honourable Mr. Justice Harry McKay. President of the Haida Nation Miles Richardson Jr. represented the defendants, who chose to testify orally rather than submit written affidavits. On November 8th, the injunction was granted. The following testified at these hearings:[1]

Chief Gid Kun *Nathan Young*, who testified in Haida with Minnie Croft as his translator

Chief Skidegate *Clarence "Dempsey" Collinson*

Chief Chee Xial *Miles Richardson Sr.*

Chief Iljuwaas *Reynold Russ*

Chief Gaahlaay *Watson Pryce*

Percy Williams

Lilly Bell

Diane Brown

Marina Jones

Bill Reid

Gladys Gladstone

Russ Jones

Paul Pearson

Gary Russ

Phil Watson

Robert Davidson

Guujaaw

Pansy Collison

Lavina Lightbown

ARRESTS

Between November 16th and 29th seventy-two arrests were made at Lyell Island. Sixty-six arrests involved citizens of the Haida Nation, of which one person was arrested twice. The other six arrests concerned Indigenous and Canadian allies invited to stand on the line by Haida citizens.[2]

November 16

Kamee *Ethel Jones*

Chief Gaahlaay *Watson Pryce*

Jaadsankinghliiyas *Ada Yovanovich*

November 18

Brad Collinson

Fred Davis

Mervin Dunn

Andy Edgars

Lawrence Jones

Colin Richardson

Ron Russ

Noel White

Martin Williams

John Yeltatzie

November 20

Harold Yeltatzie

Willard Wilson

Diane Brown

Rose Russ

Laura Williams

Richard Williams

Reg Wesley

James "Bussy" McGuire

Merle Adams

Henry Wilson

Barbara "Babs" Stevens

Kim Yovanovich

November 22

Kenny Davis

John Jones

Christopher Collison

Barry Bell

Teddy Williams

November 25

Valerie Jones

LaVerne Davies

Jackie Hans

Pat Gellerman

Paulette Robinson (née Pearson)

Marni York

Colleen Williams

Audra Collison

Dave Brock

James Stelkia

Mervin Dunn

Joey Parnell

Vince Pearson

Jody Russ

Giitsxaa, Ron Wilson

Lawrence Drager

Sally Edgars

Kathleen Pearson

Russell Edgars

Harold Wilson

Herman Collinson

Clayton Gladstone

Gordon Russ

Stuart McLean

Michael Allan

Troy Pearson

Frank Baker

Mitch Richardson

November 27

Marchel Shannon

Shelley Hageman

Waneeta Richardson

Jennifer Davidson

Ron Souza

Alfie Setso Jr.

James Stanley

November 28

Dorothy Russ

James Young

November 29

Linda Day

Beatrice Drager

Ronald George

Nigel Pearson

Harold Williams

CRIMINAL CONTEMPT OF COURT CHARGES 1985

Vancouver Registry File No. C854987 and C854988

On November 22, 1985 Western Forest Products and the BC Attorney General filed in the BC Supreme Court to increase charges from mischief to that of criminal contempt, punishable up to two years in jail upon sentencing, identifying 18 people: seventeen Haida and an NDP MP who was invited to stand on the line by citizens of the Haida Nation.

The case was heard November 28, 1985 at the Supreme Court of BC in Prince Rupert by the Honourable Chief Justice Allan McEachern. President of the Haida Nation, Miles Richardson Jr. represented the Haida defendants. Sentencing for those convicted was held December 6, 1985 at the Supreme Court of BC in Vancouver.[3]

Noel White: charges dropped

Brad Collinson: charged and acquitted.

Mervin Dunn: charged and acquitted.

Andy Edgars: charged and acquitted.

Ron Russ: charged and acquitted.

Fred Davis: charged and acquitted.

Kim Yovanovich: charged and acquitted.

Colin Richardson: charged and convicted; received suspended sentence of five months imprisonment.

Lawrence Jones: charged and convicted; received suspended sentence of five months imprisonment.

John Yeltatzie: charged and convicted; received suspended sentence of five months imprisonment.

Diane Brown: charged and convicted; received suspended sentence of five months imprisonment.

Willard Wilson: charged and convicted. Before sentencing, at the express request of President of the Haida Nation Miles Richardson Jr.—in order to have Mr. Wilson continue overseeing the administration of the Athlii Gwaii stand—Mr. Wilson agreed not to return to Lyell Island for a period of four to six months and, as such, was not sentenced.

Guujaaw: charged and convicted; received suspended sentence of five months imprisonment.

Roberta Olson: charged and convicted; received suspended sentence of five months imprisonment.

Michael Nicoll Yahgulanaas: charged and convicted; received suspended sentence of five months imprisonment.

Arnie Bellis: charged and convicted; received suspended sentence of five months imprisonment.

Martin Williams: charged and convicted; received suspended sentence of five months imprisonment.

NDP MP Svend Robinson: charged and fined $750. Robinson would not apologize to the courts but agreed not to return to the Lyell Island blockade.

CRIMINAL CONTEMPT OF COURT CHARGES 1986

New charges were laid against 11 Haida, again raised from mischief to that of criminal contempt and punishable up to two years in jail upon sentencing. Charges were later dropped.[4]

LaVerne Davies

Christopher Collison

Clayton Gladstone

Kamee *Ethel Jones*

John Jones

Shelley Hageman

Chief Gaahlaay *Watson Pryce*

Noel White

Colleen Williams

Henry Wilson

Jaadsankinghliiyas *Ada Yovanovich*

1 Names have been edited to reflect a person's common name and/or to correct names as recorded in legal documents.

2 See footnote 1.

3 See footnote 1.

4 See footnote 1.

TIMELINE

While not exhaustive, this timeline aims to chronicle events leading up to and during the Athlii Gwaii stand, and some events that have happened since.

ACRONYMS

AAC	Annual Allowable Cut
Athlii Gwaii Stand	Upholding Haida law at Lyell Island
BC	British Columbia government or the nation-state of British Columbia (depending on context)
Canada	Government of Canada/or the nation-state of Canada (depending on context)
CHN	Council of the Haida Nation
ELUC	BC Environment and Land Use Committee
Haida Gwaii	Haida territory (Haida Gwaii, her surrounding waters and airways)
IPS	Islands Protection Society
Lyell Island	Tllga Kun Gwaay.yaay
MOF	Ministry of Forests
TFL	Tree Farm Licence
SBC	Skidegate Band Council
SMLUA	South Moresby Land Use Alternatives report
SMRPT	South Moresby Resource Planning Team
SMWP	Southern Moresby Wilderness Proposal
South Moresby	Gwaii Haanas Haida Heritage Site (her land, surrounding waters and airways)
WAC	BC Wilderness Advisory Committee
WPP	Western Pulp Partnership

BEFORE WE ARE HERE

It is both light and dark; the world is covered in water. The Supernatural Beings are floating there, the most powerful rest on K'il Gwaay.

Haida Gwaii and the mainland are created. The pieces Nangkilsdlaas bites from two rocks before they become land are to be trees.

Jiila Kuns is brought over from the Mainland by Nangkilsdlaas. She becomes the greatest of all Creek Women on Haida Gwaii.

Tlaajaang Kuunaa causes a massive flood.

Xaagyah, a reef, is the first land to appear after the flood. SGuuluu Jaad sits upon the reef, eventually allowing the other Supernatural Beings to rest with her.

WE ARE HERE

In the first cycle of human beings we come out of the air but do not survive. In the second round, we come from the Earth, but only the Supernatural Beings remain after Tlaajaang Kuunaa's flood. Finally, we come out of the ocean. The Supernatural take pity on us and we become the Haida we are today. While each clan has their own origin story, SGuuluu Jaad is respected as the common Ancestress of most Raven clans, Jiila Kuns for most Eagle clans.

30,000+/- YEARS BEFORE PRESENT

Kalga Jaad hovers over Skidegate Inlet as glaciers descend. Parts of Haida Gwaii remain unglaciated.

12,500 YEARS BEFORE PRESENT

The first tree to appear after the last Ice Age is the Ts'ahl *Lodgepole pine* on Xagyaah. Spruce and hemlock follow.

6,000-6,500 YEARS BEFORE PRESENT

Ts'uu *Red cedar* appears on Haida Gwaii; the rest of the trees follow.

1763

The Royal Proclamation of 1763 recognizes Aboriginal Rights and Title.

1774

Spanish explorer Juan Perez and crew are found floating in Haida waters off K̲'iis Gwaay, aboard the *SV Santiago*. Decades of trade with Europeans follow.

1787

British sailor Captain George Dixon "names" Haida Gwaii the "Queen Charlotte Islands."

1858

The British Columbia Act establishes "British Columbia."

1862

A major outbreak of Smallpox occurs on the Northwest Coast. Purposefully introduced to the Haida Nation with vaccines withheld, our population, which ranged over 10,000 to upwards of 30,000 is reduced to 600 on Haida Gwaii by the turn of the century.[1]

1865

The BC mindset in a 2012 report on the history of "Timber Tenures" is:

> From its founding as a Crown colony until the early 1900s, government's focus was on attracting labour and capital to develop virtually untouched timber resources. From the early1800s until 1865, Crown grants were the only means of allocating timber to potential users. Early grants were fee simple, with no restrictions on land or timber use. Much of the private land that exists today was granted during this period, including most of the private lands of southeastern Vancouver Island ... The 1865 Land Ordinance established the policy of granting rights to harvest timber without alienating the land from the Crown—the basis of today's tenure system that preserves public ownership [sic].[2]

1867

The British North America Act, later known as the Constitution Act, 1867 creates the "Dominion of Canada." Section 91 (24) "gives" Canada's parliament "authority" over "Indians and Indian Reserves."

1871

"British Columbia" joins "Confederation" and officially becomes part of "Canada."

1876

Canada consolidates all laws relating to "Indians" into the "Indian Act."

1884

The Indian Act is amended to ban the Potlatch, making Indigenous legal, social and economic systems of the Northwest Coast illegal in the eyes of Canada.

BCs Timber Act introduces its first "stumpage fees."[3]

1885

BC begins to issue "Timber Licences."[4]

1892

Canada and the Church enter into a formal partnership to create the Residential School System.

1908

The American owned Moresby Island Lumber Company purchases 49 square miles of "Crown timber;" 8,000 acres of "private timberland" on Graham Island; and another 40 square miles on Moresby Island, spurring the building of the first big sawmill in Queen Charlotte.[5]

1909

The British American Timber Corporation has tenures for tracts of timber throughout Masset Inlet.[6]

1910

Approximately 800 Special Timber Licences have been issued to date in the "District of Queen Charlotte," representing a total of 12,783 hectares.[7]

The Queen Charlotte mill is put into operation, with a capacity of cutting just under 200 cubic meters per day (about five logging trucks).[8]

1911
The American owned Graham Island Lumber Company builds a mill in Masset for coal mining operations and wood for settlers.[9]

1912
BC introduces its first "Forest Act," establishing a system of "forest reserves," designated for timber harvesting, and a "Forest Service" to administer the reserves, protect them from forest fires, promote their commercial use, and collect government revenues. The Act also establishes a new tenure called the Timber Sale Licence, which grants a one-time "right" to harvest a specific stand.[10]

1913
Canada's McKenna-McBride Royal Commission hear from Haida testifiers who stand firm on the Haida Nation's Rights and Title to Haida Gwaii.

1914
An agent of the British American Timber Corp. tries to stop and prosecute Haida citizens for cutting timber on the company's "claim."[11]

1914-1918
World War I brings the logging of "airplane" spruce (Sitka spruce). The main logging camp on Haida Gwaii is based at Talunkwan Island.[12]

1916
In response to the McKenna-McBride Commission, numerous Indigenous Nations organize the Allied Tribes of BC to pursue legal cases on Indigenous Rights and Title. Haida citizen Peter Kelly serves as both President and Treasurer.

1918
Small mills exist across Haida Gwaii including Queen Charlotte, Port Clements, Sewell Inlet, Masset and Buckley Bay. Nine hundred men are working in sixteen camps on Moresby Island and 1500 men working in twenty camps in Masset Inlet.[13]

1919
The Allied Tribes formally reject the McKenna-McBride findings.

1927
Canada amends their Indian Act, making it illegal for Indigenous Peoples to obtain funds or legal counsel for the purpose of pursuing Aboriginal Title.

1930s
Two A-framing operations exist on Lyell Island. T.A. Kelley in Takelley Cove, Morgan Logging in Sedgewick Bay.[14]

1940s
With changes in technology from A-framing to truck logging, and demand for wood due to World War II, logging operations move from shorelines into valleys.[15]

Lyell Island is included in the Alaska Pine Company's operations.[16]

1943
BCs forest industry reaches the limits of its timber supply. BC appoints the Sloan Royal Commission to analyze BCs tenure system.[17]

1947
The Sloan Commission's recommendations lead to major changes in BCs tenure system and amendments to BCs Forest Act. "Forest management units" are established to manage for a long-term sustained yield of timber using a regulated harvest rate: the "Public Sustained Yield," predecessor to the "Timber Supply Area" and the "Forest Management Licence" predecessor to the "Tree Farm Licence" (TFL).[18]

1949
"Indians" can vote in BC elections.

1951
Canada revises its Indian Act, removing the prohibition against the Potlatch and the pursuit of Aboriginal Title.

1958
May 2: BC awards TFL 24, then known as Forest Management Licence No. 24, to Alaska Pine & Cellulose Ltd. as a 21-year licence comprised of five supply blocks totalling 115,521 hectares on

Moresby Island. The company is authorized to harvest 212,376 cubic metres per year, including certain blocks of timber in the South Moresby area.[19]

LATE 50s
The "Sixties Scoop" begins. Canada takes Indigenous children from their families and puts them in foster homes or adopts them out.

1960
"Registered Indians" are granted the right to vote in Canada's federal elections.

1961
Alaska Pine changes its name to Rayonier Canada Ltd.[20]

May 1: TFL 24 is assigned to Rayonier's subsidiary, subsequently known as Rayonier Canada (BC) Ltd.[21]

1964
The Annual Allowable Cut (AAC) for TFL 24 sits at 232,198 cubic metres with a net operable area of 50,433 hectares.[22]

1968
A "re-inventory" of TFL 24 by BC identifies a "45-percent increase in net operable area from that assumed previously."[23]

1969
Canada's Prime Minister Pierre Trudeau introduces the White Paper. Indigenous Nations organize and push back.

Based on the 1968 inventory, BC increases TFL 24's AAC to 305,822 cubic metres of which 72,971 hectares are operable.[24]

1970s
Haida and other Islanders' concerns over the rates and results of commercial logging and fishing, the threat of the oil and gas industry, and Canada and BCs avoidance of Haida Title come to a head. Residents convene several times to address these concerns.[25]

1971
BC raises TFL 24's AAC to 410,594 cubic metres.[26]

Canada formally withdraws the White Paper.

1972
BC logging guidelines state, "Holders of TFLs shall apply for cutting permits two years in advance of operations."[27]

1973
In their ruling of the Calder case, the Supreme Court of Canada recognizes the existence of Aboriginal Title in principal.

1974
A timber supply analysis included "lower than previous estimates of physical inaccessibility and smaller losses due to fire, insects and disease." TFL 24's AAC is increased to 436,079 cubic metres with an operable area of 73,706 hectares.[28]

Canada establishes an "Office of Native Claims" to receive claim submissions.[29]

October: Rayonier presents a five-year logging plan to BC, proposing to move their contract operation (Frank Beban Logging Ltd.) south from Block 2 of TFL 24 on Talunkwan Island to Block 4 on Burnaby Island. The Skidegate Band Council (SBC) objects due to Haida reliance on the area for sustenance, art, and culture. Haida citizens and our neighbours on Haida Gwaii come together to form the Islands Protection Committee (later the Islands Protection Society) to voice environmental concerns of the general public. Together, SBC and the Islands Protection Society (IPS) draft the South Moresby Wilderness Proposal (SMWP), proposing all areas south of the Tangil Peninsula be preserved as a wilderness area, and submit it to BC, whose premier, Dave Barrett, promises to take action.

November: SBC holds the first meeting at which the Council, Rayonier, IPS, and Canada's Fisheries and Forestry ministries discuss "resource conflict" in the SMWP area.[30]

December: Rayonier's logging plans for Burnaby Island are deferred for five years. The company applies to BC for permission to log in Block 3 on Lyell Island.[31]

December 7: The Council of the Haida Nation (CHN) is formed: "BE IT RESOLVED THAT this Convention direct the Executives in the formulation of a proposal for negotiating a land settlement, the Executive seek the formalization and retention of Aboriginal Title rather than surrender their Aboriginal Rights forever."[32]

1975

February: A petition with signatures from over 500 residents of Haida Gwaii, calling for an immediate moratorium on all cutting within the SMWP area until environmental impact studies are completed, is delivered to BC, which promises to have their Environmental Land Use Committee (ELUC) place the SMWP on its agenda.[33]

April: ELUC instructs its Secretariat to prepare an overview study of South Moresby.[34]

BC Forest Service issues the cutting permit for Lyell Island, in direct contravention of its own 1972 logging guidelines.[35]

1976

Canada adopts the Comprehensive Land Claims policy.

June: The ELUC study of South Moresby commences.[36]

Rayonier is given assurances by the BC Minister of lands, forests and water resources that the new BC government will not interfere with "their TFL" while ELUC studies the SMWP.[37]

July: ELUC tours South Moresby and holds meetings with Rayonier, IPS and SBC to discuss "resource conflict." A provincial park team also tours the area.[38] Over the next year, several studies of the area are conducted by the Royal British Columbia Museum and Canadian ministries, both provincial and federal, to assess environmental protection assessments; inventories of birds, mammals and freshwater fish; mineral potential; and potential ecological reserves. Parks Canada indicates South Moresby is a natural area of Canadian significance. Considering the area as a potential national park, it commissions a study of the area's natural history.[39]

November: The Graham Island Advisory Planning Commission sponsors the first all-Island symposium at the Haida Gwaii Museum

with the theme: "The QCI: where we are now, what course to the future?" One of the major concerns to emerge is the SMWP.[40]

1977

May: An independent research team compiles field studies of the SMWP for the book Islands at the Edge (1984). Parks Canada assesses the SMWP as an area of high national significance in a 137-page report.[41]

September: IPS and the book collaborators present slide shows and open dialogue sessions at Rayonier's Powrivco and Sewell Inlet logging camps.[42] The presentations eventually show straight across the country.[43]

October: Exactly three years from the date the SMWP was first drafted, the Queen Charlotte Islands Forest Advisory Committee opens deliberations on the issue.[44]

November: The IPS sponsors the second All-Islands Symposium, focusing on "Resource conflict in the South Moresby Wilderness Proposal." Participants include representatives from industry, various governments and numerous public interest organizations. The event results in a resolution calling for public hearings into the replacement of TFL 24.[45]

1978
January: As attention on South Moresby continues to rise in the media, the general public, and their elected representatives, BC Ecological Reserves Unit accepts a proposal to create an ecological reserve in Windy Bay and Dodge Point on Lyell Island, creating further conflicts with logging activities in TFL 24.[46]

Summer: BCs new Forest Act is debated and adopted amid intensifying call for the public hearings regarding TFL 24.[47]

November: A Canadian MP and BC MLA call for hearings into the replacement of the TFL; Canada's Minister of Forests does not.[48]

1979
January: Gid Kun, Nathan Young, hereditary chief and traditional trapper; Guujaaw, representing Haida hunter-gatherers; Glenn Naylor, holder of a registered trapline on Burnaby Island; and the IPS file a joint petition in the Supreme Court of BC. Citing the Judicial Review Procedures Act, they claim BC Minister of Forests Tom Waterland hadn't fairly considered their interests regarding pending replacement of TFL 24.[49]

March: In a precedent-setting decision, Judge Murray grants standing to all petitioners (except the IPS, who sponsored the petition) but denies the petition, saying the TFL had not yet been replaced and that there is still time for BC to act in good faith.[50]

ELUC releases their overview study, recommending a "five-year multiple land use planning program" and a two-year study of the Windy Bay Ecological Reserve Proposal. The report suggests BCs Ministry of Forests (MOF) act as lead agency to the program.[51]

April: Chief Gid Kun and Guujaaw file a new petition, citing evidence that BC did not respond to their requests for a meeting and are granted a court date of April 30. BC decides they better meet with Guujaaw, who invites Paul George, a long-standing supporter of protecting Lyell Island, along. They negotiate several modifications to the licence. At the court hearings, BC presents to the court a sworn affidavit regarding the meeting, presenting it as evidence of acting "fairly." The judge rules in BCs favour. A few days later BC scraps the agreed-upon modifications.[52]

May: MOF organizes the South Moresby Resource Planning Team (SMRPT) to address conflicting issues.[53]

May 2: BC issues a 25-year replaceable TFL to Rayonier.[54] The petitioners return to court, but the action is dismissed on the grounds that the TFL had been renewed. The petitioners apply for leave to appeal the decision to the Supreme Court of Canada under the sponsorship of the CHN. The action is dismissed on the grounds that the Judicial Review Procedures Act was a provincial law applying only to BC.[55]

December 28: Rayonier changes its name to ITT Industries of Canada Ltd.[56]

1980
Canadian MP Ian Waddell introduces a private member's bill to create a national park in South Moresby.[57]

October 31: ITT assigns TFL 24 to Western Forest Products Ltd. (WFP), to which ITT has changed its name.[58]

November: SGang Gwaay is "declared" a Provincial Heritage Site under BCs Heritage Conservation Act.[59]

November 19: The Haida Nation files its comprehensive land claim with Canada.[60]

December: SGang Gwaay is nominated as a UNESCO World Heritage Site.[61]

December 11: Canada acknowledges receipt of the Haida Nation's land claim.[62]

First and foremost, it's a human rights issue.

Rev. Peter Hammel (in light coloured togue), Anglican Church of Canada's consultant on national affairs. The Globe and Mail, November 27, 1985.

1981

Skidegate community members volunteer to look after old villages in the southern portions of Haida Gwaii, creating the Haida Gwaii Watchmen Program.[63]

To accommodate Forest Service concerns over terrain stability, streamside protection, wildlife protection, archaeological site protection and local aesthetics, TFL 24s AAC is reduced to 432,375 with an operable area of 75,450 hectares.[64]

October 30: Duu Guusd is designated a Haida Tribal Park by the Haida Nation.[65]

October: SGang Gwaay is recognized by UNESCO as a World Heritage Site.[66]

1982

The Canadian Constitution is amended to include Section 35, which recognizes and affirms existing Aboriginal and Treaty Rights.

January: The Nature of Things broadcasts "Windy Bay" and gets the greatest response the television program ever received in its 25-year run.[67]

June 18: The Western Canada Wilderness Committee holds "The Wilderness Auction," an evening of entertainment at the Empress Hotel's Georgian Room to raise monies for saving South Moresby.[68]

1983

The SMRPT submits their final report, South Moresby Land Use Alternatives (SMLUA), to ELUC.[69]

June 30: In a letter to Haida Nation President Percy Williams, Canada accepts the Haida land claim for negotiation, acknowledging it meets "federal policy criteria of acceptance for negotiation purposes," and that Canada's "resolve to negotiate" is "contingent upon the Province of British Columbia agreeing to participate in tripartite negotiations."[70]

December 10: Stephan Fuller, president of the Federation of Mountain Clubs of BC, which represents 30 regional clubs with about 3500 members, informs the Sun newspaper that they have voted unanimously in support of complete preservation of South Moresby. Fuller notes that while there is a need for adequate land base for the forest industry, there are many cases in which other natural values must take precedence and that this is recognized in the Forest Act.[71]

1984

The CHN holds a series of meetings with Federal and Provincial ministers who are interested in helping develop a solution to the Athlii Gwaii stand.[72]

No new logging areas on Lyell Island are to be approved while the "fate of South Moresby" is before cabinet.[73]

Canada's Environment Minister Charles Caccia publicly proposes South Moresby become a national park.[74]

Islands at the Edge is published by the Islands Protection Society, over 15,000 copies are sold.[75]

Spring: In an internal report, BCs lands, parks and housing ministry recommends to their cabinet that South Moresby become a provincial park.[76]

June: Canada's Progressive Conservative party invites BC to discuss the establishment of a national park in the South Moresby area.[77]

November 22: A landslide destroys Landrick Creek. Slides continue through the following year.[78]

1985

The Haida Nation declares Gwaii Haanas a Haida Heritage Site.

January: Prominent Canadians such as David Suzuki, Colleen McCrory, Farley Mowatt, Robert Bateman, and Canadian MPs Jim Fulton and Charles Caccia form the National Committee to Save South Moresby in support of halting logging in the region.[79]

February 6: Canada says it wants to further discussions with BC regarding the possibility of establishing a new park in South Moresby. Canada's Fisheries Minister John Fraser references the invitation his party extended to BC the previous June, saying he'd discussed the matter with BC Environment Minister Tony Brummet before Christmas and had reminded BC Premier Bill Bennett of the invitation the prior week. The SMLUA report is being studied by ELUC, which is chaired by Brummet.[80]

April: The Canadian Constitution is amended to include Bill C-31.

April 24-25: The Haida Nation and BC meet to discuss the SMLUA report. Discussions remain polarized. Brummet, now BC Minister of lands, parks and housing, wants emphasis on resource development in South Moresby and states he doesn't have a mandate to represent BC on Aboriginal Title; President of the Haida Nation Miles Richardson Jr. states the Haida Nation's position is based on Haida Title and on the maximum preservation of the region. "Our willingness to continue negotiations will be directly proportional to our perception of the sincerity of the BC government," writes Richardson Jr. then gives BC three weeks to respond to the discussions had in the meetings.[81]

June 20: Richardson writes a letter to Brummet re-asserting the Haida Nation's position, that "maximum preservation can be the most politically beneficial position for your government to put forth," and that the Haida Nation looks forward to "keeping our dialogue open, as it is important to cooperation and progress."[82]

August 8: BC Deputy Forest Minister Al MacPherson confirms logging will continue on Lyell Island, saying forest companies have run out of trees in the area.[83]

August 15: The CHN meets in Skidegate with BC Minister of Environment Austin Pelton and several other BC representatives, giving them 40 days-notice to resolve the conflict on Haida Gwaii. In an official release put out by the CHN, Haida Nation President, Miles Richardson Jr. states, "Any logging activities [occurring after this period] will be construed as an act of aggression to which we will have to defend ourselves and our homeland ... we can't keep playing their games. If Gwaii Haanas is going to be saved, we will have to do it ourselves ... I cannot keep telling my people that this matter can be resolved around a table when they keep pulling stunts like this."[84]

September 7: Politicians from all three of Canada's political parties are speaking out against logging in South Moresby, putting their support behind it becoming a national park. Several politicians have visited the area in the last month, including Canada's Liberal leader John Turner; Fisheries and Oceans Minister John Fraser, who says he will use the Fisheries Act as a last resort to stop logging on South Moresby and protect salmon runs; Canada's Liberal environment critic Charles Caccia, who proposed a national park in 1984; and BC Environment Minister Austin Pelton, who promises to return with the rest of ELUC.

Canada's new Environment Minister Tom McMillan says he is "personally predisposed" to a national park. Haida Nation President Miles Richardson Jr. says the Haida Nation is not pushing for a national park because there is no provision in Canada's legislation that would accommodate the interests of the Haida, pointing out that Native land claims remain unresolved.[85]

September 14: The creation of Bill Reid's 50-foot canoe, *Loo Taas*, is begun. The first cuts are made by Hereditary Leaders of the Haida Nation.[86]

October 9: Members of the CHN and greater Haida Nation meet with Canada's Minister of Environment Tom McMillan and others. Richardson begins his opening remarks, addressing the ongoing battle with different issues and governments, stating that, "until [the] issue of Aboriginal Title [is addressed] there will always be a difference. We own the whole thing in law and fact." The attendees discuss the preservation of Gwaii Haanas, BCs lack of willingness to enter into discussions, and the need to find a common ground.[87]

October 12: With no new logging permits issued to WFP since June 1984, the last of the loggers at Lyell Island are laid off.[88]

October 18: BC Environment Minister Austin Pelton announces that a Special Advisory Committee, later called the Wilderness Advisory Committee (WAC), has been struck to study and make recommendations on 16 wilderness areas and eight park boundaries, including the southern region of Moresby Island. In the meantime, Pelton says logging will continue at Lyell Island.[89]

October 22: BC forests ministry announces the approval of new logging areas for WFP. Haida Nation President Miles Richardson Jr. says the trust and dialogue the Haida had been trying to establish with BC has been destroyed. Beban and his loggers say the provincial government is partly to blame. "This issue should never have come to the fore," said Emma Hougen, wife of one of the loggers. Beban concurs, "We're not pleased with the provincial government, let's put it this way."[90]

October 26: Frank Beban meets with personal friends and chiefs of the Haida Nation.[91]

October 27: The Haida meet in Massett, expressing their unanimous opposition to logging Lyell Island.[92]

October 28: A planning meeting is held at the Skidegate Band Council office; that evening a feast for the crew heading to Lyell Island is held at the Skidegate Community Hall.[93]

October 29: Workers from Frank Beban Logging Ltd. start falling trees to make roads into the new cutting areas approved by BC.[94] Fishing boats, carrying the first Haida crew of twenty-plus people and enough building supplies to build their cabins, depart from the Queen Charlotte dock to Lyell Island. States Haida Nation President Miles Richardson Jr., "We are going down there to prevent any logging, to ensure the position our people took many years ago."[95]

October 30: The *Haida Warrior*, *Haida Raider*, and the *Haida Spirit* arrive at Sedgewick Bay. The media arrives as well. Led by Chief Clarence "Dempsey" Collinson, around twenty Haida hike from camp up to the logging road and begin the Nation's stand against logging on Lyell Island. Beban's crew turn back to their camp. Asked for comment by news reporters, Beban says, "I don't want to have a confrontation. They are my friends. We're not going to cause violence. We won't log as long as they are stopping us." Chief Skidegate states, "Frank's my friend. I told him I didn't want to confront him, but I have to. He can't go through us now."[96]

October 31: The US National Parks and Conservation Association wants logging at Lyell Island halted. President Paul Pritchard says, "Probably the worst forestry management in the world is being practiced by Bennett in that area right now."[97]

November 1: WFP and its sub-contractor, Frank Beban Logging Ltd., file suit for damages against the Haida, applying for interlocutory injunctions against the line being held at Lyell Island. Haida Nation President Miles Richardson Jr. says a political solution is the only "long-term positive way" to solve the problem. Frank Beban states, "The land claim issue is in the hands of our prime minister of Canada; he should address it. Premiere Bill Bennett should address it, it's serious business."[98] BC defends their non-negotiation stance on "Indian claims."[99]

November 5–8: Injunction hearings are held at the BC Supreme court. Lawyers for the logging companies make their submission in about 40 minutes. One argument references the Meares Island judgement where the BC Supreme Court prohibited logging until a Native land claim is heard, saying it does not apply to this situation because the Haida don't have an asserted land claim before the court. Haida Nation President Miles Richardson Jr. counters in the news that Canada had accepted the Haida's land claim, that the Haida Nation has worked diligently for 12 years to resolve the conflict by seeking justice in the courts and dialogue with BC but were constantly pushed aside. "I don't think you can talk about justice when it's constantly delayed."[100]

The final argument of WFP lawyer Edward Chiasson's ends with him agreeing with the Haidas' sentiment that the court was being used as a political scapegoat. "The real dispute is between the Haida and the government. My client cannot resolve that dispute."[101]

The Haida choose to not seek legal counsel nor present written affidavits. Instead, they are represented by Haida Nation President Miles Richardson Jr. and deliver oral testimonies. Between November 6th and 8th, Justice Harry McKay listens to nineteen Haida testimonies, including that of Chief Gid Ḵun, Nathan Young, who spoke in Haida with Minnie Croft as his translator.[102]

Agreeing with the Haida, Justice Harry McKay notes, "Many of the things being said belong in the political arena, not a court of law."[103]

Hundreds of letters of support, financial donations and offers of other support from organizations and individuals from around the world begin to flood in to the CHN; others write letters to newspapers, Canada and BC, calling for protection of South Moresby and supporting the Haida stand. These actions continue for several years.[104]

November 6: Canada's Environment Minister Tom McMillan announces Canada is willing to buy some "timber rights" on Lyell Island from WFP, saying the cost, that would be split between Canada and BC, will not be known until the company submits a bill, but suggesting it could be between ten and twelve million dollars.[105]

November 8: The applications filed by WFP and Frank Beban Logging Ltd. for injunctions are granted. Justice Harry McKay concludes:

... I have been on the bench a good many years and I can tell you that the last few days have been about the roughest that I have ever had on the bench. Sometimes people think that judges have great powers and we can do what we want. Of course, that is not the case. We must act according to law.

... Much of the evidence I have heard from the Haidas would not in the usual case have been considered or led on an interlocutory application. I sensed, however, the frustration of the Haidas and I felt that they should be heard.

I could reserve my decision, but I feel it necessary to face those Haidas who have travelled so far and who have spoken with such deep feeling, reverence and eloquence of the lands they cherish and of their concerns for the future of those lands and of the Haida people. I have heard a great deal in the last few days and I am sure you appreciate that I have been very moved, very impressed, and I want some time to prepare my formal reasons ... I will deliver them as soon as I reasonably can.... I have concluded, however, that on the law which I am sworn to uphold, I have no alternative but to grant the injunctions sought.[106]

November 9: After the ruling, Haida Nation President Miles Richardson Jr. challenges BC Premier Bill Bennett and his government to a public debate on the Native lands claims. Haida artist Robert Davidson states, "I felt kind of sad for humanity because I feel if we don't start preserving wilderness areas, we are dwindling away our own spirit. It's the same way people flock to Stanley Park to seek refuge. The irony of it is that the people who are destroying it are losing it in the end because they will have no place to seek refuge beyond the overpopulated Stanley Park."[107]

November 12: Flying to Haida Gwaii to stand with the Haida Nation, NDP MP Svend Robinson becomes the first Canadian politician to become directly involved in the Athlii Gwaii stand. "As a lawyer, and as the NDP justice critic, it wasn't easy for me. [The companies] have the court order but there is a point where you have to stand up for what you believe in."[108]

November 13: Eleven Haida stand on the line. Richard Bourne, hired by WFP and Frank Beban Logging Ltd., reads both companies' injunctions to Haida Nation President Miles Richardson Jr. and

12 Haidas arrested in renewed Lyell blockade

Another 25 Haida Indians blocked a logging road on Lyell Island today in defiance of two court injunctions and 12 of them were arrested by RCMP.

After the arrests, the loggers moved down the road and started work.

RCMP Supt. Bob Currie said from Prince Rupert that those arrested were taken to Queen Charlotte City and charged with mischief.

Currie couldn't say what happened to the other 13. "They could have stood aside after the original confron-

tation, in which case they would not be arrested," he said.

Like their colleagues arrested during earlier block-ades, the 25 stood with their arms linked and refused to move when asked to do so by logging crews.

RCMP officers then moved in and arrested them. Cur-rie said there was no resistance or violence. "It was all very peaceful."

Thirteen Haidas were arrested before today for defying the two injunctions granted Nov. 8 by a B.C. Supreme

Court Justice prohibiting the blocking of logging roads on the island.

Logging crews were given Tuesday off to let tempers cool.

Today's confrontation came after native leaders in Kamloops put Premier Bill Bennett "on notice" Tuesday that they won't be used as pawns in a land-claims elec-tion-issue battle.

The native leaders said all Indians should support the Haida people who are opposing logging on Lyell.

That support, they said, should include travelling to Lyell and joining the Haidas in confronting the loggers.

The Haidas' fight for what they say is their ancestral home grabbed most of the attention at the all-day meet-ing in Kamloops of the Shuswap Nation Tribal Council, attended by more than 60 chiefs, elders and tribal mem-bers of the 17-band council.

"We challenge Premier Bill Bennett and the British Columbia government to stop using issues like Lyell Is-
—More Haidas A2

More Haidas arrested in blockade of road

Continued from page 1
and the Stein Valley to gain pre-elec-tion public support," the native lead-ers said in a press release.

National Assembly of First Nations leader George Erasmus charged the provincial government "is virtually making an election issue out of Indian people" and warned that the natives have "a lot of eloquent people ready to take action.

"It's very obvious if we're going to win these battles we can't let the peo-ples of the first nations stand by them-selves. Our very strength is doing things together."

Spallumcheen Band Chief Wayne Christian said "I'm no stranger to confrontation with the provincial or

the federal governments. If perso-nally called on, I will go there (Lyell Island) and stand with them and be put in jail."

Frank Collison, of the Council of Haida Nations said the Haidas have rescheduled a strategy meeting to later this week because of a death in the Haida village in Skidegate.

He said there are about 30 Haidas encamped on Lyell, and more are ex-pected to arrive whenever arrests are made.

"I expect this whole thing will con-tinue like this. It doesn't look like any-thing has changed," Collison said, and Haidas will likely try to block the road whenever loggers go to work.

Meanwhile, Justice Harry McKay of the B.C. Supreme Court released

Tuesday his reasons for granting the injunctions that bar the Haidas from interfering with logging on Lyell.

Justice McKay said the Haidas must take court action against the provincial government if they wish to pursue their claim to aboriginal title on Lyell.

Justice McKay said the answer to the concerns expressed by the Haidas

is that the matters lie outside the jurisdiction of the court.

"They involve matters of govern-ment policy. It is to the appropriate governments and their agencies that the Haidas must address their con-cerns."

The judge added that hearing the applications was difficult "because it was apparent to me that the Haidas

assume that the court has almost un-limited power in these matters."

He said the court's discretion "must be exercised according to well estab-lished principles of law."

Collison said he wasn't surprised by McKay's comments, saying native peoples must learn not to rely on the courts for justice because they have rarely received such justice.

another Haida citizen. When they fail to respond, Bourne serves each Haida on the line. None respond. Beban and his loggers start back to their trucks. A Haida man catches up saying, "Frank you can go to work now. The road is clear." With that, the Haida move aside.[109]

November 14: Led by one-year-old Nicole Stephenson from Massett, a solidarity demonstration is held by the Haida and their allies outside the BC legislature. Christian White says his people will not give up despite the injunction.[110]

November 15: The Right Reverend Robert Smith of the United Church of Canada urged in a strongly worded telegram that Canada and BC intervene in the Lyell Island dispute. "Our concern [is] based on long tradition and ministry with the Haida ... and our consistent position is that aboriginal claims be justly settled before development by government or industry."[111]

November 16: **Three Elders are first to be arrested at Lyell Island**: Chief Gaahlaay, Watson Pryce; Jaadsangkinghliiyas, Ada Yovanovich; and Kamee, Ethel Jones. Flown to Sandspit by helicopter, they are fingerprinted, charged with mischief and released on the condition that they not interfere with loggers or use the roadways on Lyell Island. The Haida say their issue is not with the loggers, it is with BC. NDP MP Svend Robinson states in the media that it is " ... a day of shame for British Columbia."[112] Ernie Wilson hosts a potlatch in Skidegate, taking the name Niis Wes and the hereditary chieftainship of the Gakyals KiiGawaay.[113]

November 18: **Ten arrests at Lyell Island.**[114] In the news, Canada's Opposition leader John Turner says that Haida lands are being despoiled and tells Mulroney the Haida interests should be paramount in any negotiations; Canadian MP Jim Fulton says the conflict is grave and dangerous, suggesting that negotiations on the claims settlement should be started immediately;[115] Canada's Environment Minister Tom McMillan says Ottawa would be pleased to assist in creation of a national park but that Canada is powerless to act without BCs support because the land in question is "BC Crown land;"[116] Ottawa has offered to spend up to $10 million to buy out timber rights in the area, while an officer of WFP said their "rights" are worth far more than that;[117] and, Brian Williams, chairman of WAC says he told BC Environment Minister Austin Pelton that he wasn't happy the logging was taking place but that "the minister's answer was that a decision had been made and [we'll] have to proceed on those terms.".[118]

November 19: Loggers take the day off as Frank Beban meets with WFP executives to update them on the Athlii Gwaii stand. The Haida convene as well. In the House of Commons, NDP MP Jim Fulton states Haida claims are "as clear-cut a case of Aboriginal Title as you can find anywhere on Earth."[119]

November 20: **Twelve arrests at Lyell Island.** WFP is preparing documents to seek contempt of court charges against the Haida, which carry a possible two-year jail term, instead of charges of mis-chief. Attorney General Brian Smith also thinks the charges should be "more severe."[120] Haida Nation President Miles Richardson Jr.

A 2 The Sun FRI., NOVEMBER 22, 1985 ★★★★C

Ottawa offers to aid Moresby mediation

responds, "Everyone [on Lyell Island] knows what we're doing is right and nothing will change because of the severity of any court penalty ... We'll deal with the contempt charges when they come. As this gets more challenging, our resolve seems to get stronger."[121]

Echoing demands made for the last two days by NDP MP Jim Fulton, NDP MP Svend Robinson calls on both the Canadian and BC governments to begin immediate negotiations with the Haida, saying, "The Constitution recognizes and affirms existing Aboriginal and Treaty rights. And that includes land claims."[122]

November 22: **Five arrests at Lyell Island. Seventeen Haida and a Canadian MP are charged with criminal contempt.** When asked by reporters if the Haida were prepared to go to jail, Haida Nation President Miles Richardson Jr. responds, "Our people have always been very law abiding. We've survived on our islands for thousands of years only because of our own very stringent laws." When asked about the Haida perspective, WFP Executive R. P. Manning said, "If I were a Haida, I'd probably be doing the same thing, wouldn't you?"[123] RCMP Superintendent Bob Currie says "I think the Haida people have made it clear what their position is. It's not my position to say the government should step in, but it would certainly be a welcome step. Anything to get us out of this would be helpful."[124]

Canada's Indian Affairs Minister David Crombie and Minister of Environment Tom McMillan send out a press release indicating that they are willing to meet with interested parties concerning South Moresby.[125] The offer is refused by BC Attorney General

Brian Smith who says no negotiations will take place because the dispute is going before the courts. George Erasmus, national chief of the Assembly of First Nations, representing approximately 350,000 people; James Gosnell of the Nisga'a Tribal Council; and Haida Nation President Mile Richardson Jr. say Bennett broke a promise the Social Credit party made ten years earlier when the party passed a resolution that would "recognize and rectify past and present grievances" of Native people and set up a "mechanism" for negotiations. Bennett denies he went back on the promise.[126]

November 24: Twenty-five Mounties are reported on Lyell Island.[127]

November 25: **Twenty-eight arrests at Lyell Island.** Temperatures fall to minus 28 degrees overnight.[128]

November 27: **Seven arrests at Lyell Island.**[129] In the news, Canadian and world church organizations offer moral and financial support to the Haida. "First and foremost, it's a human rights issue," says Reverend Peter Hammel, Anglican Church of Canada's consultant on national affairs. Seven Canadian churches have agreed to send telegrams in support of the Haida to BC Premier Bill Bennett and Attorney General Brian Smith, urging BC to negotiate Aboriginal Title, emphasizing the importance of protecting the unique environment, and stressing it is not fair of BC to argue jobs will be lost if Native Rights and the environment are protected. "We really feel strongly that the Haida have title to that land and need to be involved in decision-making [about] that land," said Project North spokesman Lois Kunkel. The policy of the United and Anglican churches is that no development should take place on un-surrendered Aboriginal land until land claims have been justly settled. Financial contributions from churches include the Geneva-based World Council of Churches ($5,000) and the United Church ($2,000).[130]

November 27: It's reported that Prime Minister Brian Mulroney met with BC Premier Bill Bennett to discuss solving the controversy surrounding Lyell Island. Bennett says he's rejected the offer to mediate the dispute and won't call a moratorium on logging.[131] The BC Federation of Labor attacks BC in the news for its "cowardly use of the courts and police in a game of divide and conquer."[132]

Nine hundred BC Federation of Labor delegates attending Canada's annual federal convention give three standing ovations to speakers urging passage of an emergency resolution demanding all charges against the Haida blocking the road on Lyell Island be dropped. Calling on their government to negotiate a fair and just settlement of the Haida land claim, the resolution declares "solidarity with both the Haida and the natural resource workers." Haida citizen and BC Government Employees Union delegate Delphin Trudel says, "[My people] will not become the victims of cultural genocide ...." Industrial Woodworkers Association Regional Vice-President Jack Munro says, "... it wasn't the Indians who stopped this logging, it was the government ... they're directly responsible for this mess."[133]

November 28: **Two arrests at Lyell Island. Seventeen Haida and a NDP MP face criminal contempt charges at the BC Supreme Court in Prince Rupert.**

In court, lawyer Jack Giles urges the Haida "to perform their duty and agree the lawbreaking will end." Haida Nation President Miles Richardson Jr. responds, "I don't have the mandate to say that in this court. I don't have the mandate to say that publicly or otherwise." During proceedings, Richardson points to the Haida charged, "These are not criminals before you." Chief Justice Allan McEachern responds, " Oh, I know that. You don't have to persuade me of that, that they're not regular criminals."[134]

A request by the Anglican Church to intervene in the proceedings because the issues are "spiritual in nature," is denied. Anglican Bishop of northern BC John Hannen wanted to testify to the genuineness of the spiritual connection the Haida have to their lands. Judge McEachern is reported as repeatedly saying the case was technical, concerned exclusively with determining whether the accused had defied the injunction, and that "the religious, moral, social or other kinds of concepts are not anything I can do anything about here. The larger questions are not before me. I wish they were."[135]

November 28: The Native Brotherhood begins its annual convention in Massett. More than 70 leaders gather for three days, the theme being the environment. "There will definitely be strong support for the Haidas, there's no question of that," says Cliff Atleo, Executive Director of the Native Brotherhood of BC.[136]

November 29: **Five arrests at Lyell Island. At the Supreme Court of BC in Prince Rupert, ten Haida are convicted of criminal contempt of court.** In Haida Nation President Miles Richardson Jr.'s final summation, he states his people know in their hearts that Lyell Island belongs to them despite the fact that BC has refused, for more than 100 years, to acknowledge or negotiate the Haida Nation's land claim. He continues on, saying the Haida are under a religious obligation protect the land that has provided them with their livelihood and culture. Chief Justice A. E. McEachern is considering prison sentences of four to six months but would suspend the sentences if the Haida promised not to block logging on Lyell Island.[137]

November 30: A province-wide poll commissioned by The Sun newspaper finds three out of five British Columbians want Premier Bennett to negotiate land claims.[138]

Loggers on Lyell Island go to work. Frank Beban says operations will be suspended over Christmas.[139]

December 2: BC is reported to have applied for an injunction that will vastly extend police powers to keep the Haida from blocking logging operations on Lyell Island. If approved, Haida citizens can be stopped by police before they reach Lyell Island. If a person refuses to not participate in the blockade, they can be arrested or diverted by police. Attorney General Brian Smith says the injunction would let police "work outside the arena of conflict—stop Haida in fishing boats or wherever found. We want the logging on the island, and the policing elsewhere—interrupting logging to remove Indians is very time-consuming and expensive." Supreme Court Justice Allan McEachern reserves his decision on the request.[140]

December 3: WFP is expecting approval of seven new logging sites on Lyell Island; if approved, their logging area will increase from about 50 hectares to over 150 hectares.[141]

It is reported that BC has spent over $200,000 in police costs on Lyell Island.[142]

December 6: At the BC Supreme Court in Vancouver, Chief Justice Allan McEachern assigns nine of the Haida convicted suspended sentences "as long as they do not return to Lyell Island for a period of six months from this date." One has their sentence reprieved and Svend Robinson is charged $750. McEachern says:

> It is obvious that there is an escalating dispute between the elected government of this province and the Haida people over title or property rights to the Queen Charlotte Islands. It is obvious that this dispute cannot be resolved in these proceedings. It is also obvious that these proceedings are being used for political purposes, that being the stating and restating of the Haida's claim to the Queen Charlotte Islands. Whether they have been driven to this strategy or whether it has been deliberately chosen as a tactic in their overall strategy, it is not for me to say.

> It is further obvious that the court has been placed in the invidious position of dealing with a specific problem arising in a much larger dispute. The Haidas particularly base almost all their arguments and submissions in these proceedings on the assumption that their claims justify their actions, when they know that that is something I cannot take into account. In short, the Court is being used for political purposes without there being any possibility that the Court can do what the Haidas ask...

> Reverend Hannon agreed with me that there is no earthly point to be served by any of these defendants going to jail ... The Court has no choice, however, but to respond to breaches of the law, but my intention is to go as far as humanly possible to avoid sending anyone to jail if such can be avoided.

> With that in mind, I informed the defendants last week that I had in mind imposing a term of imprisonment of from four to six months, and to suspend sentence on condition that the order of this court not be further breached.

> It has been suggested that this is a harsh sentence, but I do not think it is, considering the position of most of the defendants. They will not give me any assurance that they will obey the law.[143]

December 10: The Haida Nation, Canada and BC meet. BC Attorney General Brian Smith says he'll ask the BC cabinet to review its decision to allow logging on Lyell Island. Speaking to the meeting, "I've never heard it in that detail before. Hearing it first hand was very helpful. It impressed me ... It doesn't represent a change of heart. I think it represents a renewed resolve to try to deal with matters cooperatively."[144]

1986
The AAC for TFL 24 remains at 432,375 cubic metres, with an operable base of 73,802 hectares.[145]

January 8: With logging expected to begin again, it's reported that four Haida have returned to Lyell Island.[146]

January 10: In brief to WAC, Canada's Environment Minister Tom McMillan says President Miles Richardson Jr. has indicated the Haida Nation would be willing to consider a national park *reserve* and have requested further discussions with Canada's federal officials. The brief describes a "reserve" as a mechanism to protect lands without prejudicing Aboriginal land claims.[147]

January 16: The WAC begins two days of public hearings in Skidegate and Sandspit. Diane Brown tells the committee Gwaii Haanas has deep spiritual meaning for the Haida and that, "the thing that is inside of me to protect the land is a lot stronger that the laws of this society—of your society today." In Sandspit, John Ulinder says, "Timber is a crop. It must be harvested, like wheat is harvested in the Prairies."[148]

BC Minister of Forests Tom Waterland, whose ministry granted the cutting permits on Lyell Island, is accused of a conflict of interest. In 1983 Waterland invested $20,000 in Western Pulp Partnership (WPP), a tax-deferral scheme, which owns pulp mills worth $400 million and has a timber supply agreement with WFP.[149]

January 17: Tom Waterland resigns. It is revealed BC Energy Minister Stephen Rogers also has shares in WPP, worth $100,000. Roger's portfolio includes oil and gas "rights" in the South Moresby area. Both ministers sit on ELUC. WAC Chair Brian Williams says he dumped his shares on December 9, 1985 once he learned WPP was connected to WFP.[150]

January 20: After a five-week break, logging resumes on Lyell Island. Haida on the line call for an immediate end to logging then step aside for the loggers, demonstrating the Haida Nation's intent to negotiate their Title in good faith. In discussing the park reserve proposal, Haida Nation President Miles Richardson Jr. suggests it could be a workable interim measure while land claims are resolved. Nine more cutting permits for WFP are pending.[151]

January 21: The news reveals BC Energy Minister Stephen Rogers signed a cabinet order giving BC Hydro (of which Rogers is a board member) authority to grant energy discounts. Port Alice Mill, owned by WPP, is one of the companies benefitting—paying only 1.3 cents per kilowatt hour rather than the regular rate of four cents per kilowatt.

Industrial Woodworkers of America's International Vice President Jack Munro says, "Rogers has to resign, and if he doesn't, the premier has to ask for that resignation. If the premier doesn't do that, it makes a mockery out of the system." Munro also brings to light that two BC cabinet orders in the past year-and-a-half have granted lower stumpage rates for WPP and other companies getting wood from Haida Gwaii, reducing costs from the usual $1.50 per cubic metre to 10 cents per cubic metre.[152]

Broadcaster Jack Webster, who has aired several editorials against the Haida, also has shares in WPP. Webster claims there is no conflict between his investment and his news coverage of the industry.[153]

January 22: BC Premier Bill Bennett says Stephen Rogers can keep his job because he has had no direct dealings with the lumber industry or WPP.[154]

January 29: **The BC Crown upgrades charges against 11 more Haida** to breaching a court order, punishable for up to two years in jail upon conviction. Included in the charges are the three Elders arrested on November 16, 1985: Watson Pryce, Ethel Jones and Ada Yovanovich. Haida Nation President Miles Richardson Jr. says the act "flies in the face of [BCs] promise to sit down and talk," saying the Haida are surprised BC would lay more serious charges against three Elders. "If this is an indication of their attitude I don't know what to expect of them anymore. This episode has certainly increased our readiness."[155]

The Nature of Things airs Windy Bay again.[156]

January 30: At WAC hearings in Vancouver, WFP President Rodger Manning, cynical at the "very coincidental" timing of the Windy Bay airing, proposes over an eight percent reduction in the company's timber cut. IPS spokesman John Broadhead says it does "nothing

to keep South Moresby a wilderness," and that the company was making "no sacrifice in terms of foregoing revenues."[157]

February 5: Canadian Fisheries official Chris Dragseth says Frank Beban Logging Ltd. and ITT Industries of Canada Ltd. (predecessor to WFP) have been jointly-charged under Section 31(1) of Canada's federal Fisheries Act with the "harmful destruction and alteration" of fish habitat, alleging logging practices between 1977-1980 resulted in the 1984 destruction of Landrick Creek on Lyell Island. Company representatives are due in court on February 26 in Queen Charlotte, the same day 11 Haida face charges of breaching a court order for protecting Lyell Island. The charges against the Haida are later dropped.[158]

February 7: After a two-hour meeting with Haida Nation President Miles Richardson Jr., BC Attorney General Brian Smith announces no new cutting permits will be granted on Lyell Island until BC acts on the recommendations of WAC, whose report is due March 3rd. Frank Beban says company layoffs will happen within two weeks. Haida Nation President Miles Richardson Jr. says BCs move is an "opening" that will allow talks to continue.[159]

February 10: BC Progressive Conservative leader Peter Pollen formally charges BC Energy Minister Stephen Rogers with violating the Financial Disclosure Act, paying for the action out of his own pocket. Pollen says while Rogers has no direct interest in the South Moresby issue, that as a cabinet minister he's "collectively responsible" for every decision BC makes.[160]

February 23: The news reports Canadian musician Bruce Cockburn presented a $35,311 cheque to Haida artist and President of the CHN Vancouver Region, Robert Davidson, for the Haida's fight to save Gwaii Haanas. Davidson gifted Cockburn one of his paintings in appreciation.[161]

March 4: The Save South Moresby Caravan leaves Newfoundland.[162]

March 7: WAC's report, The Wilderness Mosaic, is submitted, recommending a national park in South Moresby, with negotiations to be completed before 1989. Excluded from the areas would be the islands of Lyell, Richardson, T'aanuu and Kunga, except for an ecological reserve on Lyell Island and a buffer strip on the west side of both Richardson and Lyell Island. WAC also recognizes the Canada must "consult the Haida Nation to identify their interests and provide them with a voice and a share in the management of such a park."[163]

March 15: The Save South Moresby Caravan arrives in Vancouver.[164]

March 21: US folk singer Pete Seeger holds a benefit concert in Vancouver for the Lyell Island Defence Fund. CHN Vancouver Region President Robert Davidson helps organize the event.[165]

July: Basing their decision on the WAC report, BC again issues logging permits on Lyell Island, causing nine Haida to renounce their Haida citizenship. "This clarifies what the lack of a formal relationship between Canada and the Haida Nation means to our people," states Haida Nation President Miles Richardson Jr.[166]

October 24: BC Ministry of Forests and Lands writes Haida Nation President Miles Richardson Jr., noting they'd learned in the press that the Haida will be building a longhouse on Lyell Island and advising "to do so without first receiving formal approval is contrary to the laws of British Columbia."[167]

1987

Bill Reid halts production of the Black Canoe sculpture commissioned for the Canadian Embassy in Washington, DC due to Canada and BCs lack of addressing the issues surrounding Lyell Island.[168]

January 13: Canada and BC meet, agreeing to discuss three major issues when they reconvene on February 19: a national park boundary, compensation for third party forest and mining interests, and the establishment of an adjacent national marine park.[169]

February: Canada's Minister of Indian Affairs and Northern Development responds to an inquiry from Haida Nation President Miles Richardson Jr., advising that the logging plan for Lyell Island has been recommended but has not yet received final approval.[170]

March: The Haida host a Loggers Feast at Lyell Island for Frank Beban and his crew.[171]

March 22: At a public meeting held in Skidegate, Haida Nation President Miles Richardson Jr. addresses the room: "Contrary to

[the] position of the Haida Nation, logging is still taking place. The CHN is proposing that we return to Lyell Island and shut everything down ... [Canada] has accepted our position in principal but [has] not been able to help us. The most effective way to change that to our advantage is to go back down to Lyell Island and stop the logging. Not four months down the road, now. A national park reserve will protect [the] area, but the Haida Nation is not interested ... if all of Lyell Island is not included."[172]

May: The Haida Nation potlatches the opening of Looking Around Blinking House at Windy Bay.[173]

May 14: Canada's three political parties unanimously adopt a resolution put forward by NDP MP Jim Fulton, calling on BC to cooperate in the creation of a national park reserve; to call on Canada to provide compensation to interests affected by its establishment, and for the continued participation of the Haida in matters affecting South Moresby.[174]

June 21: *Loo Taas* leaves Vancouver, embarking on journey up the Northwest Coast and over to Haida Gwaii. Throughout the trip, paddlers wonder if they'll be heading to Lyell Island for another stand-off, or to Skidegate for a celebration.[175]

June 22: Canadian MP Charles Caccia speaks in Canada's House of Commons:

> Mr. Speaker, the issue of South Moresby demonstrates that, when we come right down to it, the provinces place their own objectives above national objectives ... The federal government is perceived as a pushover at the negotiating table. The Premier of British Columbia has proven he wants to exploit the situation to the limit, a form of 'environmental hostage taking' ... Environment Canada and the Minister should become ardent advocates for the protection of South Moresby ... I call upon every Member of this House to help in building up such pressure. South Moresby should not be held for ransom and the Premier of BC should not be allowed to make a mockery of the new cooperative federalism proclaimed on May 1 by the Prime Minister.[176]

June 24: It's reported that BC has rejected Canada's offer of $106 million, the most Canada has ever offered a province to "set aside land" for a national park.[177]

The Islands community came together in November of 2010 to mark 25 years since the Stand, to celebrate the achievement.

July 11: The Canadian and BC governments sign the South Moresby Memorandum of Understanding (MOU) to stop the logging in Gwaii Haanas. *Loo Taas* arrives in Skidegate, a gigantic feast is held to welcome the canoe and her paddlers home. Tom McMillan flies in by helicopter to join the festivities, announcing the freshly signed South Moresby MOU.[178]

End of July: Frank Beban dies from a heart attack while dismantling his camp. "He was an honorable man," says Haida spokesman Ernie Collison in the news, "We are a people protecting our heritage, and he was a man fighting for his livelihood and his workers' jobs."[180]

October 28: Haida Nation President Miles Richardson Jr. and Canada's Environment Minister Tom McMillan meet to discuss the many issues surrounding the development of a national park reserve.[181]

1988

"Indians" working on reserve are "allowed" to pay into Canada's Pension Plan.

January 26: Haida Nation President Miles Richardson Jr. receives a letter from Canada's Environment Minister Tom McMillan, referencing their October 1987 meeting. McMillan recognizes the importance Richardson placed on both Haida Title and the necessity of Haida management of the Islands. He continues, "My goal is to forge a partnership, based on mutual respect, between the Government of Canada and the Haida in protecting and managing the South Moresby lands and waters as park reserves. In so doing, I believe we will be advancing the resolution of the comprehensive claim of the Haida Nation." He also agrees with Richardson's stance that interim measures between the governments are necessary while waiting for Haida Title to be addressed. McMillan advises he expects an agreement to be signed soon between Canada and BC assuring the "ultimate protection of South Moresby as a national park reserve, with funds for its development along with regional development."

July 12: Canada and BC sign the South Moresby Memorandum of Agreement (SMA) which, through the lens of these two governments, provides Canada the ability to establish a national park and national marine park, as well as financial compensation for interests affected by the protection of Gwaii Haanas (via the creation of a Regional Economic Development Initiative fund (REDI) and South Moresby Forest Replacement Account fund (SMFRA)).

July 25: Environment Canada's P. Thompson sends Haida Nation President Miles Richardson Jr. a copy of the SMA, writing "We will now be moving forward to implement the many commitments contained in the Agreement and look forward to working with Queen Charlotte Islands residents and organizations in the planning, developing and operating of the park reserves and in implementing [REDI]. Staff at the Canadian Parks Service will start the park planning very soon ..."[185a]

September 17: In an open letter to the residents of Haida Gwaii, Haida Nation President Miles Richardson Jr. writes:
The Gwaii Haanas/South Moresby issue has been the focus of much attention on Haida Gwaii for many years. The recent "South Moresby Agreement" between Canada and BC will trigger much direct government action, both politically and economically, on Haida Gwaii. To date there has not been a formal agreement between Canada and the Haida Nation. It is not acceptable that development related to the "South Moresby agreement" proceed without a formal Haida/Canada Agreement in place.
The position of the Haida Nation has been clear and consistent. The position of the Council of the Haida Nation regarding the [REDI] initiative is that none of these dollars be spent until a Haida/Canada Agreement regarding the Gwaii Haanas Archipelago is in place.[185b]

1989
January 1: With the anticipated loss of over 52% of the TFL 24 land base to the creation of the Gwaii Haanas National Park Reserve, the AAC is reduced by 73 percent. The new AAC is set at 115,000 cubic metres, with an operable area of 23,514 hectares.[184]

April 11: BC Park Projects Coordinator J. Christakos writes to Haida Nation negotiator Guujaaw, recounting their meeting of March 23rd, writing, "I explained my appreciation and understanding of your position with respect to the issue of land ownership and I sensed that Colin [Richardson, also a Haida Nation negotiator] too appreciated my position as the matter now stands." Christakos goes on to summarize issues discussed at the meeting.[185]

April 15: A meeting between Haida Nation President Miles Richardson Jr. and Canada's new Minister of Environment Lucien Bruchard is held to discuss Canada's involvement in the management of Gwaii Haanas. Meeting notes record Richardson giving a background on Gwaii Haanas then addresses the current climate, saying:

We went through a lot of torment, a lot of conflict in stopping the logging. Now we have a proposal from [Canada] to create a national park in that area. That concerns us a lot.
If we are going to be successful in [coming to an agreement] it is preferable to us that we address the long outstanding business of a formal relationship between the Haida Nation and Canada ... We have no formal relationship and yet Canada continues to assert sovereign unilaterally assumed jurisdiction over these Islands.
We have sat down with representatives in your department ... and tried to come to an agreement that encompassed and reflected the broad consensus we share in terms of our mutual objectives for that area ... We tried to go ahead without prejudice to the question of ownership, but at every step down the road we were stymied.
We need to have trust if we are going to carry out this very worthwhile task ... Any initiatives that are taken in this relationship must be acceptable to our view of things.

The fundamental recognition is that the Haida people are the status quo in that area and any new initiatives must be agreeable to us. From there we can build an agreement. It is important and critical to us proceeding if we have this and a mutually acceptable agreement in place.

When asked by Richardson if he is "prepared to steer that through to the agreement stage personally," Bruchard responds, "I personally will convince the government to enter into an agreement with you where your principles, where our principles, where the imperatives of the [integrity] of the land will be respected ... I am ready to meet you, work with you at any time ...." Richardson responds, "If that's the case, then I believe we can get to work immediately on putting in place an agreement regarding Gwaii Haanas."[186]

October 18: WFP is acquired by Doman Forest Products Ltd., but continues to operate under WFP.[187]

November 29: Responding to recent negotiation discussion around the development of the Gwaii Haanas Agreement, Haida Nation negotiator Guujaaw writes to Canada's Deputy Minister of the Environment Jim Collison. Asserting Haida Rights and Title, Guujaaw states that the ongoing use of Gwaii Haanas by the Haida Nation will continue. He also states that Canada cannot decide the citizenship of the Haida, writing, "Some of our people resent being called 'Canadian' ... While some of our people are happy to be called Canadians, it is their right in our constitution as well as yours to have additional citizenship as they choose. Citizenship cannot be imposed on anyone however and this agreement isn't from Canada's little Indians, it is between the Haida Sovereign authority and Canada's authority ... [The Agreement] should simply read 'all people of Haida Ancestry' ... that is what our people put themselves on the line for, certainly not to lock themselves out."[188]

1990

Canada forms a Planning and Coordination Committee to oversee the spending of the SMA's REDI fund.[189]

March 23: A special meeting between Haida Nation President Miles Richardson Jr. and Canada's Minister of Environment Lucien Bouchard is held to address a major outstanding issue in negotiations around the Gwaii Haanas Agreement: the definition of "Haida." Richardson states that " ... only the Haida can define who Haida are and that the only options acceptable to the Haida [are] to use the Haida definition 'all people of Haida ancestry,' or to be silent" and that "the Haida are not prepared to change their constitution or prejudice their position on sovereignty." The parties discuss the differing views on citizenship as being set out in parallel statements in sub-section 1.1 of the Gwaii Haanas Agreement.[190]

May 4: Richardson receives a letter from Bouchard saying, "I am pleased that we have succeeded in resolving all the outstanding issues in the Agreement during our three meetings in February and March ... Together we have crafted a truly innovative and creative approach ... During our meetings, I felt that we shared the same strong desire to have the Agreement ratified by the Special Haida Assembly, now scheduled for May 5, so that we could move ahead in the spirit of cooperation that characterizes the Agreement. I understand from your [May 2] letter that you wish to resolve a number of additional issues before the agreement is signed. Moreover, it is your view that nothing should proceed beyond some preliminary planning until the Agreement is signed." Bouchard goes on to clarify his position on the key issues Richardson raised, including who manages and distributes the REDI funds.[191]

August 30: Watching the Oka Crisis unfold, Haida Nation President Miles Richardson Jr. writes the Quebec Premier R. Bourassa, stating the Haida Nation's solidarity with the Mohawk people, urging the army be replaced by peaceful talks.[192]

1991

Bill Reid's Black Canoe is unveiled at the Canadian Embassy in Washington, DC.

1993

It is agreed that the REDI fund be transferred to residents of Haida Gwaii for independent management and distribution.[193]

January 30: The Gwaii Haanas Agreement is signed in Old Massett.

1994

September: The Gwaii Trust is formalized, REDI funds are handed over to Haida Gwaii.[194]

1996

The Report of the Royal Commission on Aboriginal Peoples is released.

Canada's last federally funded residential school is closed.

1997

November 7: In the BC Court of Appeal, three judges led by Mr. Justice William Esson rule that BC does not have exclusive control over its forests as long as Aboriginal land claims remain unresolved.[195]

December 11: In a ruling on the Delgamuukw case, the Supreme Court of Canada acknowledges the continued existence of Aboriginal Title.[196]

The Haida Nation designates SG̱aan K̲inghlas (the Bowie Seamount) as a Haida Marine Protected Area.

2002

The Council of the Haida Nation files a Statement of Claim, launching the Haida Title case.

2004

November 18: The Haida Nation brings BC to court over TFL 39. A summary of the Supreme Court of Canada's ruling is provided by EAGLE Law, the Haida Nation's legal firm at the time:

> The Supreme Court of Canada affirmed that the Haida have a good case in support of Aboriginal Title and a strong case for the Aboriginal Right to harvest red cedar. Therefore, the Court held that the Province has a legally enforceable duty to consult the Haida with respect to TFL 39 and that the Province failed to fulfill this duty when replacing and approving a transfer of TFL 39. The Haida are not required to prove their Rights or Title in court before the duty of consultation arises: a key clarification of the law. The court also held that the Honour of the Crown requires interim protection of Aboriginal interests pending proof or resolution. The Court found that Weyerhaeuser does not have a duty to consult the Haida, because 'the ultimate responsibility for consultation and accommodation rests with the Crown' but did hold that there are some circumstances where third parties could be liable to Aboriginal Peoples.[197]

2005

The Haida Nation and other Island residents again oppose commercial logging practices on Haida Gwaii, resulting in the Islands Spirit Rising stand. Negotiations between the Haida Nation and BC begin.

A protocol agreement is signed between the CHN and the municipalities of Masset and Port Clements.[198]

2006

A protocol agreement is signed between the CHN and the Skeena-Queen Charlotte Regional District Electoral Area D.[199]

A protocol agreement is signed between the CHN and the Village of Queen Charlotte.[200]

2007

The Haida Gwaii Strategic Land Use Agreement between the Haida Nation and BC is signed.[201]

The SG̱aan K̲inghlas MoU between the Haida Nation and Canada is signed.[202]

The SMFRA fund is handed over to Haida Gwaii to become the Athlii Gwaii Legacy Trust.[203]

The United Nations Declaration on the Rights of Indigenous Peoples (UNDRIP) is adopted by the General Assembly. Canada votes against adoption.

2009

The Kunst'aa Guu—Kunst'aayah Reconciliation Protocol between the Haida Nation and BC is signed.[204]

Enbridge's proposed Northern Gateway pipeline is on the radar of Coastal and Interior Indigenous Nations, and our Canadian neighbours.

2010

The marine component of the Gwaii Haanas Agreement is formalized by the Haida Nation and Canada.

The Haida Nation respectfully repatriates the name "Queen Charlotte Islands" back to the Crown.

2013

The Gwaii Haanas Legacy Pole is raised at Windy Bay to celebrate the twenty year anniversary of the Gwaii Haanas Agreement.

2014

Canada approves the Northern Gateway Pipeline proposal.

2015

The Truth and Reconciliation Commission releases its report with ninety-four calls to action.

The Haida Nation and BC release the Haida Gwaii Marine Use Management Plan.[205]

2016

Enbridge's Northern Gateway Pipeline is shut down.

Canada approves the Pacific Northwest liquified natural gas (LNG) project with 190 legally binding conditions. Less than a year after receiving approval, the companies behind Pacific Northwest pull the plug on the deal.

Canada approves the Kinder Morgan Trans-Mountain Expansion project.

2017

BC approves the Site C hydroelectric dam.

2018

Canada passes Bill C-48 (The Oil Tanker Moratorium Act) in their House of Commons.

Indigenous Peoples, Canadians and their various governments, including the government of BC, oppose Kinder Morgan. Several Indigenous Nations file legal suits. Blockades and arrests begin.

BC offers new conditions and tax incentives for LNG projects in a move to attract investment.

With investors of Kinder Morgan on the verge of pulling out, Canada announces it will buy the pipeline for $4.5 billion of taxpayers money with a further $3M bonus to top executives.

Canada passes a private member's bill, Romeo Sanganash's Bill C-262, to bring UNDRIP into Canadian law. Five days later the Liberal and Conservative parties vote that UNDRIP shouldn't be applied to the Kinder Morgan Pipeline Expansion project.

**WE ARE STILL HERE
AND SO, IT CONTINUES …**

TIMELINE ENDNOTES

1   "The Smallpox Issue," Haida Laas Journal, March 2009.
2   Pioneer Era: 1800s-1911. *Timber Tenures in British Columbia, Managing Public Forests in the Public Interest*. BC Ministry of Forests, Lands and Natural Resource Operations, 2012: Section 2.
3   Evolution of Timber Tenures in British Columbia. *Timber Tenures in British Columbia, Managing Public Forests in the Public Interest*. BC Ministry of Forests, Lands and Natural Resource Operations, 2012: Section 2.
4   See footnote 3.
5   Nick Reynolds, Stewardship Planning Coordinator, Council of the Haida Nation. Personal communication with the editor, February 20, 2018.
6   See endnote 5.
7   See endnote 5.
8   See endnote 5.
9   See endnote 5.
10 Early Regulation and the Founding of an Industry: 1912-1946. *Timber Tenures in British Columbia, Managing Public Forests in the Public Interest*. BC Ministry of Forests, Lands and Natural Resource Operations, 2012: Section 2.
11 See endnote 5.
12 Pearson, Audrey and Challenger, Derek. *Old-growth Forests 1937-2007 for TllGa Kun GwaanyYaay (Lyell Island) Haida Gwaii (Queen Charlotte Islands) British Columbia, Canada* 2009: 9.
13 See endnote 5.
14 See endnote 12.
15 See endnote 12.
16 See endnote 12.
17 See endnote 10.
18 Sustained Yield and Industrial Growth: 1947-1978 in *Timber Tenures in British Columbia, Managing Public Forests in the Public Interest*. BC Ministry of Forests, Lands and Natural Resource Operations, 2012. Section Two.
19 *TFL History Summary*, Council of the Haida Nation, 2018; Pederson, Larry. *Tree Farm Licence 24, Rationale for Annual Allowable Cut (AAC) Determination*. British Columbia Ministry of Forests, 1995: 3; and *South Moresby Land Use Alternatives*. Final report to the Environment and Land Use Committee. South Moresby Resource Planning Team. Victoria, BC: The Queen's Printer for British Columbia, 1983: 15.
20 Pederson, Larry, Chief Forester. *Tree Farm Licence 24: Rationale for Annual Allowable Cut (AAC) Determination*. British Columbia Ministry of Forests, 1995: 3.
21 *TFL 24 History Summary*, Council of the Haida Nation, 2018; and Pederson, Larry. *Tree Farm Licence 24: Rationale for Annual Allowable Cut (AAC) Determination*. British Columbia Ministry of Forests, 1995: 3.
22 *TFL 24 History*, Council of the Haida Nation, 2018.
23 Pederson, Larry. *Tree Farm Licence 24: Rationale for Annual Allowable Cut (AAC) Determination*. British Columbia Ministry of Forests, 1995. Page 4.
24 *TFL 24 History Summary*, Council of the Haida Nation, 2018; and Pederson, Larry. *Tree Farm Licence 24: Rationale for Annual Allowable Cut (AAC) Determination*. British Columbia Ministry of Forests, 1995: 4.
25 John Yeltatzie, Captain Gold and John Broadhead. Personal communication with the editor, 2015-2018.
26 See endnote 24.
27 Islands Protection Society. A brief submitted to the QCI Public Advisory Committee to the BC Forest Service, re: The Southern Moresby Wilderness Proposal. October 2, 1977: 2.
28 See endnote 24.
29 Islands Protection Society. A brief submitted to the QCI Public Advisory Committee to the BC Forest Service, re: The Southern Moresby Wilderness Proposal. October 2, 1977: 2; and *South Moresby Land Use Alternatives*. Final report to the Environment and Land Use Committee. South Moresby Resource Planning Team. Victoria, BC: The Queen's Printer for British Columbia 1983: 16.
30 See endnote 27.
31 *South Moresby Land Use Alternatives*. Final report to the Environment and Land Use Committee. South Moresby Resource Planning Team. Victoria, BC: The Queen's Printer for British Columbia 1983: 16.
32 CHN Executive Meeting minutes, December 7, 1974.
33 See endnote 27.

34 See endnote 31.
35 See endnote 27.
36 *South Moresby Land Use Alternatives*. Final report to the Environment and Land Use Committee. South Moresby Resource Planning Team. Victoria, BC: The Queen's Printer for British Columbia 1983: 17.
37 See endnote 27.
38 See endnote 27.
39 See endnote 36.
40 Islands Protection Society. A brief submitted to the QCI Public Advisory Committee to the BC Forest Service, re: The Southern Moresby Wilderness Proposal. October 2, 1977: 4.
41 See endnote 27.
42 See endnote 27.
43 Broadhead, John. *All Alone Stone*, in this publication: see page 91
44 See endnote 27. see page133
45 See endnote 36. see page 97
46 *South Moresby Land Use Alternatives*. Final report to the Environment and Land Use Committee. South Moresby Resource Planning Team. Victoria, BC: The Queen's Printer for British Columbia 1983: 18
47 See endnote 46.
48 See endnote 46.
49 *South Moresby Land Use Alternatives*. Final report to the Environment and Land Use Committee. South Moresby Resource Planning Team. Victoria, BC: The Queen's Printer for British Columbia 1983: 18; and Broadhead, John. *Islands at the Edge*. Islands Protection Society, ed. Vancouver, BC: Douglas & McIntyre 1984: 134.
50 Broadhead, John. *Islands at the Edge*. Islands Protection Society, ed. Vancouver, BC: Douglas &McIntyre 1984: 134-135; and Gill, Ian. *All that we Say is Ours: Guujaaw and the Reawakening of the Haida Nation*. Vancouver: Douglas & McIntyre Publishers, 2010: 96.
51 *South Moresby Land Use Alternatives*. Final report to the Environment and Land Use Committee. South Moresby Resource Planning Team. Victoria, BC: The Queen's Printer for British Columbia 1983: 19.
52 Gill, Ian. *All That We Say Is Ours*. Vancouver, BC: Douglas & McIntyre, 2010: 96-97
53 See endnote 51.
54 See endnote 24.
55 *TFL 24 History Summary*, Council of the Haida Nation, 2018; and *South Moresby Land Use Alternatives*. Final report to the Environment and Land Use Committee. South Moresby Resource Planning Team. Victoria, BC: The Queen's Printer for British Columbia 1983: 18.
56 See endnote 24.
57 Bohn, Glenn. *Politicians seek to preserve South Moresby*. The Sun, Sept 7, 1985.
58 See endnote 24.
59 No author. *Totems declared Heritage Site*. Provincial Secretary, Volume 25, Number 10, November 1980.
60 Terri-Lynn Williams-Davidson, White Raven Law Corporation. Personal communication with the editor, May 7, 2018.
61 *World Heritage List No. 157*. International Council of Monuments and Sites, Paris, 1981.
62 See endnote 60.
63 Boyko, Cindy. *Watching Over Village Sites—The Haida Gwaii Watchmen*, in this publication: XX.
64 See endnote 24.
65 Council of the Haida Nation. *Let it be known* public announcement, stamped December 8, 1981.
66 *Report of the Rapporteur*. World Heritage Committee: 5th Session. Sydney, 1981.
67 Suzuki, David. *The Nature of Things*, in this publication: XX.
68 Islands Protection Society. *Save a Little Something*, 1982.
69 *South Moresby Land Use Alternatives*, final report to the Environment and Land Use Committee. South Moresby Resource Planning Team. Victoria, BC: The Queen's Printer for British Columbia 1983.
70 See endnote 60.
71 Fuller, Stephan. Letter to the editor. The Sun, December 10, 1983.

72 Council of the Haida Nation, Vancouver Local. *An Evening for Athlii Gwaii.* Pete Seeger Benefit Concert information package. March 21, 1986.

73 Bohn, Glenn. *Confrontation has been building for years.* The Sun, October 29, 1985.

74 Bohn, Glenn. *Politicians seek to preserve South Moresby.* The Sun, September 7, 1985.

75 Broadhead, John. *All Alone Stone*, in this publication: see page 91; and Farrow, Moira. *Island Wilderness, Stories of the Queen Charlottes.* The Sun, December 29, 1984.

76 Bohn, Glenn. *Creation of Moresby park urged by ministry last spring.* The Sun, October 24, 1985.

77 Rose, Chris. *Ottawa urges preservation of south Moresby as parkland.* The Sun, February 7, 1985.

78 No author. *Two firms face Lyell charges.* The Sun, February 5, 1986; and No author. *Fisheries gets tough with loggers.* The Sun, February 6, 1986.

79 McLaren, Christie. *Committee aims to save BC islands.* The Globe and Mail, January 29, 1985; Rose, Chris. *Ottawa urges preservation of south Moresby as parkland.* The Sun, February 7, 1985; and *Save South Moresby A Retrospective.* Share BC — Citizens' Coalition For Sustainable Development, 1990.

80 Rose, Chris. *Ottawa urges preservation of south Moresby as parkland.* The Sun, February 7, 1985.

81 Meeting minutes, CHN & BC. Victoria, April 24-25, 1985.

82 Richardson Jr., Miles. Letter to A. J. Brummet, June 20, 1985.

83 Fitterman, Lisa and Shaw, Gillian. *Victoria said stalling on South Moresby Logging.* The Sun, August 9, 1985.

84 CHN official release, c. late summer, 1985.

85 Bohn, Glenn. *Politicians seek to preserve South Moresby.* The Sun, September 7, 1985.

86 Athlii Gwaii photo records, Skidegate Band Council.

87 CHN/Environment Canada minutes. Skidegate Longhouse (SBC Band Office). October 9, 1985.

88 Bohn, Glenn. *Creation of Moresby Park urged by ministry last spring.* The Sun, October 24, 1985.

89 Bohn, Glenn. Confrontation has been building for years. The Sun, October 29, 1985; and Wilderness Advisory Committee records, BC Archives Series GR-1601.

90 Bohn, Glenn. *Forest firm vows to log Lyell.* The Sun, October 26, 1985; Bohn, Glenn. *Indians halt Lyell logging.* The Sun, October 30, 1985.

91 No author. *Haidas out to halt logging on Lyell.* The Sun, October 29, 1985.

92 See endnote 91.

93 Athlii Gwaii photo records, Skidegate Band Council.

94 Fournier, Suzanne. *Haida head for sunrise showdown.* The Province, October 30, 1985.

95 Athlii Gwaii photo records, Skidegate Band Council; Fournier, Suzanne. *Haida head for sunrise showdown.* The Province, October 30, 1985; and Glavin, Terry. *Haidas to sail to stop fallers.* The Sun, October 29, 1985.

96 Athlii Gwaii photo records, Skidegate Band Council; Glavin, Terry. *Indians Halt Lyell Logging.* The Sun, October 30, 1985.

97 No author. *US group wants logging halt.* The Sun, November 1, 1985.

98 Transcript. *Proceedings at Trial.* Vancouver Registry No. C854987 and No. C854988. Justice Harry McKay. Supreme Court of British Columbia, November 18, 1985; and Bohn, Glenn and Needham, Phil. *Forest firms suing over Haida protest.* The Sun, November 2, 1985.

99 No author. *BC's no-negotiation stance reasserted on Indian claims.* The Sun, November 2, 1985.

100 Transcript. *Proceedings at Trial.* Vancouver Registry No. C854987 and No. C854988. Haida testimony heard by Justice Harry McKay. Supreme Court of British Columbia. November 6-8, 1985; and Bohn, Glenn. *Haidas, loggers vie in court.* The Sun, November 7, 1985.

101 Odam, Jes and Rose, Chris. *Loggers win – Haida challenge Bennett on land claims.* The Sun, November 9, 1985.

102 Transcript. *Proceedings at Trial.* Vancouver Registry No. C854987 and No. C854988. Haida testimony heard by Justice Harry McKay. Supreme Court of British Columbia. November 6-8, 1985.

103 Bohn, Glenn. *Lyell logging political issue, judge tells court.* The Sun, November 8, 1985.

104 CHN archives.

105 Canadian Press. *Ottawa bids to purchase timber rights.* The Globe and Mail, November 7, 1985.

106 Transcript. *Proceedings at Trial.* Vancouver Registry No. C854987 and No. C854988. Haida testimony heard by Justice Harry McKay. Supreme Court of British Columbia. November 6-8, 1985.

107 Odam, Jes and Rose, Chris. *Loggers win, Haidas challenge Bennett on land claims.* The Sun, November 9, 1985.

108 No author. *Haidas maintain blockade as loggers ready to move.* Winnipeg Free Press, November 13, 1985.

109 Canadian Press. *Haida allow loggers to pass road barrier.* The Globe and Mail, November 14, 1985.

110 Mason, Gary. *Protest parade at Legislature: 'Injunction not end of battle.'* Times Colonist, November 15, 1985.

111 Hume, Mark. *Loggers to test Haida blockade.* The Sun, November 16, 1985.

112 Lyell Island arrests records, Royal Canadian Mounted Police; News Services. *'3 arrests shameful.'* The Province, November 17, 1985; and Baldrey, Keith. *10 more Haidas arrested.* The Sun, November 18, 1985; and Cruickshank, John. *3 Haidas charged with defying order on island logging.* The Globe and Mail, November 18, 1985.

113 See endnote 112.

114 Lyell Island arrests records, Royal Canadian Mounted Police.; and Baldrey, Keith. *10 more Haidas arrested.* The Sun, November 18, 1985.

115 Canadian Press. *AP140.* Indian and Northern Affairs Canada, Communications Branch Press Monitoring, November 18, 1985.

116 Canadian Press. *Haidas expecting long fight.* The Globe and Mail, November 19, 1985. The Sun, November 18, 1985.

117 See endnote 116.

118 Pynn, Larry. *Pelton rebuff claimed on Moresby logging halt.* The Sun, November 18, 1985.

119 Baldrey, Keith. *Lyell loggers get cool-off time.* The Vancouver Sun, November 19, 1985; and Canadian Press. *AP110.* Indian and Northern Affairs Canada, Communications Branch Press Monitoring, November 19, 1985.

120 Lyell Island arrests records, Royal Canadian Mounted Police; and Canadian Press. *BC firm going back to court to thwart blockade by Haida.* The Globe and Mail, November 21, 1985.

121 Baldrey, Keith. *Haidas take a day off from Lyell Blockade.* The Sun, November 21, 1985.

122 Canadian Press. *AP062.* Indian and Northern Affairs Canada, Communications Branch Press Monitoring, November 20, 1985.

123 Lyell Island arrests records, Royal Canadian Mounted Police; *Notice of Motion.* Vancouver Registry No. C854987. Submitted by Western Forest Products to the Supreme Court of British Columbia, November 22, 1985; Cruickshank, John. *Haida not criminals, judge tells BC Court.* The Globe and Mail and Mail, November 24, 1985; and No author. *Log Jam.* The Sun, November 23, 1985.

124 Baldrey, Keith. *Mountie urges talks. Logging peace sought.* The Sun, November 25, 1985.

125 Government of Canada news release. *Federal Environment and Indian Affairs Ministers offer to meet on South Moresby dispute,* November 22, 1985.

126 Cruickshank, John. *Haida promised aid in Lyell Island stand.* The Globe and Mail, November 22, 1985; and No author. *Moresby mediation rebuffed by Smith.* The Sun, November 22, 1985.

127 Middleton, Greg. *At loggerheads.* The Province, November 24, 1985.

128 Lyell Island arrests records, Royal Canadian Mounted Police; and No author. *Logging crews back at work in Lyell Island woods.* The Sun, November 26, 1985.

129 Lyell Island arrests records, Royal Canadian Mounted Police; and Baldrey, Keith. *Native session expected to endorse Haida stand.* The Sun, November 28, 1985.

130 McLaren, Christie. *Churches back Haida in forestry feud.* The Globe and Mail, November 27, 1985.

131 No author. *Haida Nation pleads for aid as cost of blockade mounts.* The Sun, November 27, 1985.

132   No author. *BC Fed backs Haidas, loggers in Lyell dispute.* The Sun, November 28, 1985.

133   See endnote 132.

134   *Notice of Motion.* Vancouver Registry No. C854987. Submitted by WFP to the Supreme Court of British Columbia, November 22, 1985; Baldrey, Keith. *Haidas refuse to knuckle under on blockade.* The Sun, November 29, 1985; and. Baldrey, Keith. *Haida leader refuses to vow blockade end.* The Sun, November 29, 1985.

135   Sun staff reporter. *Church refused standing in court.* November 29, 1985; and Cruickshank, John. *Haidas convicted for defying court in logging protest.* The Globe and Mail, November 30, 1985.

136   Baldrey, Keith. *Native session expected to endorse Haida stand.* The Sun, November 28, 1985.

137   Lyell Island arrests records, Royal Canadian Mounted Police, received 1998; Transcript. *Reasons for Judgement.* Re: File No.: C854987 and C854988. Chief Justice McEachern. The Supreme Court of British Columbia, Nov 29, 1985; Cruickshank, John. *Haidas convicted for defying court in logging protests.* The Globe and Mail, November 30, 1985; and Baldrey, Keith. *Haidas refuse to knuckle under on blockade.* The Sun, November 29, 1985.

138   Pynn, Larry. *Talk land issue, poll tells Bennett.* The Sun, November 30, 1985.

139   No author *Lyell Island quiet.* The Sun, December 3, 1985; and Pynn, Larry and Cox, Sarah. *Lyell progress leaves parties hopeful."* The Sun, December 10, 1985.

140   Fournier, Suzanne. *Haida ban asked.* The Province, December 2, 1985.

141   Glavin, Terry. *Logging company seeking seven new Lyell Island sites.* The Sun, December 3, 1985.

142   No author. *$200,000 police bill mounts in Lyell clash.* The Sun, December 3, 1985.

143   Transcript. *Reasons for Sentencing.* Vancouver Registry No.: C854987. Chief Justice McEachern. The Supreme Court of British Columbia, December 6, 1985.

144   Pynn, Larry and Cox, Sarah. *Lyell progress leaves parties hopeful.* The Sun, December 10, 1985; Danylchuk, Jack and Gory, Brian. *Discussion helpful, BC minister asserts after meeting Haida.* The Globe and Mail, December 11, 1985; and Baldrey, Keith and Fitterman, Lisa. *Smith says he'll ask cabinet to reconsider logging Lyell.* The Sun, December 11, 1985.

145   *TFL 24 History Summary,* Council of the Haida Nation, 2018.

146   Pynn, Larry. *Four Haidas back on Lyell.* The Sun, January 8, 1986.

147   Bohn, Glenn. *South Moresby pushed as Park.* The Sun, January 9, 1986.

148   Canadian Press. *Committee hears please to save South Moresby.* The Globe and Mail, January 17, 1986; and Bohn, Glenn. *Cheering, clapping crowd backs Moresby logging.* The Sun, January 18, 1986.

149   Staff Reporter. *Minister in hot water over conflict charge.* The Province, January 17, 1986.

150   Cruickshank, John and Danylchuk, Jack. *Holds investment in forest company, BC minister quits.* The Globe and Mail, January 18, 1986; Larsen, Bruce. *A conflict remains.* The Sun, January 18, 1986; and Bohn, Glenn. *Wilderness committee chief dumped shares.* The Sun, January 18, 1986.

151   Canadian Press. *Haida step aside for Lyell loggers in bid for better land-claims talks.* The Globe and Mail, January 21, 1986; and Bohn, Glenn. *Moresby reserve sparks interest.* The Sun, January 21, 1986.

152   Baldry, Keith and Mason, Gary. *Hydro rates for mill cited as conflict.* The Sun, January 21, 1986; and Cruickshank, John. *BC firm with ties to minister seeking rate cut.* The Globe and Mail, January 22, 1986.

153   No author. *Broadcaster defends investment.* The Sun, January 21, 1985; and Guujaaw, personal communication with the editor, 2011.

154   Cruickshank, John. *BC firm with ties to minister seeking rate cut.* The Globe and Mail, January 22, 1985.

155   Baldrey, Keith. *New Charges imperil talks, Haida claims.* The Sun, January 30, 1986; and Trask, Peter. *Smith defends altered Haida charges.* The Sun, January 31, 1986.

156   Bohn, Glenn. *Company offers to lower timber cut.* The Sun, January 31, 1986.

157   Bohn, Glenn. *Company offers to lower timber cut.* The Sun, January 31, 1986.

158   No author. *Fisheries gets tough with loggers.* The Sun, February 6, 1986; and LaVerne Davies, personal communication with the editor, May 25, 2018.

159   Bohn, Glenn. *Cutting permits freeze means layoffs, logger says.* The Sun, February 8, 1986; and No author. *New logging put on hold.* The Sun, February 7, 1986.

160   Fitterman, Lisa. *Pollen charges energy minister.* The Sun, February 11, 1985.

161   Wong, Todd. 1986. *Cockburn helps Haidas.* The Ubyssey, February 25, 1986

162   ammsa.com/publications/windspeaker/heros-welcome-indian-caravan

163   Wilderness Advisory Committee records, BC Archives Series GR-1601; *South Moresby A Retrospective.* Share BC–Citizen's Coalition For Sustainable Development, 1990; Henley, Thom. *Save South Moresby National Caravan.* Special Issue, Spring 1986.

164   http://ammsa.com/publications/windspeaker/heros-welcome-indian-caravan.

165   News Services. *He'll Sing for Lyell.* The Province, February 20, 1986; Terri-Lynn Williams-Davidson, White Raven Law Corporation. Personal communication with the editor, March 16, 2016.

166   CHN News Release, July 14, 1986; and *Blockades or Breakthroughs? Aboriginal Peoples Confront the Canadian State.* Belanger, Yale D. and Lackenbauer, P. Whitney, editors. Montreal & Kingston. London. Ithaca: McGill-Queen's University Press, 2014: 80.

167   Edgell, F. Letter to Miles Richardson Jr., October 24, 1986.

168   *Bill Reid, the grand old man of Haida art.* www.cbc.ca/archives/entry/the-grand-old-man-of-haida-art

169   Thompson. P. Letter to Michael Nicoll, February 10, 1987.

170   McKnight, Bill. Letter to Miles Richardson Jr., received February 2, 1987.

171   Miles Richardson Jr., personal communication with the editor, November 21, 2015; and Jeff Gibbs, personal communication with the editor, May 8, 2018.

172   Public meeting minutes. Skidegate Community Hall, March 22, 1987.

173   Guujaaw, personal communication with the editor January 11, 2017; and Jeff Gibbs, personal communication with the editor, May 10, 2018.

174   Fulton, Jim. Open letter announcing passing of resolution, May 22, 1987.

175   Editor, personal experience.

176   Caccia, Charles. Statement Pursuant to S. O. 21, National Parks South Moresby—Federal-Provincial Relations, June 22, 1987.

177   McLaren, Christie. *Chretien asked to intercede in BC park dispute.* The Globe and Mail, June 24, 1987.

178   Editor, personal experience.

179   Pynn, Larry. *Lyell Island: 25 years later* Vancouver Sun, November 17, 2010.

180   Burns, John F. *With Logging Banned, The Logger Is Mourned.* Special to the New York Times, August 15, 1987.

181   McMillan, Tom. Letter to Miles Richardson Jr., received January 26, 1988.

182   See endnote 181.

183   a: Thomson, P.A. Letter to Miles Richardson Jr., July 25, 1988.
       b: Richardson Jr., Miles. Open letter to *The Residents of Haida Gwaii,* September 17, 1988.

184   See endnote 24.

185   Christakos, J. C. Letter to Guujaaw, April 11, 1989.

186   Meeting minutes, re: Gwaii Haanas. Skidegate Band Office, April 15, 1989.

187   See endnote 24.

188   Guujaaw. Letter to Jim Collison, November 29, 1989.

189   Dale, Norman. *Finding (the) Trust,* in this publication: see page 125

190   Environment Canada Canadian Parks Service Memorandum, March 27, 1990.

191   Bouchard, Lucien. Letter to Miles Richardson Jr., stamped May 4, 1990.

192   Richardson Jr., Miles. Letter to R. Bourassa, August 30, 1990.

193   Dale, Norman. *Finding (the) Trust,* in this publication: see page 125

194   Dale, Norman. *Finding (the) Trust,* in this publication: see page 125; and www.gwaiitrust.com/about/history/

195   Hauka, Don. *Haida claim victory in ruling on forests.* The Province, November 12, 1987.

196   www.thecanadianencyclopedia.ca/en/article/delgamuukw-case

197   EAGLE Law TFL 39 legal team: Cheryl Sharvit; Louise Mandell, QC; Michael Jackson, QC; Terri-Lynn Williams-Davidson.

198   Documents and agreements available for viewing at: www.haidanation.ca.

199   See endnote 198.

200   See endnote 198.

202   See endnote 198.

202   See endnote 198.

203   Cowpar, James. *The Gwaii Trust Society,* in this publication: see page 125; and www.aglt.ca

204   See endnote 198.

205   See endnote 198.

ACKNOWLEDGEMENTS

This book started out as a "simple project" that would be completed in one year, but the stories kept coming and there are still many more to tell. For those patiently waiting for the past two years, we say an extra special haawa. Following are the direct contributors to this publication:

NEVER-ENDING RESEARCH
Nika Collison, Simon Davies, Candace Weir-White and two researchers who wish to remain anonymous.

RESEARCH SUPPORT
Jaskwaan Amanda Bedard, Lawrence Bell; Arnie Bellis; Marianne Boelscher Ignace; John Broadhead; Diane Brown; Robert Cross; LaVerne Davies; Warren Foster; Jeff Gibbs; Lisa Gordon; Guujaaw; Michael McGuire; Miles Richardson Jr.; Lois Rullin; Gary Russ and Barbara J. Wilson.

Council of the Haida Nation Communications Committee: Jason Alsop, Tyler Bellis and William Russ.

Council of the Haida Nation Communications Team: Mare Levesque, Graham Richard, Leah Mattice, Rhonda McIsaac, Tanisha Salomons, Sharon Williams.

Council of the Haida Nation Heritage and Natural Resource Dept.: Nick Reynolds.

Gwaii Haanas/Parks Canada: Heather Ramsey, Patrick Bartier and Joanne Collinson.

Haida Gwaii Museum at Kay Llnagaay: Lynn Hughan, Nathalie Macfarlane, Jennifer Pigeon, Leah Sankey, Cherie Wilson and Sean Young.

The Lyell File team: Greg, Alar, Miles, John, Kelly, Lorenda and Walrus, for Earth Embassy.

Ravens & Eagles Productions: Marianne Jones and Jeff Bear.

Skidegate Band Council: Barbara Stevens and Doris Rosang.

Skidegate Haida Immersion Program: Lorna Berekoff, Diane Brown, Lilly Brown, Jackie Casey, Don Collinson, Elizabeth Collinson, Kathleen (Golie) Hans, Kathleen Hans Sr., Bea Harley, Roy Jones Sr., Grace Jones, Laura Jormanainen, Gertrude Kelly, Doreen Mearns, Mr. Moody, Becky Pearson, Jack Pollard, Norman Price, Watson Pryce, Betty Richardson, Miles Richardson Sr., Agnes Russ, Eleanor Russ, Freddy Russ, Rose Russ, Grace Stevens, Hazel Stevens, Gladys Vandal, Charlie Williams, Harvey Williams, John Williams, Mabel Williams, Percy Williams, Susan Williams, Ernie Wilson, Sally Wilson, Solomon Wilson, Audrey Young, George Young, Henry Young, James Young and Nathan Young, Ada Yovanovich with Kevin Borserio and Denver Cross.

White Raven Law Corporation: Terri-Lynn Williams-Davidson, Liz Bulbrook, Suzanne Redmond, Carmen Pollard, Emily Bell, Laverne Hamilton, Fallon Crosby, Megan Dorrington and Wanda Bernaka.

SPECIAL HAAWA
Percy Crosby, Fanny Aisha, Deanna Bayne, Patrick Bell, Juul Collison-Robertson, Kuuyas Collison-Robertson, Beth Carter, Conrad Collinson, Jenny Cross, Robert Cross, Jennifer Davidson, Cynthia Davies, Karen Dean, Sean Griffin, Kwiaawah Jones, Lawrence Jones, Dan Keeton, Richard Krieger, Yvonne Laviolette, Michaela McGuire, Jacquie Miller, Robert Mills, Len Munt, Seraphine Pryce, Colin Richardson, Danny Robertson, Denise Russ, Frank Russ, Cynthia Samuels, Scott Steedman, Christian White, Daphne White and Nadine Wilson.

Friesens Corporation: Jorge Rocha

Gwaii Haanas Archipelago Management Board: Jason Alsop, Robert Bennett, Cindy Boyko, Ernie Gladstone, Colin Masson, Tyler Pete.

Gwaii Haanas/Parks Canada: Ernie Gladstone and Terrie Dionne.

Gwaii Trust Society: Staff: Carla Lutner, Errol Winter and Dana Bellis; Board: James Cowpar, Bret Johnston, Cecil Brown, Clyde Greenough, Warren Foster, Robert Bennett, Jason Alsop, Billy Yovanovich, and Berry Wijdeven.

SFU Special Collections and Rare Books, W.A.C. Bennett Library: Melanie Hardbattle and Allison Moore.

Secretariat of the Haida Nation: May Russ, Lisa Edwards, Denise Thiessen and Valerie Thiessen.

All those contributed to the success of the Athlii Gwaii stand in all ways; those who've shared their stories here and all of those who are keeping the story alive.

We've done our best to acknowledge everyone involved and are so very appreciative to all who've contributed.
Haawa dalang 'waadluuxan!

Haawa id Kuuniisii, our Ancestors;
haawa SGaanaGwas, the Supernatural Beings;
haawa Haida Gwaii; haawa to those yet
unborn for keeping us on our path.

The line that the Haida Nation drew in Gwaii Haanas, and stated
that this area will be protected, stands to this day. They didn't
move over it. And I give our people a heck of a lot of credit,
but I also give credit to Canadians and British Columbians,
and people around the world for understanding, for
listening and, above all, for bringing themselves to
a point where there was a mutual respect.

Kilsli Kaji Sting, Miles Richardson Jr.,
in Athlii Gwaii: The Line at Lyell,
Ravens and Eagles Productions, 2003.